MULTICULTURAL EDUCA

James A. Banks, Series Editor

Learning to Teach for Social Justice
LINDA DARLING-HAMMOND, JENNIFER FRENCH, AND
SILVIA PALOMA GARCIA-LOPEZ, EDITORS

Culture, Difference, and Power
CHRISTINE E. SLEETER

Learning and Not Learning English:
Latino Students in American Schools
GUADALUPE VALDÉS

Culturally Responsive Teaching:
Theory, Research, and Practice
GENEVA GAY

The Children Are Watching:
How the Media Teach About Diversity
CARLOS E. CORTÉS

Race and Culture in the Classroom:
Teaching and Learning Through Multicultural Education
MARY DILG

The Light in Their Eyes:
Creating Multicultural Learning Communities
SONIA NIETO

Reducing Prejudice and Stereotyping in Schools
WALTER STEPHAN

We Can't Teach What We Don't Know:
White Teachers, Multiracial Schools
GARY R. HOWARD

Educating Citizens in a Multicultural Society
JAMES A. BANKS

Multicultural Education, Transformative Knowledge, and Action:
Historical and Contemporary Perspectives
JAMES A. BANKS, EDITOR

Learning to Teach
for
Social Justice

Linda Darling-Hammond
Jennifer French
Silvia Paloma Garcia-Lopez
EDITORS

Teachers College, Columbia University
New York and London

Published by Teachers College Press, 1234 Amsterdam Avenue, New York, NY 10027

Library of Congress Cataloging-in-Publication Data

Learning to teach for social justice / Linda Darling-Hammond, Jennifer French, Silvia Paloma Garcia-Lopez, editors.
   p.   cm.   (Multicultural education series)
   Includes bibliographical references and index.
   ISBN 0-8077-4209-0 (cloth : alk. paper).— ISBN 0-8077-4208-2 (pbk. : alk. paper)
   1. Multicultural education—United States. 2. Teaching—Social aspects—United States. 3. Teachers—Training of—United States. I. Darling-Hammond, Linda. II. French, Jenmnifer C. III. Garcia-Lopez, Silvia Paloma. IV. Multicultural education series (New York, N.Y.).
LC1099.3 .L45 2002
370.117—dc21   2001-060361

ISBN 0-8077-4208-2 (paper)
ISBN 0-8077-4209-0 (cloth)

Printed on acid-free paper

Manufactured in the United States of America

09 08 07 06 05 04 03 02   8 7 6 5 4 3 2 1

In memory of Ryan Caster,
whose efforts to learn and teach
"The Big Lesson"
inspired and taught us all.

Contents

Series Foreword, by *James A. Banks*   ix

Preface: We Wish We Could Teach Like Our Eyes Can See,
    by *Jennifer French and Silvia Paloma Garcia-Lopez*   xiii

1. Learning to Teach for Social Justice   1
    Linda Darling-Hammond

Part I: What Is Diversity?   **9**

2. What Is Diversity?   13
    Todd Ziegler Cymrot

3. Acknowledging Diversity in the Classroom   18
    Jennifer Steele

4. Swimming Against the Mainstream: Examining Cultural
    Assumptions in the Classroom   22
    Kristy Garcia

5. From the Margins to the Center: Reconstructing the Canon
    in Social Studies Curriculum   30
    Winter Pettis-Renwick

Part II: Does Who We Are Influence How We Teach?   **39**

6. Survey Says...: Can White Teachers Effectively Teach Students of Color?   43
    Kristin Traudt

7. Finding Myself in My Students: A Step Toward Transforming Social
    Dynamics in the Classroom   52
    Carlo Corti

8. Idealism Meets Reality   59
    Jennifer French

9. The *Big* Lesson   66
    Ryan Caster

10. Watching Words and Managing Multiple Identities   71
    Grace MyHyun Bang

11. Whose Rally Comes First?   79
    Silvia Paloma Garcia-Lopez

Part III: Who Are Our Students and What Do They Need?   89

12. Depending on Success   93
    Susan Park

13. "I Ain't Doin' That": Why "Doing Good in School" Can Be So Hard   103
    Leah Anderson

14. Navigating a New World: The Development of an Immigrant Student in an
    American Middle School   116
    Roman H. Garcia

15. Drop Out or Push Out? Succeeding in Spite of the System   128
    Sandra Navarro

16. Beyond Cultural Relevance   139
    Claudia Angelica Narez

Part IV: What Is the Problem and What Can We Do About It? 149

17. Finding the Right Track   153
    Suzanne Herzman

18. To Track or Not to Track: That Is Still a Question   163
    Erin Hays

19. Unity and Division: Working Through the Issues of Equity
    in School Reform   171
    Laura Blythe

20. Checking In: Bridging Differences by Building Community   184
    Allison Rowland

21. Wanted: Teachers with *Conciencia*   192
    Ana Louisa Ruiz

22. Educating a Profession for Equitable Practice   201
    Linda Darling-Hammond

References   213
About the Editors and Contributors   217
Index   221

Series Foreword

The nation's deepening ethnic texture, interracial tension and conflict, and the increasing percentage of students who speak a first language other than English make multicultural education imperative in the 21st century. The U.S. Bureau of the Census estimated that people of color made up 28% of the nation's population in 2000 (U.S. Census Bureau , 1998). The census predicted that they would make up 38% of the nation's population in 2025 and 47% in 2050.

American classrooms are experiencing the largest influx of immigrant students since the beginning of the 20th century. About a million immigrants are making the United States their home each year (Martin & Midgley, 1999). More than 7.5 million legal immigrants settled in the United States between 1991 and 1998, most of whom came from nations in Latin America and Asia (Riche, 2000). A large but undetermined number of undocumented immigrants also enter the United States each year. The influence of an increasingly ethnically diverse population on the nation's schools, colleges, and universities is and will continue to be enormous.

In 1998, 34.9% of the students enrolled in U.S. public schools were students of color; this percentage is increasing each year, primarily because of the growth in the percentage of Latino students (Martinez & Curry, 1999). In some of the nation's largest cities and metropolitan areas, such as Chicago, Los Angeles, Washington, DC, New York, Seattle, and San Francisco, half or more of the public school students are students of color. During the 1998–1999 school year, students of color made up 63.1% of the student population in the public schools of California, the nation's largest state (California State Department of Education, 2000).

Language diversity is also increasing among the nation's student population. Sixteen percent of school-age youth lived in homes in which English was not the first language in 1990 (U.S. Census Bureau, 1998). Most teachers now in the classroom and in teacher education programs are likely to have students from diverse ethnic, racial, and language groups in their classrooms during their careers. This is true for both inner-city and suburban teachers.

An important goal of multicultural education is to improve race relations and to help all students acquire the knowledge, attitudes, and skills needed to participate in cross-cultural interactions and in personal, social, and civic action that will help make our nation more democratic and just. Multicultural education is consequently as important for middle-class White suburban students as it is for students of color who live in the inner-city. Multicultural education fosters the public good and the overarching goals of the commonwealth.

The major purpose of the MULTICULTURAL EDUCATION SERIES is to provide preservice educators, practicing educators, graduate students, and scholars with an interrelated and comprehensive set of books that summarizes and analyzes important research, theory, and practice related to the education of ethnic, racial, cultural, and language groups in the United States and the education of mainstream students about diversity. The books in the Series provide research, theoretical, and practical knowledge about the behaviors and learning characteristics of students of color, language minority students, and low-income students. They also provide knowledge about ways to improve academic achievement and race relations in educational settings.

The definition of multicultural education in the *Handbook of Research on Multicultural Education* (Banks & Banks, 2001) is used in the Series: "Multicultural education is a field of study designed to increase educational equity for all students that incorporates, for this purpose, content, concepts, principles, theories, and paradigms from history, the social and behavioral sciences, and particularly from ethnic studies and women studies" (p. xii). In the Series, as in the *Handbook*, multicultural education is considered a "metadiscipline."

The dimensions of multicultural education, developed by Banks (2001) and described in the *Handbook of Research on Multicultural Education,* provide the conceptual framework for the development of the books in the Series. They are content integration, the knowledge construction process, prejudice reduction, an equity pedagogy, and an empowering school culture and social structure. To implement multicultural education effectively, teachers and administrators must attend to each of the five dimensions of multicultural education. They should use content from diverse groups when teaching concepts and skills, help students to understand how knowledge in the various disciplines is constructed, help students to develop positive intergroup attitudes and behaviors, and modify their teaching strategies so that students from different racial, cultural, language, and social-class groups will experience equal educational opportunities. The total environment and culture of the school must also be transformed so that students from diverse groups will experience equal status in the culture and life of the school.

Although the five dimensions of multicultural education are highly interrelated, each requires deliberate attention and focus. Each book in the Series focuses on one or more of the dimensions, although each book deals with all of them to some extent because of the highly interrelated characteristics of the dimensions.

In this skillfully crafted and engaging book, a group of insightful and committed students who are learning to become teachers share their personal struggles, triumphs and joys of teaching in classrooms that are diverse in terms of race, class, gender, language and sexual orientation. A key goal of their teacher education program is to help them acquire the knowledge, attitudes, and skills needed to teach for social justice. The contributors to this book not only read and talk about diversity in the university classroom; they apply the concepts and theories they are learning in highly diverse classrooms and schools.

Students preparing to become teachers will find the reflections, revelations, and insights described in this book challenging, motivating, and a source of inspiration and hope. The honest and sometimes poignant reflections, case studies, lessons, and projects described by the student teachers in this book document how teaching sensitively about diversity is a challenging but deeply rewarding and important endeavor.

Many of the contributors to this book are themselves members of cultural, ethnic, and language communities that are marginalized within U.S. society. Diversity for them is not an abstract concept but an integral part of their lives. The candid ways in which these students share insights about diversity they have acquired from experiencing discrimination and racism in American society is one of this book's unique strengths. They also describe how they have used their insights about diversity to intervene on behalf of victimized and marginalized students.

This book is a singular contribution to the multicultural education literature because it is one of the first publications to describe the voices, perspectives, and experiences of students learning to become teachers in diverse classrooms. It consequently enriches and extends the important multicultural education research and theoretical literature that present the voices of researchers (Banks & Banks, 2001) and those of veteran teachers (Nieto, 1999).

I am especially pleased to welcome this book to the MULTICULTURAL EDUCATION SERIES because the students who took the leadership for its conceptualization and development—Jennifer French and Silvia Paloma Garcia-Lopez—were under the tutelage of Linda Darling-Hammond, a teacher educator who has for the last two decades been an important leader of the movement to educate and acquire high quality teachers for all of the nation's students. The publication of this book by Darling-Hammond and her teacher education students documents how she "walks the talk" of diversity in her own classroom and in the teacher education program for which she is responsible. I hope the excellent and powerful examples she and her students exemplify in this book—of thoughtfully integrating diversity within a teacher education program—will serve as both model and inspiration for teacher educators who are seeking ways to transform their teacher education programs so they will prepare teachers to work effectively in diverse classrooms and schools.

James A. Banks
Series Editor

REFERENCES

Banks, J. A. (2001). Multicultural education: Historical development, dimensions, and practice. In J. A. Banks & C. A. M. Banks (Eds.), *Handbook of research on multicultural education* (pp. 3–24). San Francisco: Jossey-Bass.

Banks, J. A., & Banks, C. A. M. (Eds.). (2001). *Handbook of research on multicultural education.* San Francisco: Jossey-Bass.

California State Department of Education. (2000). On line [http://data1.cde.ca.gov/dataquest]

Martin, P., & Midgley, E. (1999). Immigration to the United States. *Population Bulletin, 54*(2), 1–44. Washington, DC: Population Reference Bureau.

Martinez, G. M., & Curry, A. E. (1999, September). *Current population reports: School enrollment-social and economic characteristics of students* (update). Washington, DC: U.S. Census Bureau.

Nieto, S. (1999). *The light in their eyes: Creating multicultural learning communities.* New York: Teachers College Press.

Riche, M. F. (2000). America's diversity and growth: Signposts for the 21st century. *Population Bulletin, 55*(2), 1–43. Washington, DC: Population Reference Bureau.

U.S. Census Bureau. (1998). *Statistical abstract of the United States* (118th edition). Washington, DC: U.S. Government Printing Office.

We Wish We Could Teach Like Our Eyes Can See

Last summer we began a year-long adventure in a teacher education program. Wide-eyed and optimistic, we jumped into our education classes and student teaching positions with enthusiasm and high hopes. Both of us wanted to create a social awareness among our students and, more important, be part of reforming our educational system so that it meets the needs of all students. With fire in our bellies and passion in our eyes, we looked forward to getting the tools from our program to help us in this challenge.

Jennifer was a social worker in Portland, Oregon, and New Mexico before coming to a teacher education program. During this time, her eyes had been opened to the inequalities faced by women and children who encounter violence in their lives. Through guest presentations in classrooms, she tried to empower youth to help stop the cycles of violence in their homes and communities. While doing this work, she also became involved in supporting gay and lesbian youth. This experience echoed what she had experienced in high school 10 years earlier: many gay and lesbian youth were silenced in schools and faced verbal and physical abuse from their peers. In addition, Jen discovered that few teachers interrupted anti-gay language and even fewer teachers included gay and lesbian culture in their curriculum. Troubled by how her observations mirrored her own experiences as a gay youth and young adult, she felt a strong need to become a teacher to work toward making school a safe place for all students.

Paloma, on the other hand, had spent years throughout high school and college doing volunteer service with a Latino youth organization based in southern California. This program intervened when she was 16 to help her build self-esteem, motivation for academic achievement, and preparation for the university and financial aid applications. She came to resent schools for not helping thousands of others like herself and felt strongly that schools, not an outside organization, should be filling this void. This experience, along with witnessing injustice and oppression though her family's work with Cesar Chavez and the United Farm Workers union, drove her to become a teacher who would empower students to overcome their educational and societal obstacles. Not only did she want them to navigate the system, she wanted students to become leaders in their communities and change that system to make social institutions more equitable for all children.

We both participated in countless classroom discussions within the education program, listening for other voices with similar visions for social change as new teachers. This eagerness turned into frustration as few of our peers expressed concern about remedying the inequities in our system of education. Soon, we found each other in the same informal group that lingered after classes as a forum to fill in the missing pieces. Though these sessions were comforting for a moment, we quickly realized that everyone in these groups was a member of a racial or sexual minority group. Was it really true that only minorities could see the need for social change? We didn't want this to be the case. But, if it was, what would this mean for our experience in the program and as teachers?

Although we knew early on that we were being idealistic about the social change we could create as teachers, we jumped into the task expecting our peers to follow with the same wave of passion in their hearts. As time went on, we found that there were different responses to the reality that we saw in our own experiences as students, and again as student teachers. These frustrations turned into anger, anxiety, silenced voices, and disillusionment. At different times we knocked on our professors' doors to complain or cry on their shoulders. How are we going to acquire the tools to accomplish our dreams? How can we live knowing that our peers will someday teach our children? How could we alleviate the oppression that many of us felt as racial and sexual minorities? There had to be a way to infuse discussions and training to meet the challenge of social change in schools. Moreover, we wanted to find a means by which we could educate our peers so that they better understood the experiences of minority educators and students.

One answer came to us from another teacher education program. During a weekend gathering with a friend from Harvard, Jen was introduced to an anthology that the students in the education program created. This anthology, *Meet Me at the River*, was a collection of voices from students of color enrolled in a school of education. When she returned from this weekend trip, Jen shared this idea with Linda Darling-Hammond and her peers. This seemed like a productive step to unleash the silenced voices in our program. What if we too could create an anthology that addressed the issues that we felt were missing and so vital to our education and to that of our students?

The opportunity to express our views and experiences in an anthology was timely. Halfway through the program and our student teaching, those of us interested in social change were in need of a venue to address what we saw in local schools on a daily basis. We formed and co-chaired a committee, and we began to make the book a reality.

Throughout this process we were keenly aware of the sense of privilege we all had as Stanford students. One of our primary concerns at this point was that educators across the country might not sympathize with the struggles of student teachers from Stanford. This posed an interesting paradox because the majority of the contributors were raised in underprivileged communities and were themselves trying to find a balance between these two very different realities. As we discussed these issues of privilege in our group, we remembered that we walked into the teaching profession with intentions of using our power as educators in a positive way. This was a special opportunity to make the choice to use the power and resources that we had at Stanford to make positive changes in education. Linda Darling-Hammond's educational work and activism was an excellent role model for us. We could not pass up this unique opportunity to learn from a professor who was well acquainted with the problems of social justice and who could also guide the process of getting published to document our collective struggles. We, too, wanted to use our power and education to influence and inspire teachers across the country.

We were also concerned about the reception that this project would get among the rest of our peers. To our surprise, a large number of our peers became interested in contributing experiences from which others could learn. This made us realize that not all of our peers were oblivious to issues of equity, and that something tangible like this book could serve as an excellent vehicle for people to come together to create a dialogue and share their experiences. Why do people need something tangible? Why did it seem that so many people in our program had difficulty confronting issues of diversity and social change? We came into the program expecting solutions and practical results; we had overlooked some very real issues that arise when individuals raise questions about social justice. Issues of inequality, oppression, and racism often invoke feelings of fear, guilt, helplessness, and anger. These feelings are what make the discussion about social change so difficult: Each one of us came into the program with different kinds of understanding and experience.

With the book, we now had a common ground that brought together the diverse perceptions and experiences that created so much friction at the beginning of the program. Now there was a specific venue for student teachers to come together. This helped break down many of the assumptions and stereotypes by providing a safe and more personal forum for sharing and writing. We realized that the process of creating this book was, in essence, an act of social change. We watched in awe, as the feelings of helplessness and frustration shifted to empowerment during this process.

The process that we went through in writing this book is what we want to replicate for those who read this anthology. We hope that the book will open a window to help other educators examine the obstacles teachers and students encounter in working toward social and educational equity. Perhaps these problems can be more easily confronted when people read the stories of others and then probe them to expose issues of equity, discrimination, and social justice.

Perhaps these stories can serve to revitalize dreams and visions held by teachers across the country. The stories can also be used to generate awareness among teachers who have struggled to connect to diverse students. Through our experiences working with veteran teachers, we know how easily the multiple pressures placed on teachers can dampen the sense of idealism we share. New ideas and voices were what kept us going in our program, and we hope that these perspectives can help other teachers remain inspired to continue to develop their skills and pedagogy as professionals.

It is our hope that this book will serve as a powerful educational tool that has the capacity to start the fire for some, and for others, to rekindle the fire in our bellies as teachers for social change. We believe that teachers make a difference in the lives of their students every day. We believe that we can teach like our eyes can see.

Jennifer French and Silvia Paloma Garcia-Lopez
STEP Library, Stanford University

CHAPTER 1

Learning to Teach for Social Justice

Linda Darling-Hammond

As we move into the 21st century, the demographics of the United States continue to evolve rapidly, and schools reflect these changes. In the year 2000, more than 35% of public school students were students of color. In most large cities and some states, such as California, "minority" students have become the majority in public schools, a trend that will characterize the entire nation by the year 2020. With growing immigration, mainstreaming, and awareness of student differences, schools and classrooms represent a greater range of ethnic groups, languages, socioeconomic status, sexual orientations, and abilities than ever before in our history.

As student diversity in schools becomes the norm, not the exception, teachers, administrators, and students are looking for strategies to successfully negotiate these changes. Teacher education programs are looking for ways to sensitize and enable prospective teachers to understand diversity and to develop an equity-oriented pedagogy. These issues are widely discussed, but there are few forums in which teachers who are entering teaching have shared their candid questions, concerns, dilemmas, and learnings about how to teach for social justice and social change.

The book is written by student teachers in the Stanford Teacher Education Program (STEP) who studied in a program aimed at helping teachers develop an equity pedagogy and who student taught in the extremely diverse communities of the San Francisco Bay Area. It is intended to provide a forum in which new teachers address difficult issues of diversity in our schools and society and reveal how they are considering and constructing their role in addressing these issues. Teaching is a moral and political act, and teachers can play a key role in facilitating positive social change. Each teacher is shaped by his or her own experiences and observations of diversity. This book offers a tool to help teachers engage in productive dialogues about both the inequities and the possibilities for social reconstruction in the communities within which they and their students are developing.

THE DIFFICULTIES AND DILEMMAS OF LEARNING TO TEACH FOR SOCIAL JUSTICE

The process of learning to teach for social change is not an easy one, even for those already committed. When Jennifer French and Paloma Garcia-Lopez came to see me in the early fall of 1999, they had already felt the frustration of holding discussions with classmates who had had little personal experience with the issues of inequity, marginalization, discrimination, and oppression that are regularly experienced by students whose race, income, language, sexuality, or learning abilities place them outside the mainstream. They could not understand why all of their classmates were not aware of the issues that seemed so obvious to them and why not all of these future teachers were mobilized to fight for social justice as the central core of their commitment to teaching. Jen, Paloma, and many of their colleagues were encountering firsthand the conservative forces in education—that is, viewpoints that conserve an inequitable status quo because it is seen as nonproblematic, as just the "way things are"—and they felt stunned and hurt.

This is a common story in schools of education—indeed in institutions of education everywhere—but it takes on special significance in those programs that prepare the practitioners who will, one way or another, shape the schools of the future and, thus, the life chances of millions of children and youth. Lisa Delpit has written eloquently about how students of color often feel silenced in teacher education programs, as though their knowledge and understandings, hard-won in years of experience, do not count. Some of the reasons for this silencing exist in the failure of programs to become conscious about the differences in life experience that initially divide their participants and to create a common ground in which these experiences can be more fully shared and the divide bridged. Other sources of silencing are the choices of readings, course topics, and field experiences that are constructed for prospective teachers, which may either choose to open up issues of diversity and equity or to close them down and ignore them.

I knew when Paloma, Jen, and I first talked only weeks after the start of the year-long STEP program that the process of opening up these experiences and conversations would be a long and necessarily difficult one; that their colleagues' comments were not deliberately meant to offend but were a function of their more limited experience base and perspectives over their own years of often-segregated and unexamined educational opportunities. I knew that those experiences and perspectives would change a great deal over the coming year, as we read and talked (and talked and talked) and as they student taught in diverse schools where they would work with a range of students under the guidance of often insightful and courageous mentors, where they would be asked to inquire into the lives and learning of their diverse students, and where they would critically evaluate the equity outcomes of school policies and practices.

I also knew that the transformations in understanding for STEP teachers would not be easy or painless for anyone, that some students would bear the brunt of explaining how injustices work from their own life experiences, and that others would struggle to find a way to become agents of social justice when they found that they had been beneficiaries in their lives of the system which produces so much educational injustice. Instructors, too, would struggle to learn from their students and to continue to develop their own ways of working for equity both in the teacher education program and in the schools. I knew that the process of change takes a great deal of time, effort, perseverance, and trust, and that all of us would have to work to support and understand one another as it unfolded and deepened over the course of the year. A critical part of this effort would be our efforts to embed these conversations again and again in the warp and woof of everything we worked on together, in every course and in every learning experience—not backing away from or compartmentalizing the uncomfortable dialogue that is a precursor to deeper understanding and growth.

Some critics of multicultural education fear that focusing on diversity will create separatism. They fail to understand that finding out what we have in common requires that we begin communicating from the vantage points of our separate experiences. Each of us has to find a way to express and locate our own experiences within that conversation in order to be validated as learners and human beings. This allows us then to connect with new knowledge and with the experiences of others. Far from encouraging separatism, acknowledgment of diverse experiences helps create new associations that helps us ultimately to build the common ground on which a more inclusive and powerful learning community can rest.

Crossing boundaries is essential to social learning. This is true for learning across disciplines and methodologies, across communities and cultures, across ideas and ideologies, and across the many groups of individuals—parents and teachers, students and staff—who make up a school, or for that matter, a teacher education program. Teachers and schools that educate well actively strive to understand rather than to suppress diversity. In this way they build a larger and stronger common ground.

HOW WE TRY TO SUPPORT LEARNING TO TEACH
FOR SOCIAL CHANGE

Stanford's Teacher Education Program, like many others across the country, tries to work consciously and systematically to help prospective teachers develop the empathy and vision that will help them truly "see" their students, the skills to address their learning needs, and the commitment to keep working for students when obstacles are encountered, as they inevitably will be. There are several aspects of this endeavor that we believe are important.

First, we find a variety of ways for STEP teachers to inquire into the lives of their students, to understand how the adolescents they teach see and experience the world. Rather than trying to teach about race and ethnicity in ways that stereotype individuals as representatives of groups, we weave readings about language and culture in the context of classrooms, schools and communities throughout courses on literacy development, adolescent development, equity and democracy, principles of learning, teaching methods, and school reform. Students conduct case studies of individual students, observing, interviewing, and shadowing them to better understand their lives and their learning. Many agree that the experience of reading about and studying young people in this way "has exposed and named the struggles that I might not have faced and made me more aware and reflective of the differing experiences of my students," as one student teacher put it.

Because STEP teachers complete a full year of student teaching while they are taking courses, they always have the opportunity to apply what they are learning directly to the classroom in real time. This helps to prevent concerns about race, class, and culture from becoming objectified, oversimplified, or an abstraction that could result mostly in "otherizing" students. Furthermore, it is critical that students develop an appropriate lens for learning from their own experience and for looking at the experiences of others—one that does not reinforce prejudices or miss critical factors that could support greater success. We try to guide the looking and learning process so that multiple perspectives are considered and so that productive insights are available. Among others things STEP teachers do to develop these insights is to conduct guided inquiries that consistently ask them to see the world from the perspective of their students, their parents, and the communities of which they are a part. In addition to case study assignments in which STEP teachers assess English Language Learners, follow a special education student, and interview and shadow an adolescent different from themselves, STEP teachers place calls to parents in which they share positive news of students' work in class, especially for students who have previously struggled, and learn more from the parents about their child.

Like many programs, STEP has struggled to find student teaching placements that enable new teachers to work with expert veterans who are knowledgeable, skillful, and committed to all of their students. We believe that it is impossible to learn to teach well by imagining what good teaching might look like or by positing the opposite of what one has seen. By being aggressive about seeking out teachers who are both technically skillful and culturally responsive we have been fortunate to find a large number of extraordinary mentors who are willing to share their expertise. In recent years, we have gone further to begin to develop professional development school relationships with middle and high schools that have been working explicitly on an equity agenda. Increasingly, the kind of schooling STEP teachers observe firsthand is schooling that seeks to confront the long-standing barriers created by tracking, poor teaching, narrow curriculum, and unresponsive systems. Clearly, however, inequities are not solved overnight. STEP teachers critically examine current school structures, practices, and outcomes as they visit and study schools and evaluate school policies and reforms. Future plans for Stanford's new 5-year teacher education program include a full-term guided internship in a community-based organization so that teachers will come to understand children and their families in contexts other than schools—contexts where service goals provide an alternative to the superordinate/subordinate relationship constructed between teachers and families in most schools.

Finally, we work on the development of specific knowledge and concrete, practical skills for teaching diverse students well. It is not enough to believe that all children can learn. Many well-intentioned people with strong values are mediocre or poor teachers. Others are able to teach those who are like themselves and who learn easily in the way that they teach, but they are unable to teach other students well, especially young people who have struggled with literacy, have lost confidence in their abilities, have experienced poor teaching, have gaps in their understandings, have specific language learning needs, have identified or unidentified learning disabilities, or have lost interest in a curriculum that does not appear to include them. Eventually, well-meaning but unskilled teachers give up on students whom they have not learned to teach. Often these teachers wind up blaming the children for their failures rather than reflecting on how they can transform their teaching. Of course, inadequate teacher education contributes mightily to this problem.

Enabling learning for all students requires knowledge about how people learn and how different people learn differently, about how to organize curriculum so that it connects to students' prior knowledge and experiences and so that it adds up to powerful learning, about what motivates people to engage and put forth effort for learning, about language and literacy development across the curriculum, about how to assess learning, and about particular teaching strategies that enable different kinds of learning in different contexts. These issues are raised in extensive year-long study of content pedagogy; in studies of language, literacy, and learning (including learning difficulties); in studies of classroom management and organization; and in studies of group work and other strategies for teaching in heterogeneous classrooms. As they develop particular skills, prospective teachers also develop the capacity to reflect on and change their practice. Examining which students participated and who learned what is as important to these reflections as examining what was taught and what was learned by the class as a whole. In the nexus where theory meets practice, we believe that a new praxis for social justice can be born.

BECOMING AN AGENT OF SOCIAL CHANGE

Teachers who are also students are in a unique position to address diversity issues. They are both transmitters and receivers of messages in the classroom. Many are keenly aware of the responsibility teachers and schools have to foster an educational environment that transforms the existing social order and empowers all of their students. Others come to their teacher education experience with little personal experience of diversity and without having considered the role of teachers and schools in either perpetrating or confronting inequality. In class discussions, readings, student teaching placements, and social interactions with peers and instructors in both the university and the schools, teachers who are students witness both positive and negative messages about diversity. As students, they process what they hear and must grapple with a range of implications before returning to face their own classroom full of students.

Many questions arise, and many often go unanswered in this process. What does it mean to teach for social change? How can we transmit what we receive in a more positive and proactive way to bring awareness, not only to our students but also to our colleagues? How do we see our individual roles as facilitators of social change?

This book uses personal experiences, case studies, and discussions of curriculum and teaching methods to reflect on these and other issues of diversity and social change. The authors discuss the dilemmas they are confronting and the ways in which they are constructing their roles as social change-agents in a variety of contexts: reaching out to students, role modeling, critiquing the status quo, developing curriculum, managing instruction, teaching to take social action, learning about oppression, practicing what you preach, being a change agent from the role of the "White teacher" or the "teacher of color," recognizing sexuality, race, and gender privilege, recognizing "reverse" privilege from a marginalized group, understanding responsibility and obligation, forming alliances, reconciling personal issues with multiculturalism, and developing pedagogy that enables all students to succeed.

The chapters that follow are organized into an anthology that raises several different aspects of diversity awareness and social action for consideration by student teachers and experienced teachers in schools and universities. The book is organized into four sections: Part I provides a range of answers to the question of "What is diversity?" It suggests a number of different lenses for considering diversity and reflects on their implications for classroom practice. Part II treats questions of identity—both teachers' and students'—as they frame classroom work. It asks how who we are influences how we teach and provides an opportunity for readers to think about how they might manage the intersection between their personal identities and their practice as educators with *conciencia*. Part III asks "Who are our students and what do they need?" Using case studies of individual students and classrooms, it provides a window into the life experiences of different kinds of students and what they may often experience in school. Part IV looks at what teachers and schools can do to make a difference. It examines "What is the problem and what can we do about it?" with an eye toward beginning to unpack solutions to the social injustices schools can too often reinforce.

We hope that providing this forum will empower teachers to define for themselves what it means to be personally affected by social issues involving equity and diversity, as well as what it means to become efficacious in their teaching for social change. We hope that the volume can also be used as a learning tool to support teachers as they form and transform their views about social justice into their teaching.

We felt that working together as a community of educators to help each other through this process of awareness would help us on our journey to become agents of social justice. This book was part of that journey. We trust that it will also assist others as they undertake their own pilgrimage.

NOTE

All proper names of students and schools in this book are pseudonyms.

Part I

WHAT IS DIVERSITY?

Linda Darling-Hammond
Silvia Paloma Garcia-Lopez

"Okay, okay. We've talked enough about the diverse kids. When are
we going to start talking about the 'normal' kids?"

—A student teacher

Many will recognize this voice of frustration from teachers who have "had
it" with discussions of culture and politics in the classroom. They want to focus
on the "normal" kids: White, middle class, heterosexual, and at least outwardly
well adjusted to school—the presumed majority. Others will recognize a sense of
frustration at the fact that there is a lot of talk about diversity, but there often
seems to be little apparent action to remedy the achievement gap between the
educational haves and the have-nots, the so-called *normal* kids and those who
are *different*. As a predominantly White, middle-class, suburban America is
becoming less and less the norm, what some think of as the "good old days"—
and others recollect as the days of separatism and vastly differential access to
school—is fast disappearing.

Dealing with diversity is one of the central challenges of 21st-century
education. It is impossible to prepare tomorrow's teachers to succeed with
all of the students they will meet without exploring how students' learning
experiences are influenced by their home languages, cultures, and contexts; the realities of race and class privilege in the United States; the
ongoing manifestations of institutional racism within the educational system; and the many factors that shape students' opportunities to learn within individual classrooms. To teach effectively, teachers need to understand
how learning depends on their ability to draw connections to what learners
already know, to support students' motivation and willingness to risk trying,
and to engender a climate of trust between and among adults and students.

Although these fundamentals are in some respects common to all successful learning environments, they take on different forms and pose dis-

tinctive demands for students with different backgrounds and life conditions. These include strategies to address language learning needs and sensitivity to cultural modes of communication to awareness of the psychological dimensions of learning—for example, the many ways in which students' construct knowledge from their very different life experiences and prior learning opportunities, as well as the ways in which students' beliefs about intelligence mobilize or paralyze their efforts. Developing an "equity pedagogy" (Banks, 1993) will also often mean confronting injustices that shape students' self-esteem and opportunities to learn in both society and schools. Teachers unaware of the structure and substance of inequality will find it difficult to understand students whose experiences do not resemble what they remember from their own necessarily limited experience.

In a typical classroom in the heart of the Silicon Valley, a teacher can find herself facing a room of students less than half of whom were born in this country. In addition to historical minority groups such as African Americans, Mexican Americans, and Chinese Americans, there are likely to be students from places like Zambia, South Africa, Russia, Bosnia, Brazil, Cambodia, Vietnam, Samoa, and the Philippines. Diversities in learning styles, interests, developed abilities, sexual orientations, and socioeconomic status are also evident for teachers who have developed eyes to see the many facets of each of their students' lives and identities.

The pieces that are included in this anthology come from the STEP students' explorations of these issues of learners and learning, content and curriculum. They begin at the very beginning, with questions of how we, as teachers, might conceptualize the issues of diversity, and why we might see the world in these ways. In the first section, each author answers the question: What is diversity? The first two chapters present different conceptions of diversity and put a real face on the many concerns faced by educators in the 21st century. The next two pieces reflect upon the implications for students of the treatment of diversity issues in the classroom. What are the potential outcomes and side-effects of teaching with an awareness of diversity? What are the pros and cons of different approaches to infusing multicultural content in the curriculum? How can new teachers transmit not only skills and knowledge but also self-awareness and respect for others?

In the first chapter, Todd Ziegler Cymrot responds to those who wonder what diversity has to do with them, noting that teaching is, at its foundation, a form of cultural exchange and that issues of diversity are part of a vast ongoing conversation about who we teach, how we teach, and why we teach. In the second chapter, Jennifer Steele examines how the human tendency to find comfort in the familiar can lead to segregation and exclusion in our schools and society, arguing that teachers and students need to address diversity explicitly and organize for inclusion in order to foster their students' participation and learning.

Kristy Garcia then takes up the sensitive issues of *how* to treat issues of diversity in the classroom, describing her own identity development as a biracial student and teacher, and deliberating about how to approach multicultural infusion without inadvertently creating the equivalent of racial profiling in the classroom. Winter Pettis-Renwick provides her own answers to these questions about implementing multicultural curriculum. As a teacher she wanted to avoid repeating her experience as a student who was denied access to information about multiple cultures and their role in history. Her article provides insight into what it means to transform the canon by recentering it on the contributions of all peoples.

All of these chapters support in different ways the idea that students learn best in an environment that is supportive and respectful of their identities. As Sonia Nieto (1999) argues, it is critical that teachers not look at difference among their students in negative terms. Teachers need to build on what children *do* have, because all children have some experiences that can help them learn (p. 7). By making the diversity discussion a priority, it is possible that teachers will better understand that learning is socially mediated and develops within a given culture and community. If diversity is what this nation is all about, then a broad view of its implications for our methods of instruction, curriculum, and classroom environment is important.

As you read this section, you may want to consider what diversity means to you. What are the implications of human diversity for learning and teaching and for the work of educators? What are the dilemmas posed by diversity in schools? Suggested questions for discussion in this section include:

How does rhetoric about inclusion match reality in schools you have experienced as a student or a teacher?

How do our own backgrounds shape how we view diversity?

How do individuals internalize an identity and use it to construct possible futures?

Why is it important to examine the individual students and groups that we, as teachers, gravitate toward or feel distanced from?

How might teaching the canon affect students from nonmainstream groups?

How might teaching about the contributions of nonmainstream groups affect students from the majority culture?

How can multicultural education be pursued so that it enhances understanding rather than supporting stereotyping?

 ѯ many ways a multicultural perspective can shape class-
 tice?
 ' do White teachers and teachers of color bring to the
 ⸗ı ϲ ⸤o create inclusive classrooms?
How can teachers work together on issues of diversity?

From these readings and discussion on diversity, we hope that you uncover answers as well as action plans for yourself. As Todd Ziegler Cymrot
puts it,

> Somewhere within the answer must be the idea that good teaching is
> about an exchange of cultures. Somewhere must be the notion that
> we, as new teachers, are inheriting a rich tradition of educational his-
> tory and wisdom, but one that has an equally long history of exclusion
> and failure. Somewhere there must be a vision of hope, a vision of
> what teaching can be within an individual classroom and within the
> larger institutions of public education.

CHAPTER 2

What Is Diversity?

Todd Ziegler Cymrot

"What does this diversity thing have to do with me?" is a frequent question. In this chapter, Todd Ziegler Cymrot discusses education as a form of cultural exchange that has everything to do with diversity, raising issues of who we teach, how we teach, and why we teach. Readers may want to consider how they think about both the concept of diversity and the nature and purposes of teaching.

The gods of language must moan every time educators appropriate another word for their lexicon. There exists, perhaps, no better way to rob a word of its power then through its overuse in an academic debate. Is it too late to save *diversity* from this fate?

"I just don't understand what this diversity thing has to do with me!" I have heard this sentiment phrased in one way or another numerous times over my past few years as a teacher, and I heard it once again most recently in a classroom at Stanford University where I am now enrolled as a student in the Stanford Teacher Education Program. What does it mean when a fellow teacher-in-training does not know her connection to *diversity*? Has the word lost its meaning, or has it taken on an identity so elusive that it is rendered foreign?

Diversity has been an omnipresent word throughout the days of my newfound career as an educator. At the middle school where I taught eighth graders for 3 years, we had a "Diversity Committee" and "Diversity Training," and I worked as part of a team of educators to draft the school's "Diversity Statement." We even sponsored a "Diversity Day" sandwiched somewhere in between our more traditional celebrations of Thanksgiving and the New Year. *Diversity* is a catchphrase, a code word that signifies not a single meaning but a vast ongoing conversation about who we teach, how we teach, and why we teach.

To me, ground zero of this conversation is the assumption that teaching is fundamentally a form of cultural exchange. It is not, as we are sometimes prone to think, the pouring of ideas into the empty heads of students. Instead, I have come to see the process of "educating" students as a complicated endeavor involving the initiation of young people into a whole new world of assumptions and habits. The classroom is a meeting ground of cultures where the worlds of the students meet the worldview of schools and teachers.

The diversity conversation, it seems, grows out of the recognition that this process works more easily for some students than it does for others. For some, schooling is a steady process of refinement and maturation, a relatively smooth transition into the world of education. For others, it is a process marked by cultural dissonance and struggle. And still for others, it is a process of broken dialogue and outright refusal (Phelan, Yu, & Davidson, 1994). The diversity discussion is an inquiry into whom we, as teachers and schools, systematically fail to educate.

Who are the "diverse"? They are the spectrum of students with different learning styles. They are the readers and the nonreaders. They are the young scholars and the young athletes. They are the students whose 50 or so native flags hang in my former school's cafeteria. They are the students with full bellies who are dropped off at school as their parents head to work, and the students who come to school each day hungry and malnourished. These are the diverse, and we are charged with offering them the mythical "level playing field" of the American Dream.

CROSS-CULTURAL EXCHANGE VS. CULTURAL WARFARE

It is a fascinating exercise to use the lens of "cultural interactions" to look at the daily social encounters within a school. How easy it is to open the door of the teacher's lounge and observe, with an anthropologist's cool gaze, discussions among the Teachers about that other tribe, the Students. They talk of the difficult ones, the Students who refuse to stay in their seats, those who won't learn—those who won't accept the norms and values of the Teachers. The Teachers joke about the music of the other tribe, their clothes, their ways of speaking.

On some level, though, teachers are aware of the cultural divide, and attempts are made to cross this gulf. The adults were themselves once children, and in the best classrooms they appreciate and engage the culture of the adolescents they serve. Most teachers are aware that, without such cultural exchange, learning rarely happens. To borrow Frank Smith's (1988) terminology, students need to be "invited into the club" of learning. They need to "buy in" to the overall goals of the classroom, and they need to be equipped with the language used there. Anyone who has ever taught (or even worse, acted as a substitute teacher) knows the terrible wrath of a class full of kids who have not accepted or agreed upon the terms for being "educated."

The diversity conversation is sometimes about cross-cultural exchange, but more often it is about the clash of cultures that occurs when teachers and schools are not able or willing to cross the divide. How can students be invited into the club when they cannot see themselves as members, or when they are denied the tools of membership? How many teachers are aware of the daily realities of the struggling reader, the non-native English speaker, or the student of color? How many teachers are able to invite these students with an authentic voice backed by real promises of support?

It is not even this simple. If it were simply a matter of teachers failing to cross the divide, then perhaps with more training and resources a happy ending would be in sight. The truth is that the diversity conversations probably have more to do with the failures of schools as equitable institutions than with the challenges facing individual teachers.

One of my roles as an eighth-grade teacher in a private urban middle school was to help place my graduating students into college-preparatory high school programs. Each spring I said farewell to my students as they left the intimate setting of their very diverse, very nurturing middle school. Each autumn I awaited their return visits with anxiety. The story was too often the same.

"I just don't get this place…I feel like they speak a different language!" Formerly vibrant, vocal students would return to me, stunned into silence by their new schools. My graduates, many of whom were young men and women of color, children of single parents or parents struggling to get by, felt themselves to be instant foreigners in schools that did not openly acknowledge their status.

Students left my school as conquerors of a rigorous math class and were immediately placed into the mind-numbingly low math track with most of the other students of color. They left my school as loquacious class leaders and returned as "troublemakers," sent to detention for speaking out in class. They left a place where their parents were invited to frequent conferences, to international festivals, to dinners with their teachers and administrators, and they returned with stories of conflicts and disdain.

The most frustrating aspect of these recurring problems was the persistent refusal among the high schools to acknowledge the patterns in these students' experiences. "We treat all of our students equally," was the refrain, and to some degree this was true. However, by equally they meant "the same." The teachers and administrators did not recognize that their evenhanded treatment was an institutional blindness to the different cultural experiences and needs of their students. "Equality" meant testing a Laotian-born young poet, a devourer of novels, and placing her into a remedial English class. Equality is the word of the day when schools plan parent-teacher conferences during a single weekday with no alternative scheduling, blind to the mysterious trend that those who show up are the young, suburban, stay-at-home moms. Equality is the paint-by-the numbers discipline procedure that is so "fair" and "equitable" that the fact that the detention halls are populated almost solely by the young Black boys in a multiracial school is not questioned.

The cultural dissonance between these high schools and the minority students they wanted to serve was profound. In many cases, this took the form of confused struggle—students were failing and the schools couldn't figure out why. In other cases it took the form of open cultural warfare, with the schools bound and determined to make their new charges over into their own image or die trying.

The diversity conversation touched my former school not only from the outside through the voices of graduates but also from the inside in a much more troubling voice. Despite the broad economic, racial, and academic spectrum of our students, our faculty was predominantly middle-class. More significantly, our collective pedagogy had a somewhat traditional, if not conservative, strain running through it. Our very mission was to prepare typically disenfranchised students to leave their community schools and find success in college-prep high schools (sometimes boarding, but almost always with students from the "other side of town"). Over time, a movement arose within the school to examine the implications of our own identity—were we forcing kids to abandon their own cultures in order to be ready for the more homogeneous world of "success"? What were the pitfalls of having a faculty who were not of the community that we served? Were we "skimming the cream" off the public schools, enrolling only the "better" students and furthering the process of academic inequality? These are the questions that began to push our own piece of the diversity discourse. These are the questions that we ultimately failed to answer.

INVITING TEACHERS INTO THE CLUB

It is perhaps one of the great ironies of the education world that teachers make remarkably unruly students. This was never more apparent to me than when I found myself in the position of facilitator of a faculty "diversity training" which took place one summer a few days before our school doors would open for a new year.

Over the course of the previous year, a faction of administrators and teachers had begun to coalesce around the questions of diversity. There was a genuine sentiment of frustration, a feeling that our own school was guilty of a certain degree of hypocrisy. There we were, taking high schools to task for cultural insensitivity and promoting inequity, and yet our own school seemed to be touched by complicity.

Everyone in the group agreed that these were important issues, but consensus was not reached on how to begin the discussion as a whole faculty. Some of us felt that things had to be taken slowly; others felt that no ground would be gained unless we talked frankly about the things we observed around us. None of us were prepared for the degree of resistance that we would eventually meet.

It is not necessary for me to go into all of the gory details. All schools have their legendary faculty meetings, events that rival either a soap opera or a WWF cage match. Ours wasn't quite this extreme, but it had its highlights of teachers walking out of the room in tears and voices being raised in condemnation. More important, the process of naming "diversity issues" within our school led to a steady degradation in the degree of trust and cohesiveness within our faculty.

I am currently in my "year off" from full-time teaching. I'm taking a step back, increasing my skills as a teacher, and reflecting on what I have learned over the past few years. One of the central questions that I find myself struggling with is how my former school's engagement with the diversity conversation could have been different.

My current conclusion is that we as a faculty missed the fundamental rule of teaching. Those of us who were already involved with issues of diversity failed to "invite" our fellow teachers into the conversation. We were the "insiders," and they were on the outside. We wielded a certain language, a vocabulary culled from our private discussions, our readings, and our experiences. Most important, we neglected to recognize the high degree of uncertainty and risk that marked those on the outside. If an outsider were to speak up, he or she ran the risk of saying something wrong, perhaps even of being branded a "racist."

There are so many discussions within the world of education that touch the core of who we are and who we want to be. There are few conversations, however, that contain the vast potential for personal risk that is found in the diversity conversation. It is a conversation with no easy answers, and one that forces us to look at our own complicity in an unjust world. Most important, though, it is too often a conversation with insiders and outsiders.

I am eager to find answers to this dilemma. I have heard the warning call from a fellow student, "What does this diversity thing have to do with me?" but I have yet to hear a convincing response. I don't know what the answer is, but I have a sense of what it must contain. Somewhere within the answer must be the idea that good teaching is about an exchange of cultures. Somewhere must be the notion that we, as new teachers, are inheriting a rich tradition of educational history and wisdom, but one that has an equally long history of exclusion and failure. Somewhere there must be a vision of hope, a vision of what teaching can be within an individual classroom and within the larger institutions of public education. Finally, I'll be looking for the sentiment that *diversity* is not just a word but a vast and a vital conversation within which all of us are privileged to be taking part.

CHAPTER 3

Acknowledging Diversity in the Classroom

Jennifer Steele

Jennifer Steele reminds us how easy it is for all of us to identify with those who are most like ourselves and how important it is to reach beyond the safe boundaries of the familiar to include the experiences of others in our worldview. Readers may want to think about how the process of inclusion/exclusion has operated in their own experience and consider how "difference" can lead to unintended exclusion in the classroom. How might teachers proactively acknowledge students' diverse experiences so that they are accepted as an integral part of the community?

There is a powerful human tendency to gravitate toward people who remind us of ourselves. People who are in some way similar to make us feel safe: We understand their motives, we share some of their experiences. And because we anticipate that they will see some of themselves in us, there is less fear of rejection on the grounds that we have nothing in common.

Difference is harder to negotiate, and yet difference is an unavoidable reality in schools and in the larger society. For many students in elementary and secondary school classrooms, difference yields exclusion: Students form alliances with one another based upon ethnic, academic, or socioeconomic similarities, and even teachers can be guilty of favoring students who are similar to them (McElroy-Johnson, 1993). Because the attraction toward similarity is so strong, teachers often fight an uphill battle to persuade students to acknowledge and appreciate diversity. Before we can be convincing and effective in teaching students to embrace diversity, we have to arrive at an understanding of why it is essential that students learn to thrive in heterogeneous environments.

Teaching an appreciation for diversity should be a primary goal in the classroom for two reasons. First, the classroom is a preparation ground for the working world, and in the world of work, we often don't get to choose our colleagues. Our students have to be skilled at finding common ground for working with those who do not share their experiences or their worldviews. Second, acknowledging diversity and its value is an act of inclusion. Telling students that their uniqueness not only matters but also brings a valuable perspective to the class validates students' experiences. It conveys to them that they do not have to look or talk or think like everyone else in order to be appreciated and welcomed. Inclusion reinforces the self-esteem of all students.

So far I've used the word diversity without defining exactly *how* I'm using it. We often think of diversity in terms of ethnicity—a diverse classroom is one that contains students of many races and ethnic backgrounds. However, I am using the term more broadly here to denote differences in backgrounds (educational, socioeconomic, or geographic), personalities, and beliefs (religious and secular), as well. Our classrooms are microcosms that reflect the larger population; they contain students who differ from one another in terms of socioeconomic class, learning style, family background, religion, sexual orientation, sometimes even age.

When students enter work environments, their intellectual skills will not be the sole determinants of their success. As teachers, most of us have worked with people who thought in very different ways from how we think, who approached problems differently, who were too aggressive or passive or hostile or deferential for our tastes. Yet in order to do our jobs well, we have to learn to get along with those people and work with them toward common goals. Diversity in the workplace includes many layers of difference, but to be stymied by differences is not only inefficient, it is professionally destructive and personally frustrating. We must teach our students to be aware of all kinds of differences, because our classrooms are mirrors of the outside world. Our students will blossom if they know from experience that differences, although valid and important, do not preclude human connection and collaboration.

In addition to preparing our students for the realities of "grown-up" life, teachers need to acknowledge diversity in order to foster students' learning. Students who feel alienated in a classroom will not be productive learners while their attention is diverted from intellectual queries onto the exclusionary social structure. An experience I had as a freshman at Georgetown University illustrates this principle. I graduated from a mostly White, nonaffluent high school in northeast Arkansas, and my transition into the more ethnically heterogeneous but socioeconomically prosperous halls of Georgetown was initially turbulent. I dropped my Southern accent quickly in order to assimilate, but assimilation is not that simple. I recall a freshman honors seminar in which the priest who taught the class stated that he knew most of us hailed from New Jersey or California and that he imagined that we, like most Georgetown students, had traveled the world and experienced foreign cultures thoroughly. Perhaps he thought he was complimenting us; perhaps he was making an ironic joke. If so, the irony was lost on me. What I perceived was that his statement did not include me, and that I somehow did not belong in that classroom. The distance I felt from this professor left me feeling unable to communicate to him my questions and needs, and my grade in that course was significantly lower than my other grades that semester.

It is unfair to blame a professor for an unintended slight, and that is not my intent. Instead, I want to illustrate that when we erase students' unique struggles with broad generalizations, when we are blinded by visions of a homogeneous classroom full of people like us, we alienate those students who don't perceive themselves to be like us. As teachers we have to instead reach out to students who are different from us, ask questions about their backgrounds, and create a space in which they are free to talk from their own perspectives, with the understanding that we all can learn from the experiences and observations of each other.

The challenge for teachers lies in creating this safe space where students can be honest about their backgrounds and experiences without feeling marginalized if their experiences don't match everyone else's. When I first became an English teacher, I was not comfortable asking students to reflect on their own experiences when we talked about texts. This was especially true when I taught in a community college setting with students of widely divergent ages and races. I see this now as my failure, for issues of difference were often sublimated only to pop up unexpectedly during conversations, as when White and Black students disagreed vehemently over a reading of August Wilson's *Fences*, or when a White student told me she was embarrassed to come to class after reading racial slurs in Faulkner's "A Rose for Emily." Our experiences shape our reactions to texts, and although I believe that we can distance ourselves from texts and intellectualize their content, I do not believe that this distancing is always the best way to teach literature. Books act on us and shape us, and that is part of what makes them wonderful. If we ask students to repress their personal reactions, they will disengage. Worse still, if we don't encourage students to acknowledge *to one another* where they are coming from as thinkers and readers, then we create a space for resentment and silence to fester in the minds of those who don't share the majority perspective, whatever that perspective may be.

When we encourage students to be open about their individual experiences and biases, we do run the risk that people's feelings will be hurt. Difference is hard, but it is inevitable. The challenge and reward of acknowledging difference up front lies in realizing that once we sift through what makes us unique, we may uncover in others experiences, dreams, and attitudes that are similar to our own.

Once we discover a common ground, the differences that blanket it will make our shared ideas stronger, more complicated and complete.

By using classroom discussions as a forum for acknowledging and discussing students' diverse experiences, our students learn that difference need not be a silent subtext precluding human connection. It comes back to human nature: People connect with one another and are able to collaborate when they discover commonalities. If students are shown how to use honest dialogue to sort through layers of difference, they won't have to resort to assumptions that people who look or talk or live like they do are the most like them. As teachers, we must let our students teach each other that differences do matter—they shape our perspectives and identities. But they are not the whole story. If we encourage students to share their stories and celebrate their uniqueness, we teach them how to uncover the ties that bind us all.

CHAPTER 4

Swimming Against the Mainstream: Examining Cultural Assumptions in the Classroom

Kristy Garcia

Kristy Garcia grapples with the problems that can occur if multiculturalism is addressed by labeling students as part of a group rather than viewing them as individuals. She discusses the effects that stereotypic assumptions can have on teachers' thinking and planning. Readers may want to consider the ways in which assumptions about identity can influence teachers' actions and students' academic development. How might teachers address identity through curriculum in a sensitive and responsible manner?

Becoming a teacher is one of the hardest tasks I have ever encountered. When I decided to enroll in Stanford's Teacher Education Program, I had no idea that I would end up learning so much about myself or spend so much time grappling with the idea of race, especially the race-oriented dilemmas teachers may encounter in the classroom. I have always identified more with the mainstream, dominant culture because of my "American" upbringing, even as a biracial person who phenotypically resembles my Mexican father more than my Polish mother. This sense of empowerment remained fairly unchallenged until my time at Stanford.

Throughout my educational career, I was able to identify myself as simply a "good" student, not as a "Mexican" student who got good grades, and I gained a sense of empowerment through my learning, both in high school and at

Harvard. I felt that what I was learning was important, and what I had to contribute would be weighed seriously by my peers because we were all on a similar quest of understanding, which involved an equal sharing of ideas and thoughts among our community of learners. My success as a student and my consequential acceptance as an intelligent member of society showed me that I was a person who could make a difference and who had a voice and opinion that would be heard. I felt that I was being valued for my ideas and my thoughts, not that I was being listened to because I was part of a certain group known as Mexican American.

At Stanford, however, I suddenly found myself in an environment where diversity was closely examined and the inequalities in education were scrutinized. Ironically, this made me feel that I might be stuck in a box with all "people of color" who are disadvantaged in our society. Although the continual focus on minority communities and the different cultural attitudes they instill in their students was helpful on many levels, I worried that other Stanford students would take this information as all-inclusive, an experience that all "students of color" share. I felt that I was losing my voice because of my status as a "minority" student, and that some people viewed me as part of a cultural framework I had not claimed. I was forced to become much more aware of how my appearance plays a role in determining how people approach me or interact with me, regardless of how much I want to be judged as an individual and not just as part of a group. This realization, coupled with the fact that student teaching comes with its own set of trials and tribulations, has made the past 10 months of my life one of the most difficult and challenging times I have yet encountered.

Writing this piece has been a struggle because I am aware of the fine lines that exist in discussions about diversity and issues of race. This is not a piece that argues against diversity training or against raising awareness of diversity. It is an account of my personal struggle with the issue of diversity (a term that often comes with a myriad of meanings, but in this particular case addresses the process of examining and validating different cultures) and how these personal struggles have affected my teaching. It is a reflection on the diversity training I have experienced, the messages I think many people may receive from this training, and my fears and trepidation about where these messages could lead.

My purpose is to encourage developing teachers to think about their own approaches to and beliefs about diversity, to seriously examine how these beliefs may affect their students' sense of empowerment, and to think about how they can modify or alter these beliefs for the benefit of their students. In a society like ours that continually receives new groups of people while still harboring a lot of the old conceptions about the people it admits, it is especially important to be aware of how we, as teachers, influence these conceptions and the impact (hidden or realized) we have on our students.

IDENTITY-BUILDING AMID ASSUMPTIONS

This is not the first time I have had to struggle with issues of race and diversity, but it is the first time that I have chosen to examine them seriously and to evaluate the effect these issues have on how I feel I am viewed and how I view others. Throughout my life, I have been aware of my appearance and the difference between me and my brother, who strongly resembles my Polish mother. I have encountered the inevitable questions of "Are you two related?" and "Do you have the same parents?"—comments that I have usually attributed more to genuine curiosity than to any sort of criticism or attempted slur. I have struggled with the dilemma of what to mark for the "Ethnicity" box during standardized tests, feeling that somehow not checking "Mexican American" was dishonest, but not entirely sure that I could identify myself with a group I didn't have much connection to. (I often preferred checking "Other" and writing in "Mexican Polish American" as a way of validating both aspects of my heritage and my upbringing, trying to show whoever actually records those boxes that I was more complex than my last name suggested.)

My high school was fairly evenly divided between Caucasian students and Asian students, as was my group of close friends, and I tended to identify with the other honors and AP students in my classes, who were also primarily Asian and Caucasian. In college, I chose not to become involved with the Mexican American student groups on campus: After one or two sojourns into that arena, I realized that I did not possess the strong Mexican culture that a lot of them did and that instead of feeling as if I belonged, I felt incredibly out of place and awkward. In short, I encountered many of the difficulties that biracial people confront when they attempt to construct their identity—the necessity of choosing a group with which to identify balanced against the constant reminder that many people will automatically identify you as belonging to a certain group no matter where you place yourself.

This identity-building is a process with which our students are struggling to come to terms on a daily basis. Teachers can help in this developmental process by reinforcing positive attributes of their students and getting young people to think more deeply about who they want to be and how to get there. Adolescence is a time when young people attempt to figure out who they are and what they believe. For any adolescent, creating a strong sense of self is an incredibly difficult process, but for adolescents who are biracial or who belong to a group that is identified as "different"—because of race, sexual orientation, or religion—the process becomes even more complex. These teens are not only trying to figure out where they want to place themselves, they are also constantly confronting the assumptions that other people make about them, assumptions often based on what they look like.

Assumptions are a fact of life. People constantly make assumptions about other people, regardless of how well they know each other. We all tend to look at others and instantly place them in a category based on appearances, mentally describing them as "nerdy," "ghetto," "foreign," "stuck-up," "Beverly Hills," "sketchy," or one of numerous other categories. These assumptions usually lead us to treat these individuals in a certain way, often in ways that affect their sense of self. When I was visiting New York recently, I found myself shying away from people on the subway who looked scruffy and unkempt, and instead I situated myself near people who looked more clean-cut or student-like, people I felt were less dangerous because of their more acceptable appearance.

People have walked up to me on quite a few occasions and have started to talk to me in Spanish, assuming my darker complexion meant that I would be able to converse with them in a language I've learned solely through high school and college language classes. I've had people get angry at me when I don't understand the Spanish, indirectly accusing me of abandoning my "mother tongue," even though the only language I've ever spoken fluently is English. I've felt the frustration of being seen as a group member instead of as an individual, based primarily on my appearance, and have experienced the confusion and guilt that arise when I choose to identify with my non-Mexican side, feeling somehow I have betrayed my "true" culture even when I feel that my true culture is American.

FIGHTING ASSUMPTIONS

In my view, assumptions are the most treacherous aspect of life in a classroom. The idea of treating people as members of groups without really getting to know who they are seems counterproductive to the idea of being able effectively to create a student-centered environment by structuring lessons around the particular needs of learners. As teachers, we make dozens and dozens of decisions in a single lesson, basing these decisions on what we know about our students and what we think we know about our students, both as students and as people. We assume that every student feels safe in our classroom just because we are welcoming and sympathetic. We assume that we can create a strong classroom environment in a few months. Sometimes we assume that every student is interested in our subject as much as we are.

We may even look around our classroom and—consciously or subconsciously—separate students into separate groups, often using race as a distinguishing characteristic, and assume that each student identifies with the group he or she resembles. We use these assumptions when we plan our lessons, careful to incorporate multicultural works or perspectives into our activities and lectures, trying to forge a sense of connection between our other-cultured students and ourselves. Although incorporating diverse works and perspectives can be productive, we also need to worry about the messages that may inadvertently be sent to students when we talk and read about cultures other than the mainstream, middle-class, White American culture. These messages depend upon how individuals and cultures are portrayed, how the ensuing discussions unfold, and what classroom participants assume about the generalizability of what they have read.

As teachers, we need to think about the accompanying value judgments that can be communicated, including, perhaps, a sense that other cultures are not on par with American culture and that students "of color" are different and not part of the mainstream. In many ways, by not examining or being aware of these assumptions, we may build a subtle underlying message into our lessons, showing our students what is most valued (mainstream American culture) and what isn't valued as highly (the "others" who do not fall into the American culture category). We cannot assume that merely introducing "other" cultures into the curriculum will ensure that its members will feel more included.

Although attempts to recognize different aspects of American society should not be avoided, it is important to recognize the value judgments that shape the way that "diversity" is portrayed in the classroom. It is very easy to affect students' self-perceptions negatively if multiculturalism is misused. If "other cultures" are merely sprinkled throughout the curriculum for the sake of adding spice, then many students will get the impression that these cultures are secondary and less important than the "real" literature or history they are supposed to learn. To avoid creating assumptions about "dominant" and "subordinate" cultures, it is important that multiculturalism is conveyed consistently with an eye on issues of equity.

TREATING STUDENTS AS INDIVIDUALS, NOT STEREOTYPES

As teachers, we are responsible for giving our students a voice, not for contributing to their silencing. Students are already painfully aware of the role of power in the classroom: They know that the teacher holds the power and that they often have little voice in what goes on in the classroom. Through their classroom experiences, they also learn about the role of power in society, most notably that those who hold the power tend to be of the dominant culture. Many students conclude that if they are not a part of that culture, they will not be in a position to hold power. This can lead some students from minority cultures to try as hard as they can to be seen as individuals, eschewing the culture they've been placed in so that the teacher will acknowledge them as potentially worthy. It can also lead them to feel that they can succeed only if they embrace others' values, even if they don't identify with these values. If students feel frustrated and powerless, they may refuse to take part in the classroom because they don't see what good it can have. The classroom is one of the primary arenas where students learn the language of power and understand the nature of the culture they live in—if they aren't empowered in the classroom, they are unlikely to feel connected to the larger society either.

In my own classroom, I have become much more aware of the assumptions I make when dealing with my students, especially since I have been struggling with these assumptions as a student. I notice my tendency to look at students who more obviously fit into certain ethnic categories in a more stereotypical way, and my tendency to treat students who are more "White" as individuals. Even though I do not like being placed in a certain "box" of values, I find that I have also sometimes placed my students in these same "boxes." It is hard not to do this as a human—categorizing and sorting our environment into a more ordered pattern is a natural tendency for all of us—but we are not always aware of the implications or repercussions this instantaneous categorization may have. For example, if I look at my Chinese and Korean students and think "Asian," I may find myself automatically assigning a set of characteristics to these students in my mind: They are "model" students who are willing to work, they come from very protective families and are pushed hard by their parents, they are either completely conformist or incredibly rebellious.

However, thinking of my students in these terms doesn't help me figure out how to get them engaged in the subject I am trying to teach; it only convinces me to see them as students who will willingly do whatever I decide to assign, no matter how interesting or pointless it is, because they are only at school to earn straight As. Instead of seeing them as individuals—Jenny Kim or Joseph Lin— as I should, I may see them as part of a larger whole—the Asian community— and base my teaching methods around my assumptions about this larger whole, rather than gearing my teaching toward the individuals I have gotten to know in my class, which would be much more effective in successfully teaching them.

I am learning to be aware of these all-too-human tendencies to categorize and assume, and I am very consciously trying to view each of my students as individuals, mostly because I have become increasingly aware of how it feels to be viewed as part of this larger whole. In her book "*Why Are All the Black Kids Sitting Together in the Cafeteria?*," Beverly Tatum (1997) observes that one of the privileges members of the dominant culture enjoy is the privilege of being seen as individuals, not only as members of a larger group. We have been taught by society that there are groups ("people of color") and individuals ("people not of color"), and this is how many of us, even people outside the dominant culture, view the world. Bringing this set of assumptions into the classroom without maintaining an awareness of this worldview will merely perpetuate the distinctions, leaving many students wondering if they are less valued because of their skin color, on the one hand, or feeling guilty and unsure because they don't identify with the group they are "supposed" to belong to, on the other.

I am thoroughly grateful that no teacher looked at me during my educational years and thought about me in terms of my "group," with all of the negative stereotypes that often are assumed: Mexican student, has trouble with the language, won't get very far in life because she's inherently too lazy to apply herself. Being viewed in such a way would have devastated me and convinced me that there was no point in trying because it wouldn't matter anyway. I would have become a silenced student, one of those students who tries to hide by sitting in the back row and participating as little as possible or who starts acting out because he or she doesn't feel valued as a member of the class and is frustrated by this.

One of my strongest fears about how diversity issues are raised within teacher education programs is that developing teachers could view the information they get as applicable to all students in a certain group. The effort to develop awareness of certain issues some students may bring into the classroom – for example, language learning needs, academic difficulties, or side-effects of poverty – could evoke a set of blanket assumptions if blindly applied to students. Teachers could begin to assume that African American or Latino/a students, for example, are necessarily low-income or that they have limited skills, rather than being able to see their strengths and abilities or to acknowledge their actual family circumstances, which may be quite different from the statistical disproportions that are often emphasized.

In turn, this blind application of prejudices could continue to encourage the empowerment of certain students over others. I recognize the need for focusing energy on groups that come from less advantaged backgrounds or don't come to the classroom with certain skills other students may already have. At the same time, I fear that developing teachers could soak in information about diversity and believe that they can merely apply generalizations to their classroom without truly thinking about the students that they are trying to serve. It is important that teachers think in terms of need instead of race: If students need to improve their reading skills, focus on that, don't assume that because they are African American or Mexican American, these skills are already lacking. Take a deeper look at your classroom and truly assess the needs of your students instead of falling back on easy categorizations.

As a developing teacher myself, I understand the temptation to shortcut some areas because creating lessons and trying to keep up with all the other demands of a classroom are incredibly time-consuming and exhaustive tasks by themselves. I also understand that students are more fragile than a lot of us realize and that we have the responsibility of helping them become empowered members of society who feel that what they have to say will be heard and understood. Taking the time to pay attention to your own assumptions and the values you bring into the classroom will help you create an environment where your students feel more comfortable finding their own voice and where they are willing to speak up and explore their own identities, regardless of whether or not these identities correspond with the "mainstream" culture. We cannot expect all of our students to come into our classrooms with this voice already developed, but we must expect ourselves to keep an ear open for voices that are struggling to emerge as well as the ones that already have. As educators, we must focus on helping our students coax these voices to life and refine them so they are proud of who they are and can become empowered, not diminished, individuals.

CHAPTER 5

From the Margins to the Center: Reconstructing the Canon in Social Studies Curriculum

Winter Pettis-Renwick

Winter Pettis-Renwick argues that appreciating diversity entails not only valuing the contributions of marginalized groups but also incorporating their history at the center of a pluralistic curriculum. The chapter describes the author's approach to developing a multicultural teaching unit that accomplishes this goal while connecting to the experiences of students. Readers may want to consider how they conceptualize multiculturalism within their own teaching and how they act upon their ideals.

I began to consider teaching as a career after I changed my college major from biology to history. While I was completing my course work at a community college, I was asked to teach learning skills to small groups of students in the history department. The groups were a wonderful mix of different ages, cultures, and ethnicities. The students were all enrolled in the same American history class, and we studied history as we practiced a variety of learning techniques. We met weekly to discuss and review the class curriculum and to share and learn new study skills.

As we discussed the class's "American perspective" on history, the students were quick to share and compare stories from their own cultural histories. I realized that the sharing of each student's stories and perspectives greatly increased everyone's interest in learning about the subject matter, as they considered the roles we all play in history. By the end of the quarter I was excited by the sense of a communal history that we had created, and I wanted to try to find a way to bring that feeling to high school students.

The students had shown me a richer understanding of American history by first examining it through their own cultural knowledge and experience. Although our discussions often seemed to diverge from the subject at hand, in reality the underlying ideas embedded in the issue were still being discussed. American colonization and the struggle for independence had parallels in the histories of the countries of almost everyone in the room, and a subject like war was universally understood once a student was first given the opportunity to explore his or her own perception of it. This brief experience in the classroom caused me to reflect on my own school experience, and I realized that there were many reasons why my high school classes had failed to engage me. In large part, I was drawn to teaching as a way to keep this exciting dialogue going.

Several of the discussions in the skills class came to mind when I first read Gloria Ladson-Billings's (1994) *The Dreamkeepers*. Ladson-Billings succinctly describes a moment similar to one I felt when I finally entered college: "We sat enraptured as the greatness of Africans and African Americans unfolded for us. Why had it taken so long to learn this? What about all that stuff taught in high school? Were my African American high school classmates who had not gone on to a college that taught these truths condemned to a life of believing that their people had never made anything, had never done anything, are nothing?" (p. 87). I believe the need to learn a sense of one's self is one of the most important purposes of education. If education is to foster self-empowerment, why is the cultural education of minorities and people of color not addressed until college, if at all? Why were the voices of my own culture overlooked by my high school teachers?

As a woman of African American descent I had experienced public education at a time when there was little cultural relevancy in the classroom. In my history class, the curriculum was strong and thorough in its transmission of White American history, ideals, and attitudes; however, I learned little about people or values that I might identify as my own. I had little interest in learning about people and events that had been chosen by some hierarchical school board and that did not include the accomplishments and viewpoints of my own race. The resulting deep sense of exclusion was apparent when I dropped out of high school. Now, years later, I was returning to finish my education. My experience with the study skills class, the exposure to more diverse perspectives at college, and memories of my own school experience encouraged me to consider teaching as a way to bring equity and cultural relevance to the classroom. I realized that I wanted to work with students like myself: those who felt excluded from public education and had not been encouraged to develop a sense of their own competence.

A MULTICULTURAL CURRICULUM
AT THE CORE OF HISTORY TEACHING

How do we make classrooms more culturally relevant and inclusive of diversity? Educational standards have recently been established that support the need for multicultural curriculum. The *California Standards* and the *National Standards for United States History* both include guidelines for diversity in education—an important and belated addition. For example, the *History–Social Science Framework for California Public Schools* (History–Social Science Committee, 1997) states that to achieve the educational goal of cultural understanding and to develop cultural literacy, students must

> Develop a multicultural perspective that respects the dignity and worth of all people. Students should learn from their earliest school years that our nation is composed of people whose backgrounds are rooted in cultures around the world. They should develop respect for the human dignity of all people and an understanding of different cultures and ways of life. (p. 15)

U.S. history includes a number of movements, changes, and improvements that are the result of the efforts of women, people of color, youth, sexually diverse peoples, immigrants, language minorities, and other traditionally excluded groups. This rich history can be used to help invite students into the historical dialogue and allow them to connect with the essential ideas of history. Students can be assigned to explore the development and outcomes of a variety of historical and current events, from the role of women in the revolutionary war to the current fight to reclaim Native American water rights.

Providing a balance of culturally diverse viewpoints can also increase students' understanding of and interest in history. For example, when the students in my community college history skills class were first exposed to American history, they found little that they could understand or relate to. At our first meeting, when they found themselves frustrated with their understanding of the Puritans, we began talking instead about the different groups that we were familiar with in our communities. Several students shared their own insights and stories about groups that had suffered religious persecution, families that chose to band together economically, and individuals who judged the behavior of others. Several of the suggestions provided a starting point for a better understanding of the beliefs of the Puritans. More of the students joined the discussion and ventured views on why they felt the Puritans should be successful in the new world; others listed reasons they felt the Pilgrims did not deserve to do well.

The addition of a variety of cultural perspectives brought new facets to the topic. The Puritans had seemed one-dimensional until the students compared these early settlers' essential beliefs to their own. Now everyone had an opinion, and suddenly a topic that had earlier been dismissed as "stupid" was being debated by the whole group. The learning started to take. Later in the quarter, some of the students in the class used the Puritans in comparisons when they discussed other issues of history.

HISTORY AS THE PLACE WHERE STUDENTS CAN FIND—OR LOSE—THEMSELVES

Providing students with a sense of empowerment is another important reason for the inclusion of cultural diversity. When history is presented in an "important people only" format—that is, as the study of people from dominant cultures who accomplish acts deemed worthy of inclusion in written history—students may begin to feel excluded from their role in history.

The *National Standards for United States History* (National Center for History, 2000) describe how a lack of informational equity can affect students:

> Denied knowledge of one's roots and of one's place in the great stream of human history, the individual is deprived of the fullest sense of self and of that sense of shared community on which one's fullest personal development as well as responsible citizenship depends. (p. 2)

As a high school student in the California school system, I will always remember how the inclusion of African Americans in the subject matter seemed so disingenuous to me. There was often a sidebar mention of a famous Black American in the textbook; in February, the Black History Month bulletin board would be set up in the hallway with a few paragraphs and pictures.

This lack of access to equitable information led me to believe that there had been a deep lull in the notable achievements of African Americans somewhere between my history teacher's mention of Crispus Attucks and his discussion of Rosa Parks. My sense of historical exclusion was furthered by the teacher's presentation of both Attucks and Parks as "accidental heroes," that is, individuals disconnected from any broader struggle of their people. This devaluation of the people with whom I identified resulted in my own disillusionment with my required history courses.

Students can also find themselves in history, when teaching is organized to draw them in. Cultural inclusion can be a key to maintaining students' interest in and commitment to school. Bringing previously marginalized groups onto the center stage of the classroom can help to recreate the historical canon so that it is the study of all peoples. A beautiful example of student inclusion was demonstrated by several of my teaching program classmates in a practicum course. The five—Claudia Narez, Lynda Taylor, Paloma Garcia-Lopez, Jennifer French, and Lydia Mongia—taught a lesson that modeled a way to use multicultural sensitivity and understanding in the teaching of immigration. The lesson began with the students sharing stories about their families' moves in small groups and using colored markers to trace the destinations on a transparent map of the world. As the groups were brought back into a whole-class discussion, the maps were collected and layered atop each other on the overhead projector. The combined maps were filled with hundreds of colored lines that stretched all over the world. Projected together, the maps provided evidence of the students' own immigration while it also served to underscore the rich diversity of the students in the room. We were discussing diversity and immigration even before we realized that it was intended to be the essential idea of the lesson. Furthermore, because the teachers chose to begin with a visual representation of historical inclusion, the image on the wall made every student aware of the role that they played in the lesson to come.

Fortifying the Curriculum

Inclusive curriculum design allows students to wrestle with key ideas while studying a broad array of subjects. Grant Wiggins and Jay McTighe (1998) argue that effective lessons are best structured by choosing essential questions and layering them within the instructional content to encourage student-generated discovery or "uncoverage" of ideas. Active learning is achieved when students uncover and examine for themselves the ideas that undergird an event. Essential questions provide a framework that allows for the presentation of multiple perspectives. This premise relieves teachers from being constrained to a single historical time period when choosing to focus class study on a particular group. Thus diversity can be included in world history, government, English, and economics classes as well as other subject areas.

When history is presented as the study of a diverse society, there is a greater likelihood of student understanding and involvement. In a high school history class, my cooperating teacher, Helen Kim, designed a lesson that required students to read materials that represented the status and desires of different groups at the time of the American Revolution: women, African Americans, poor colonists, congressional members, and Native Americans. The students were given the readings in groups, and they shared the information in a round-table discussion the next day. We provided suggested questions—such as "What was your role?" "Why did you fight?" "What did you hope to gain?"—and encouraged the students to dig for more information. By analyzing the assigned readings and sharing the information, the students uncovered many of the tensions of this time period for themselves. For example, during the discussion the students uncovered some intriguing paradoxes, such as the fact that northern

Blacks tended to fight for the colonists whereas many Southern Blacks fought for the British. The students were then motivated to investigate further the reasons for these differences. The understanding of the differences in life for northern and southern Blacks or rich and poor colonists was essential for the unit. The practice of questioning helped the students to learn to identify problems by asking critical questions and then having to investigate, gather, and synthesize information to draw conclusions. Thus the students uncovered the goals of the participants in the revolutionary war while they used the occasion to further develop their analytical skills.

James A. Banks (1993) suggests that students also evaluate and reinterpret historical materials with sources of alternative perspectives to identify and understand the biases of the writer. Assigning students to create their own interpretations can improve students' analytical and research skills through knowledge construction and encourage students to examine and question the biases they may encounter in accounts from different sources. In my student teaching classroom, a 10th-grade U.S. history class, my cooperating teacher and I worked to incorporate all of these goals for our students' learning.

An assignment to create a 2-week unit for my curriculum and instruction class allowed me the opportunity to practice multicultural curriculum design. Helen worked with me to create many of the lessons in my unit on the Great Migration and the Harlem Renaissance. The first half of the unit focused on the Great Migration. I wanted to give equal time to the importance of the first large voluntary African American migration in America. I chose to use essential questions that allowed the students to consider choices that their own parents and grandparents may have made. I chose several questions because they were universal and would have relevance for students who had emigrated from other countries: Why do people move? Can migration cause change? What was it like for the people who migrated? How did it affect the places they left? How did it affect the places they came to?

My overall goal was to help the students to understand the beginnings of the African American movement to achieve freedom and opportunity for self-expression, a key ingredient to a true understanding of the creation of democracy in America. I used additional questions that focused on this particular movement: How did the Great Migration affect the lives of African Americans? What were the short-term and long-term effects? Did the Great Migration change American society?

The ongoing assessment of the unit was a collection of students' journal entries, constructed as each student created a character from a southern state and wrote about the stages of his or her life before and after the journey north. The unit began with a discussion about the reasons why people move, and several of the students shared stories about their family's moves from other states and countries. We later listened to firsthand, audiotaped accounts of life in the south and discussed the stories we heard. The students compared the descriptions on the tape with their experiences in their own community. For example, the tape described the strong sense of community that had developed among Blacks in the south, and a student mentioned that her mother had felt "a less-social change in the community" since she had moved to California.

The oral histories were also included when we examined the move north and life in the cities. One recorded story told of a northern African American store clerk who treated a recently migrated African American employee unfairly. The female speaker said, "Sometimes it's just like we were all crabs in a barrel." This comment encouraged the students to express their feelings about times that they felt betrayed or unaccepted by others. The students were asked to write in their journals about their characters' experiences when they arrived in the north and were encouraged to include details that they had learned from class readings and activities. This journal entry, typical of many others, shows how students combined imagination with the facts we had studied into interesting narratives:

> We can barely make ends meet. I have gotten work but I can't get any of the better paying jobs, because I cannot make my color go away. I am treated poorly and remain the same way. We now live in the area allowed to us as we cannot live by the white people. The laws and place may have changed, but the policy "separate but equal" still remains. We have been shuffled to a new injustice in order to be workers in factories instead of plantations.

The Harlem Renaissance curriculum in social studies was linked to the curriculum in the students' American literature class. This allowed students to extend their study on life during the Harlem Renaissance. The essential questions were: How did the Harlem Renaissance affect the lives of African Americans? What influence did it have on society as a whole? Was this movement inclusive or exclusive? Who was excluded? Were there lasting effects of the Harlem Renaissance?

In the literature class the students watched a documentary on Zora Neale Hurston, they then read the short story "Jelly's Tale" and created a slang dictionary. They also responded to several primary source readings and analyzed, memorized, and performed a poem. In the history class we listened to music, watched videos, and discussed readings to prepare for their journal entries. Each student was assigned a person from the Harlem Renaissance, and they did computer searches to explore and choose their character. As they collected information and wrote as their character in their journals, they were also preparing to portray their character at a Harlem Renaissance party.

During the party the students shared facts about their assigned people and collected the ideas of others. They used graphic organizers to collect information about W. E. B. DuBois, Jean Toomer, Langston Hughes, and Zora Neale Hurston: Where were they raised and educated? What were their responses to racism and segregation? After the party the class reviewed all of the documents that they had collected over the course of the unit. I asked the students to use their information as evidence for an essay on the changes that we still see today. We talked about rappers and church communities; famous sports stars, and poor neighborhoods with potholes.

One of my own key concerns in compiling the Great Migration–Harlem Renaissance unit was to provide the students with an opportunity to examine the relevant facts in an important time of change for a large segment of the American population. The students explored and wrote about the lives of everyday Americans just as they later examined and wrote biographies of the famous participants. They compared the effects of a small, well-known artistic movement with a large, little-known physical movement. They brought in stories from their own lives and communities to add to their understanding of these two events, and the final assessment included the opportunity to write a journal and share their opinions of how the Great Migration and the Harlem Renaissance have affected life today. One student's final essay included this observation:

> One of the changes that we still see today is African American writers are still taking a stand in what they believe in and what they write. So many poets and writers have come out to speak their minds and to write what they think about their lives and how racism sometimes gets in the way of their success.

History as the Study of All Peoples

Although the history canon is still evolving, and there is now a greater inclusion of race and segregation as topics beyond the study of slavery and civil rights, there is still a tendency simply to add a few famous minorities to the lecture notes rather than refocusing to offer a study of a time of great change for a minority group. For me, the central problem lies in the way we have traditionally chosen to incorporate diverse peoples and perspectives into the curriculum—as adjuncts to the main story rather than as a central part of the story itself. Mentioning only famous individuals ignores the true panorama of human life. Studying events that are important to different groups, and examining their worldviews and contributions, is a key aspect of providing students with a thorough understanding of history.

Addressing diversity in the curriculum is a challenging task. Teaching for diversity means more than simply presenting curriculum materials that represent the ethnic makeup of a classroom. As a teacher of U.S. history, I feel that America's culture is more than a melting pot; it is the result of the dialectic action of the many groups that make up the American landscape. The growth, movement, inclusion, or suppression of any group creates changes in the fabric of American society. These changes *are* our history.

While arguing the need for the melding of multicultural education perspectives with traditional democratic educational ideas, Geneva Gay (1997) remarks that "The lives of the citizens of the United States, individually and collectively, are inextricably interrelated and what happens to one invariably affects the other" (p. 5). U.S. History is a product of the lives and cultures of all of the people who make up the country's social fabric. The central message to our students should be that all people create history—and that includes them.

Part II

DOES WHO WE ARE INFLUENCE HOW WE TEACH?

Jennifer French

I wondered whether I, a White, middle-class, prestigiously educated woman, could have any effect teaching in an under-privileged, minority environment…

—A student teacher

Does our identity influence what kind of school—White, upper-class, underprivileged, racially diverse, rural, urban—we teach in? How much does our personal identity influence our pedagogies and our everyday practices? How do we develop a broader professional identity that extends beyond our personal experiences growing up and incorporates a commitment to teaching for social justice? Answering these questions requires teachers to think about their students, their curriculum, their instruction, and their own identity. Yet, to truly begin to answer questions about identity and teaching, a dialogue must exist among people of different races, genders, religions, and sexual orientations.

In our teacher education program, we found engaging in dialogue on identity issues to be extremely challenging. Each time a conversation on race, gender, sexual orientation, or social class began, the room temperature went up: Some people became angry, others shut down, some became defensive, others felt misunderstood, and some people didn't quite understand what was going on. How can this conflict—which is inevitable when honest sharing occurs—turn into a positive learning and growth experience for all participants?

We found that it is important to treat the examination of these questions of identity and commitment as a dynamic *process*. Over time, relationships are slowly built and the discussions move to a deeper level. In-depth identity and social change discussions require vulnerability. When people make themselves vulnerable, there must be opportunities to come back to the discussion. Otherwise, individuals who discuss their experiences and emotions may find themselves feeling isolated and less supported for who they are and what they believe in.

Our own process of engaging in dialogue on identity and social change issues is embedded in the six pieces that constitute this section. The vulnerability in each of these pieces is striking: All of the authors openly disclose their own identity and philosophies, as well as their struggles. The willingness to share personal vulnerability that you read and feel in these pieces is a result of a process that occurred over a full year in which relationship building, sharing, and listening occurred across and within races, genders, religions, and sexual orientations. These pieces—and the growth processes they represent—inform each other. Much of the thinking about the issues raised in these pieces would not have occurred without our commitment to these long, often difficult, sometimes traumatic discussions.

It is our hope that, by reading and discussing the stories of these six authors, the process of establishing a safe environment for an identity discussion can begin in schools and in teaching programs. Although each reader may not fully identify with each author's experience due to his or her race, religion, sexual orientation, gender, or class, the feelings demonstrated by each of these authors create places where all readers can connect.

Each of these pieces raises different issues, yet all speak to a common theme of working to find ways to promote social justice and equity in schools and society. They all illustrate how important identity is in teaching and within our larger communities and society. As a collection, they exhibit how vital it is for teachers to share their own stories regarding identity. It is also our intent that these pieces be used to encourage deep thought and discussion on how our own race, gender, sexual orientation, and religion may grant us privilege or subject us to oppression in different arenas of our lives.

In the first piece of this section, Kristin Traudt addresses a widely shared question, "Can White teachers effectively teach students of color?" with an examination of her students' experiences and perspectives and insights into her own process of learning to teach diverse students well.

Next, Carlo Corti, a social studies teacher, addresses how gender and race can create power dynamics that impact the classroom and how teachers can make a difference in how students treat each other. Corti, like the other authors in this section, uses his own identity and experiences as a basis for understanding his students and developing strategies to help them learn to treat each other well. Jennifer French broadens the scope of identity by addressing sexual orientation. She discusses what it means for gay and lesbian teachers and students to feel safe and included in the classroom and in the educational system.

Several authors expand the dialogue to include how our identities as teachers of subject matter can advance an equity agenda. Ryan Caster describes how the oppressive use of anti-Semitic and homophobic language in his classroom convinced him of the importance of English teachers explicitly preparing to teach the "Big Lesson"—the lesson about the power of words to connect or destroy. Grace Bang illustrates how, through her own history and identity as a Korean American, family history and identity are intertwined in her decision to become an English teacher—enabling others, like herself, to master the language of power in this society. Finally, Silvia Paloma Garcia-Lopez ends this section by focusing on her identity as a Mexican American social studies teacher. Garcia-Lopez interweaves her own story of facing inequities in education with the experiences of her students and describes her efforts to transform curriculum and school culture.

The following questions may help to encourage discussion in this section:

How do my experience and my identity influence my teaching philosophy?

How can I incorporate my own and my students' social identities into my work as a teacher of mathematics, science, English, social studies, foreign language, or other discipline and as a teacher of primary students, secondary students, or adults?

What does it mean to a student to feel safe and included in the classroom and on campus?

How might teachers act to increase all students' sense of psychological safety and inclusion?

How can teachers with differing identities build alliances for social justice?

How does language impact the classroom? What can we do about it as teachers?

How can we move beyond classroom management to teach tolerance and respect in classrooms?

What is a teacher's responsibility in confronting the way that society socializes some people to privilege and others to exclusion?

As you read and discuss the pieces in this chapter, please remember that you are not alone in grappling with issues of identity and teaching. Keep in mind that the values of this struggle are weighty and powerful. Relationships are built and alliances are formed when individuals speak openly and actively listen to one another. This process also encourages self-reflection and makes us better teachers and advocates for social change. We invite you to join us in the exciting process of engaging and exploring identity issues.

CHAPTER 6

Survey Says...:
Can White Teachers Effectively
Teach Students of Color?

Kristin Traudt

Kristin Traudt explores a common question: How can White, middle class teachers support the learning of their students from very different backgrounds? She shares what she has learned through a process of reflecting on her own identity, expanding her knowledge base, and examining the experiences and perspectives of her students. Readers may want to reflect on their own autobiographies and consider means for developing trust and understanding with students whose backgrounds are different from their own.

> A glass window stands before us. We raise our eyes and see the glass; we note its quality, and observe its defects; we speculate on its composition. Or we look straight through it on the great prospect of land and sea and sky beyond.
> —Benjamin B. Warfield, *Some Thoughts on Predestination*

At times I am Warfield's glass window, carefully examined. I notice both my qualities and defects. I know that my students, their parents, and my colleagues speculate on my "composition," as Warfield puts it, especially in terms of my abilities to teach in a diverse classroom. As a White, heterosexual female, I hope I am seen as an equitable teacher. Yet I know that some may see my race and beliefs as obstacles to my ability to teach students of diverse backgrounds. In fact, while attending Stanford University's Teacher Education Program (STEP), I encountered diversity in new ways. Many of my colleagues' stories in this book brought me new insights, not only into teaching, but also into life. For the first time I learned about struggles that minority students experience in classrooms across the United States, about ELD (English Language Development) "ghettos" that segregate English Language Learners in many high schools. Prior to STEP I had read about the disparities in treatment of African Americans, Latinos, and other ethnic groups in the United States, but it was not until discussing it with my colleagues that I began to picture the real pain and suffering involved in each case. After teaching students who fit these descriptions, I became aware of the unspoken privileges that I have had throughout my own education and life because of the color of my skin and my sexual orientation.

As part of the process, I questioned my ability to teach a diverse student population. As I examined my teaching, I felt that students and peers were making assumptions that were not true about me based on stereotypes that fit my outward characteristics. The scrutiny paralyzed me. Eventually, however, like Warfield, I began to look straight through a glass to analyze diversity in the classroom. I found it important to look beyond my "composition," at who I am inside in order to see and embrace "the great prospects of land and sea and sky beyond." I needed to understand the concept of looking through a window as it pertains to both teachers and students. If I did not look through the glass at who each of my students is as an individual, diversity would continue to separate me from my students. By recognizing and understanding my background and how my cultural experiences inadvertently affect my teaching, I am more ready and able to bridge chasms in the classroom caused by diversity that might otherwise create barriers.

My experience as a female White teacher at American High School in San Jose, California moved the theoretical discussions from my seminars at Stanford to my own high school classroom. Before I moved to Stanford, I had visited, studied and worked in Western and Eastern Europe, Mexico, and Costa Rica. After responding to a strong call to teaching, I was surprised by the culture shock I experienced in Northern California. Moving from a corporate sales position in suburban Chicago to pursue a teaching career through a West Coast teacher education program was a big change. The experience of simultaneously becoming a graduate student and student teacher in California had an enormous impact on me.

With little time to acculturate to my surroundings, I began student teaching at a diverse middle school in Sunnyvale, California. I loved my first class of students, most of them excited about attending middle school for the first time. I taught African American, Chinese, Filipino, Indian, Latino, and Caucasian students who came from a wide spectrum of local towns representing low-income and high-income families. But the 19 days together in summer school only gave me a glimpse of the adventures and exciting teaching experiences I had in store for me at my year-long student teaching placement, where I would actually learn more about my students' rich cultures.

As I discussed my placement with the student-teaching placements coordinator, I knew that, above all else, I wanted a teaching experience different from my own high school environment. I grew up in Wisconsin and attended a predominantly White high school in the rural/suburban greater Milwaukee area, and although I came from a struggling middle class family of six kids, I attended school in an affluent area. Throughout high school, I balanced working responsibilities with academic, extracurricular, and social activities. At times I felt that I did not fit in, when my friends wore expensive clothes, drove fancy cars, and were able to participate in several after-school activities—things I could enjoy only in moderation because of my part-time jobs. However, I could hide my feelings of alienation. If I chose to, I could spend my money to improve my wardrobe and mimic the lifestyles of my friends.

Although My High School (MHS) prepared me academically, socially, and, to some extent, culturally, I realized that my education was Eurocentric, from history and English classes to languages and peer interactions. Sharing the same experience, my Korean friend, Flora, hardly complained about her identity or role in a nearly all-White school. Later in life she reconnected with the Korean heritage she had undervalued and nearly forgotten. But LeCrisha, one of the two African American students at our school, spoke out about not fitting in. Most of the time, LeCrisha was funny, but sometimes teachers considered her comments disruptive and a nuisance. At times like these it seemed that the teachers saw her concerns about social disparities as complaints that could simply be dismissed. I recall an in-class discussion with LeCrisha in which she complained about her lack of companionship and camaraderie; she did not even have someone she could relate to regarding hair and cosmetic issues, and she couldn't find someone to date at our school. At cross-country practice, LeCrisha shared with me the crushes that she had on some guys at our school, but nothing would ever develop out of those crushes because students at MHS did not date interracially. From my perspective as a student, I think our all-White staff of teachers did not validate her feelings; instead of openly discussing the societal issues with which she and many others struggled, they made it seem to the class that she was complaining.

DIRECTING MY QUESTIONS TO TEACHING

Ten years later, as I began to assume responsibility for my own class, I questioned the teaching with which I was familiar. It seemed that some teachers thought diversity issues would go away if they dismissed and ignored them. But interactions with classmates, readings, and, most important, a diverse student population in which Whites represent only 13% of the student body have helped me develop a heightened awareness of diversity. I respected and appreciated each person as an individual, regardless of sexual orientation, racial, ethnic, or social background. I wanted to provide equal access to education for all students, free from biases and prejudices. However, I did not realize how complicated it can be to create a safe, equitable classroom that fosters respect, tolerance, and appreciation for all individuals. It does not happen automatically; rather, it requires patience, communication, interest, and vulnerability. Although it may sound like a cliché, it seemed that the more I read, heard, and learned from others about teaching for diversity in the classroom, the less adequate I felt at meeting my goals.

As we discussed teaching for diversity at STEP, I wondered how I was affecting my students' lives. Had I created a safe learning environment for them? Was I showing my students respect for their cultures, their individuality? I questioned whether I supported the student who wanted so badly to develop and to be herself, yet who also felt the need to conform to classroom norms and the U.S. high school culture. In my ELD classes, when I asked students to be quiet during class, was I squashing their social development? Was I silencing my students? Was I isolating them when I spoke too quickly and students like Dianne, a freshman who had recently moved to the United States from China, could not understand me? Some of these questions related specifically to teaching my intermediate ESL class, but they could also be valid in any classroom. Although I did not have answers to all of the questions, exploring them has helped me develop an awareness toward my students' needs that is reflected in the lessons and units I have planned to engage my student population.

CREATING SOLUTIONS IN CURRICULUM DESIGN

During my student-teaching assignment, my cooperating teacher and I established a safe learning environment through our recognition of students' voices, the creation of norms of respect, and our choice of curriculum materials. Throughout the year, I became more sensitive to issues of diversity in my curriculum planning. In January, my American literature class at AHS read *The Great Gatsby*, a story about young men and women from the Midwest who live on Long Island, New York. Gatsby is wealthy and hosts many parties for his "friends" as he pursues his "American Dream." I wondered whether my students could relate to him and the other characters in the book. How would my students who come from the Philippines, China, Mexico, Nicaragua, Germany, and from African American and Native American backgrounds living in San Jose,

California, identify with this book? What about their cultural texts?

In a discussion with a colleague, I realized that the biggest hurdle in teaching *The Great Gatsby* was to hook my students, to make the unit relevant to their personal lives. First, we explored general history about the 1920s through a self-designed web game. My students were comfortable with the medium and excited about the unit. As we read the story, through journal prompts I asked students to relate conflicts in the story to conflicts in their own lives. Then, through a self-reflective essay, I challenged my students to discover and examine their own American Dreams. I wanted them to realize who they are and to identify what is important to them. The project also included an interview with a parent or a mentor, in which many students realized the sacrifices their families had made for them. What were their parents' American Dreams? What had they done to achieve them? How were my students a part of their dreams?

While many of the students did well exploring those questions, during the discussions, a whole new question developed for me. As they talked about the American Dream, some removed themselves and seemed to consider themselves outsiders. Even with that unexpected reaction, students were engaged throughout the unit because they felt a connection to the themes and the people. In hindsight, though, I felt I needed to explore these questions in order to make the material relevant to my students.

THE UNIQUE ROLE: THE TEACHER AS STUDENT

As I navigated my first unit, I was caught off guard by new questions and reactions, because part of my role as a STEP student called me to explore the depths of my own personal identity. What makes me who I am? Is it my parents? Is it my background? When I wrote my personal statement in Chicago, I answered those questions with certainty; I also talked excitedly about working with a diverse student population. Now that I was in the middle of it, had I really understood what my aspirations meant? Although I may not have prejudices against my students and colleagues, what sort of preconceived ideas did I bring to them and they to me? What stereotypes did I labor under as a female, White, Stanford graduate student/teacher?

During a quick-write exercise in one of my graduate seminars, we were asked to respond to the prompt, "Who am I?" As I began to think of words that would describe me, I realized how many labels could separate me from my peers. If I labeled myself as a female, would the men in my class feel a barrier? If I said "White," would that color separate me from my colleagues and friends of different ethnic origins? What troubled me most was if I claimed the label "Christian," would I be closing a door to my colleagues who held different beliefs? This became one of the most difficult moments I had at STEP. I did not want people I had known only as acquaintances to consider me judgmental or conservative. As I struggled through the process, I wondered whether my inhibitions came from a fear of rejection or if I was denying my faith. Later I realized that I am not ashamed to admit that I am a Christian, but I prefer to have people find out through my actions or through knowing me, not by my claiming that label, because my views will be different from those of some other Christians, and I don't want to be stereotyped.

When it came time to share, I had written only two sentences and I left the adjectives out. "I am the daughter of Richard and Barbara Traudt. I am a teacher who believes in quality, equitable education for all." Although this was a very personal struggle for me, it helped me realize that I had a choice in the matter, whereas some distinguishing characteristics—like race, sex, and perhaps socioeconomic backgrounds—are not a matter of choice. I began to understand how deep the chasm separating groups can be, and I truly valued open conversations and forums that we had throughout the year as they helped us build bridges to understanding. My teacher education program was powerful in moments like these, when student teachers were able to confront issues from the unique perspective of both student and teacher. There were many times during the year that I walked away from lessons concerning diversity with more questions than answers, and with more feelings of doubt than feelings of confidence that my teaching could ever transcend the barriers of diversity in education. Now I realize that was an inevitable part of the process.

DEVELOPING STRATEGIES FOR EQUITY-BASED TEACHING

Fortunately, I had a great model to demonstrate effective teaching that honored diversity in the classroom in my cooperating teacher (CT). During first semester I helped lead an assignment where students performed skits confronting prejudice on campus. When one of my good-natured students used a stereotypical gesture to portray a gay man, I did not confront him. Instead of addressing it, I carelessly laughed with my students at his acting a different role, without realizing the hurtfulness of my response. Fortunately, my CT knew better. He asked the student, "Why did you add that hand gesture?" He then explained how this cast the person in a stereotype, which can be hurtful. The student was apologetic, but not damaged, and an important message was communicated within the classroom.

Even with the confidence I felt with *The Great Gatsby,* I still had to grow during the second semester. With so many things to be aware of while student teaching, how could I look out for and stand up for diversity in our school? At times I felt so isolated, so ignorant. Afraid that I might offend someone, especially when I may be dealing with some of these issues for the first time, myself, how could I respond or raise issues? Bombarded with articles and discussions at STEP about the cultural relevance of teaching, I was interested in hearing what my students felt I was missing, what it was that I could not see. As the year progressed and I began to feel more equipped with tools for teaching, such as pedagogical tactics, curriculum, and an understanding of adolescent and cognitive development, I gained more confidence in my ability to teach and encounter diversity. Teaching became less of a guessing game and more of a profession.

Multicultural week at the high school was a perfect opportunity to hear from my students. After an incredible assembly that celebrated the diversity at AHS, I asked my students to respond to a survey that asked how diversity, or the lack thereof, affects education. On the optional survey my students expressed a wide range of views in response to questions of how culture, ethnicity, and diversity among the teaching staff affect their relationships with their teachers. From the survey I learned that, for most students, it is more important that teachers respect and value them as individuals than that they be of the same race as the student. For example,

> I think none of those factors affect your relationship with a teacher. What affects your relationship with your teacher would be the way that he or she treats and teaches you. When a teacher respects me, I respect him [her].

> It doesn't matter as long as the teacher treats everybody equally, no matter what race they are.

Many students also acknowledged the importance of having diverse teaching staffs, so that students could bond with teachers with whom they share similar cultures, backgrounds, and values. Here again, students were clear that their main goal was to be understood and accepted, something they felt was more likely from teachers with whom they share a cultural bond, but not exclusively so. These responses were representative:

> Culture, ethnicity, and diversity amongst the staff can sympathize for the backgrounds of their students and tend a little more to their needs. It could be that the students do not know English or simply explaining a better understanding.

> A strong student-teacher bond is more convenient for both the students and teacher. If I had a teacher of the same ethnicity as I, I would be able to share a bond with them. They would know and accept my family background.

> Diversity amongst teachers and students would make student-teacher

relationships easier. A student coming from the same background as their teacher would have an easier time relating to them. Diversity shouldn't necessarily matter between teacher and student relationships, but it does. I would feel more comfortable with a teacher who understood me. It does not have to exactly be by ethnicity, but more by actions.

Unfortunately, some students also felt discriminated against and alienated by teachers.

Well, culture and ethnicity are very important to me. Because just like anyone in the student body of AHS, all want to be welcomed and respected. When we talk about ethnicity and culture that's like talking about you. And you want people to respect you, which means your culture and ethnicity. If my teacher is racist and doesn't like me very much, he/she can fail me in her class. Because she is the powerful one who holds my grade, she can fail me. This may affect my learning because of my teacher, I may cut her class all the time because she tortures me. I wouldn't want to be tortured now. So I do something to avoid him/her.

Teachers here can be prejudiced. Most teachers I know favor girls, for some reason. They also think like some kids are bad just by the way they are dressed. I know those people and they are really smart. It's just that they are like, "the teacher is hating on me so why should I do my work?" So that might be why a lot of kids drop out. [Some teachers] do not understand that they might be hurting a student inside. So diversity can be a factor in stopping a student from doing their best in school.

This perception of prejudice creates a destructive legacy throughout a school. In my own experiences, I saw that often when there could be 10 things contributing to a situation involving a student and a teacher, one of the 10 being racial differences, race was often immediately viewed as the source of the problem. If this perception is not further addressed, both teachers and students tend to back down from the real issues and accept the conflict as a nonsolvable racial divide. Fortunately, most students also reported positive experiences in which both students and teachers benefited from each other's different perspectives, experiences, and backgrounds when shared in a trusting, respecting, and caring classroom.

As I reflect on my year of teaching and at STEP, a seminar structured around context, culture, and learning impacted my teaching most significantly. Perhaps because I grew up in the Midwest and taught at a diverse school on the east side of San Jose, a reading by Gloria Ladson-Billings (1994) followed by discussions we had in a small group challenged the cultural relevancy of my teaching. From these discussions I realized that I may never be able fully to understand what my students of different ethnicities experience in the U.S. educational system, but I can be aware of the struggles, develop a curriculum that is sensitive to diverse needs, and listen—thereby mounting tiny efforts to transcend a cultural barrier and to prevent obstacles in learning.

Without the opportunity to apply these ideas immediately to practice, educational theory and controversial discussions would lose their relevance. Without feedback from students and different theoretical lenses to view teaching in practice, teaching would seem unpredictable and happenstance. Instead, through conducting this survey, reflecting on my own experiences, and applying theory to practice, I have gained new insights into diversity within the context of teaching and learning. Furthermore, I acquired a new understanding of how to teach subject matter in a way that engages and benefits every student.

BEYOND THE SURVEY

When I first considered teaching, I was discouraged by the fact that my success as a teacher depended upon the success of my students. Although I thrive on seeing students succeed, I was intimidated because I thought that so much of teaching was a matter of whether students connected with their teachers. Knowing that not every student will connect with his or her teacher—more specifically, that not every student will connect with me—I worried that diversity would construct barriers that would keep my students from learning and keep me from being successful. However, the more I learned about teaching through my peers, my courses, and my experience, the more I realized that teaching is not just a matter of connecting or not connecting. Instead, teaching is understanding that there are specific elements of learning, like cultural relevance of material, teachers' knowing their subject matter deeply, and preparing and scaffolding materials to make information accessible to students. By using technology and these teaching tools, while also focusing on establishing a community, I have learned that when accompanied with a general respect for students as individuals, teaching is no longer the guessing game I once thought it was.

While writing this chapter, I have grown as a teacher and learner. Sharing my questions and concerns about diversity in the classroom with my peers and students has not only helped me develop a sensitivity and passion for creating safe, equitable classrooms for every individual; it has also helped me better understand who I am and who my students and colleagues are. This journey continues to help me overcome my fears and inhibitions. Most important, I have learned to question my teaching in ways that will help me teach more effectively. I have learned to step back and look critically at my teaching through theoretical lenses, my peers' viewpoints, and the minds of my students.

CHAPTER 7

Finding Myself in My Students: A Step Toward Transforming Social Dynamics in the Classroom

Carlo Corti

This chapter describes how the author, through his own process of personal reflection, addresses issues of White male privilege in the classroom, confronts students
who exhibit oppressive language and behavior, and works to model tolerance,
social support, and inclusion of all his students. Readers may want to consider their
own connection to power within the constructs of society and the classroom and
the ways in which individual and social power can be used in thoughtful ways to
empower students.

I had no idea that my first year of student teaching would force me to examine so intensely who I am and what I care about. During my first few weeks of
student teaching, I realized that a group of loud boys in my class really bothered
me, almost to the verge of dislike. They were among the dominant clique in the
school—all of them White and, as a group, socially powerful. I tried to figure
out why I found these boys so troubling. They were an annoyance to be sure, but
their intentions never seemed to be to inflict harm on anyone around them.
They were always smiling and joking around in class, and they just seemed to
enjoy being the centers of attention wherever they went. They loved displaying
their power, intelligence, and wit to the class.

After a few weeks, the reasons for my discomfort became clearer to me. The
more I listened to these students, the more I realized that their interruptions and

interaction in class were for the purpose of making fun of other students. There was an air of superiority surrounding these students. As their banter escalated to include some borderline sexist and racist comments, I began experiencing more than just anger at their remarks. The boys made fun of women in the class, sometimes made rude sexual comments, and mocked the English of some of the English-language learners in the class. I had taken action to stop these comments both publicly and privately with the boys, and they tended to listen to me when I asked them to be more sensitive to the feelings of other students in the class. Yet something more bothered me.

Finally, it struck me. I disliked these kids because they were a mirror of my past. I was facing, as a student teacher, a group of students who were acting almost exactly as I had in high school. Everything that I have struggled to improve about myself was sitting in front of me in my class. It was one of those strange karmic moments when I started to believe the phrase, "What goes around, comes around."

When I was in high school, I was a very loud and talkative student. I took every opportunity to be the center of attention in a class. I got most of my support from fellow male classmates. As a group of young, White men, my friends and I were always able to team up to have fun in class. We laughed at each other's jokes, defended each other from people's verbal responses, and always sat with each other in class. Moreover, we showed no respect for teachers who made mistakes or students who were having difficulty in class. I saw school as my place and my time. Anything that did not involve my immediate learning was ridiculed or discarded. I hated it when other students took up time to learn something that I already understood. I also knew that I could make fun of people and become more popular with my friends. Teachers rarely tried to stop us. They gave us free rein to say and do whatever we wanted. I think the reason for this was that we did well in class academically, and we were usually active in class discussions. We did not spend all our time being disruptive, but we used our productivity to compensate for our disruptions. We were very aware that we had to be good sometimes to get away with what we wanted to do the rest of the time.

I loved being on stage in a classroom. I was aided by the fact that I was able to pick up information quickly. This left me with time to hone my humor and "capping" skills. Capping sessions—that is, making fun of others—could go on and on until one person folded. It was about pride. It was about popularity. It was about power. And I was really good at it.

I felt like a very strong and important person in high school. I knew that a lot of people were afraid of me. I did not have a physique that could intimidate anyone, but I usually won in a verbal joust of any kind. There were some very public occasions when I almost reduced people to tears by attacking them and their ideas. It was the one thing that I was more proud of than anything else: I had the ability to make people feel stupid.

The behavior that I was so proficient at in high school was exactly what was going on in my class at the beginning of my student-teaching year: A group of boys immediately took control of the class and dominated all conversations. When class was not interesting to these boys, they did things that would make the time more amusing for them. I understand that the need for attention, positive or negative, is part of the development of most adolescents. At the same time, I could not sit by and let these students continue to cause harm or discomfort to other students in my class. I could not be like the teachers that I had when I was in high school. I did not want students to feel left out or isolated in my classroom, so I had to put a stop to it.

As a teacher, I now had several choices. None was easy. I could continue to reprimand the students sporadically and hope that this would stop the comments. I could lay down the law and be a martinet in my class. I could also hope never to get another set of students like this in my class again. Of course, the odds of this happening were minuscule, if not nonexistent. The odds of my succeeding as a strict disciplinarian were also slim, because that kind of teaching doesn't fit my personality. I would rather be an ally to my students than set myself up as an opponent. I also thought that these options would only be successful in stopping the students' behavior in my class but would not actually get these boys to see the damage that they were doing to those around them. So I chose another route.

I decided that I would attempt to show the boys the error of their ways and try to teach them more appropriate and powerful ways to use their personalities and humor. The difficulty in this approach was that I would have to do some serious reflection about my own history and life changes to understand what actually made me start to change the way that I acted in groups of guys. When did I realize that I didn't like who I was, and what forced me to change? If I could find the answer to these questions, I would be much better equipped to deal with any future students like the group of boys I had in my class during my student-teaching year.

So I dived back into my past to try to find out what it was in my life that helped me change. How did a transformation take place that allowed me to see that having power and being the center of attention were not as important as respecting other people and treating people decently? Some would argue simple maturation and age take care of this, but when I look around the world today, I do not see convincing evidence of that view. Too many people remain ignorant and closed-minded throughout their lives. I think that people need to learn how to treat people well, and the sooner they learn, the better.

When I thought about how my attitude changed, I came up with three distinct events that changed the way I treated people around me. The earliest was right after I entered college. I got a phone call from an ex-girlfriend and we were

talking about how we felt about being in college far away from home, not knowing anyone at the schools we were attending. After a while, as the conversation
stalled, I could tell she had a more important message to give me. She asked if I
had any new friends yet. I told her that I had met a lot of new people, but basically nobody stood out as having great friend potential. She laughed and said it
would be really hard for me to make new friends. When I asked why, she gave
me one of the most blunt and honest assessments I had ever heard: "You just
enjoy playing with people, and that is messed up. If people aren't your friends
already, it is going to be hard for you to find new ones."

I almost hung up on her. I was not mad, but I had just gotten a pretty severe
wake-up call, and it was an accurate portrait. I did enjoy playing with people's
heads. Not only was that harder in college, but there were fewer people who
cared about my ability in this area. It was an immature quality, but I did not realize it until all the support I had usually received was taken away. More important, I realized that what I was doing was just mean. People were hurt by the
words that I chose, and now that my friends were not around me laughing, I
could actually see the effects that my words had on people. It was not a feeling
that I wanted to continue to duplicate.

I began the process of making friends in college when I ran into another
situation that helped me to understand the errors of my adolescence. I was
hanging out with a group of people for the first time, and we opened up to each
other a lot. All the people had different backgrounds, ethnicities, and/or sexual
preferences. We were all describing what the places we came from were like. I
heard amazing stories of struggle and success from most of the people who were
there. Some told of their financial struggles to get into college. Some mentioned
fighting racism in their high schools in order to succeed. Two spoke of the difficulty of coming out as homosexuals to their parents. Another student told how
he was constantly terrorized by students who spoke English better than he, both
inside and outside the classroom.

I started to think about why some people had to try so hard to have success
when it seemed to come so easily to others. Then I began remembering how I
treated people in high school. Gay students, students who did not speak English
well, and quiet students were all subjects of my harsh words at some point or
other. I didn't see them as people but as objects of ridicule. As I was meeting new
and interesting people that night in college, I could only be ashamed of my past.
I couldn't understand how I could have failed to see that my words could hurt
others. Here I was in a group of people whose lives I almost certainly would have
made difficult had I gone to high school with them. Now, for the first time, I was
hearing firsthand accounts of the effects of behaviors similar to mine.

Finally, I understood the real beauty and significance of life when it was
taken away from someone in my presence. One day when I attended a swim
meet at my college, I saw a swimmer get out of the pool, take a few steps, collapse

on the pool deck, and die moments later. There was no warning that this young man would have his life taken from him, and it shook me to my very core. When I saw this death up close, I realized that all of us need to look out for each other. Life is too short and unpredictable to spend hurting others. I knew that I would never be able to talk to that swimmer again. I did not want to waste any more of my time using my personality to hurt people. I wanted to learn, inform, amuse, and experience life as much as I could. This drive to improve lives, including my own, was my primary impetus to becoming a teacher, and it began in earnest that day.

After reflecting on what made me change my ways after high school and reminding myself of why I wanted to be a teacher, I began to work with the boys in my class about changing their actions as well. This was a difficult task, and I tried a number of approaches. I spoke with each of the boys individually to let them know that I would not tolerate any students' being put down in my class. I did not attack the boys when I was saying this, but I took about 20 minutes with each, explaining how their actions affected my teaching and the other students' learning. The boys seemed shocked by the realization that they might be hurting people. They knew that they might make people feel uncomfortable or embarrassed, but they had not thought about the long-term effects that their actions could have. They said that they always meant their actions in good fun, but I explained that their fun was someone else's nightmare. I shared the stories of students too frightened to talk in class for fear of being ridiculed.

I explained my own history of using verbal power to hurt others and tried to let them know the negative effects it had had on those around me. I explained that now I am aware of the effects of my words, and I quickly apologize when I say something that hurts someone. I wanted to help the boys gain an understanding of the effects of their words and to develop social consciousness. I tried to show them the power they have and help them understand that they can make choices about how to use that power. I tried to show them the option of using their strength in more positive ways.

I also restructured the way that I had discussions and debates in my class to allow for all students to speak. I did this by incorporating more time for students to write down ideas before a discussion, more guidelines about how many times someone can talk during a discussion, and more focus on the topic that was being discussed. This allowed the quieter voices in my class more opportunity to speak while also limiting how much the loud boys could control the conversations. The boys complained about this, so I let them know my motivations for taking this course of action. I complimented the boys and their verbal ability, and I explained that people do not want to hear others go on and on about a subject, but rather they want to hear short, powerful points. I let them know that once they were not surrounded by people who knew them, they would need to use their verbal prowess in a more focused manner. I let the boys know that I was trying to help everyone in the class learn the skill of honing their thoughts before speaking. This approach worked pretty well, although there were still times when the boys took over the discussion. Usually, however, one of the boys from the group would quiet the person who was talking too much. This showed me that some progress was being made.

Finally, I have tried to model inclusion in the classroom. I use a wider variety of examples when I am explaining a concept. For example, when I was teaching an economic concept, I talked about two men living together and shopping together. As I expected, a student asked if the men were gay. This allowed me to open up a discussion about the topic and to show my class that there is nothing wrong with discussing homosexuality. This is just one small example of what I try to do on a larger scale when planning my lessons. I hope that little things like this can add up to all students feeling comfortable in my class.

I have grouped students heterogeneously for projects in the class. I have also validated comments from all students in the class. I want my students to see me as a White male who respects all his students and all the people around him. I want students like the boys I worried about this year to see the contributions that everyone around them can make in a class setting as well as in their lives outside of school. The skill of seeing everyone around you as potentially valuable can assist these boys and others to get more out of life through interactions with a wider variety of people. By going beyond tokenism in my teaching, I hope all of my students can see some real value in the people around them.

I do not think what I did was special, or even unique. I just selected a group of students whom I knew I could help become better people. I wanted to make an impression on their lives to counteract their friends' support of their cruel actions. Stopping prejudice and domination in action is not something that comes easily. Some of the problem can be solved through a curriculum that is inclusive and multicultural. This allows students to be exposed to a variety of people and opinions that might help open their eyes to worlds outside of their own, often sheltered, lives. But more of the problem can be solved through one-on-one interactions with students on a regular basis. The only way that I left a mark on these students was by letting them know that I cared about them and wanted them to the best people that they could possibly be.

Teachers can initiate social change in many ways. As a teacher, I have a duty to try to make my students more aware of diversity and more prepared to be contributing citizens in their communities. If I can raise the level of social awareness and consciousness among my students, then I feel I am accomplishing part of this goal. I want all of my students to find their voices, including those who are shy or often undervalued. I want those who are advantaged by the current social structure to see the power of their actions and seize that power to help others, especially those students who are stuck in silence. Helping students find the positive power in their voices will help them to achieve well beyond what they could do either without voice or with the negative power of voice.

The most frustrating part of teaching is that you never really know how successful you are in what you are trying to accomplish. I know that by the end of the year, the boys who concerned me no longer made fun of students in my class. I do not know what they did outside of my class, but at least there was one space where they knew their unkind actions were unacceptable and they respected that. The boys also spoke to me at their graduation and told me that they respected someone taking a stand against them. They said they learned a lot from learning to listen and respect others. I think that was as good a start as I could have hoped for in my student teaching. I learned from these interactions over the course of the year that I had to understand myself before I could understand my students. I hope that process will help me become a better teacher as I enter the profession full time. It has already changed the way that I look at students when they walk into my class, which is an important beginning.

CHAPTER 8

Idealism Meets Reality

Jennifer French

Jennifer French describes her struggle to bridge the gap between her ideal teaching and learning situation that is inclusive of gay, lesbian, bisexual, and transgendered (GLBT) people, and the realities of school settings that reflect limited knowledge and frequent prejudice. Readers may wish to consider the ways in which GLBT students and teachers are marginalized in many schools and how they can be supported in achieving their ideals of equity and community.

Lately, I have been longing for the days when my theories were just theories, fitting nicely into my political agenda, identity, and self-esteem. In this utopia I could be myself completely, rather than creating a persona who lives up to what I perceive others want me to be. I could put my identity forth freely, as long as it did not cause another person harm. I could speak about my partner, my social life, and my culture without fear of emotional or physical abuse. I could be both a teacher and an out lesbian.

Why is it merely a fantasy for me to be a teacher and an out lesbian? This is the question that runs through my head on a daily basis. As I move through my student teacher experience and teacher education program, I continue to reshape my idealism of teaching and of myself as a teacher. I struggle to understand my process of negotiating identity within a system that frequently judges and ostracizes, rather than accepts and embraces, gay and lesbian people. My story—painful and extremely personal—is not easy to voice. At the same time, my story communicates a universal idea: Our identity shapes who we are as teachers. This reality affects our lives and the lives of our students.

When I was outside the education field, it was easy for me to point my finger at what I thought was wrong with schools and teachers. I was frustrated at the level of homophobia and oppression of gay and lesbian people that I observed in schools. As a social worker in New Mexico, I would walk through the halls in schools, noting how many times teachers did not intervene when discriminatory antigay statements such as "worthless faggot," "f—in' dyke," and the too-often-heard "that's so gay" were made by students. When I started a gay community-based support group outside of the local high school, the youth in my group told me that they had never had a teacher discuss gay and lesbian issues in class. I also knew, in this particular town, that there were no out gay teachers to serve as role models and advocates for these youth.

The students I worked with longed for role models and adult allies to support and validate their experiences as gay and lesbian youth. Through our conversations and interactions, I noted that the absence of this support affected their self-esteem, motivation, and academic achievement. Most gay and lesbian youth struggle with being gay in a world in which antigay slurs are commonly heard and physical safety is not assured. Unlearning negative stereotypes and finding ways to combat homophobia were particularly important for these students. Working with these young people showed me that homophobia makes it both physically and emotionally unsafe for many gay and lesbian youth to be open about their sexuality in schools, forcing them instead to hide their true selves. This is especially damaging for adolescents who are at the point in their lives where they are trying to develop a positive identity. Many of the youth who felt safe within the support group disclosed negative experiences with family members who verbally or physically abused them for being gay. Many told stories of friends who were disowned by their families because of their sexual orientation. Clearly, these brave young people needed adults in their communities and schools who could serve as role models and advocates in their struggle toward ending homophobic language and violence.

Hearing these stories and watching the youth in the support group struggle to find positive role models had a huge impact on my educational philosophy. This experience strengthened my belief that not having positive gay, lesbian, bisexual youth and adult role models in the classroom makes it difficult for sexual minority youth to discover the richness of gay history and culture and feel proud of who they are. I know from my own experiences as a young person, and from listening to young people today, that negative depictions of gays and lesbians in mainstream culture and within many schools and classrooms can have serious consequences. This reality is close to my heart: When I was 16 and filled with self-hate and feelings of isolation, I attempted suicide. Unfortunately, my experience corresponds closely with a shocking statistic: One third of teen suicides are committed by sexual minority youth. Although I had supportive and loving parents, I did not have the words to express why I felt different. Like many other troubled gay and lesbian youth, I did not have any positive gay and lesbian role models in high school and did not understand why I felt different and ashamed of myself.

When I made the decision to get my teaching credential, I vowed that GLBT (gay, lesbian, bisexual, transgendered) students would have what I didn't have in high school: role models and a sense of their own history. In my ideal classroom where gay/lesbian history and literature are integrated into the curriculum, queer students would become empowered and straight students would emerge as allies to gays and lesbians. In this idealistic vision, my students and colleagues would know that I was a lesbian, accepting me for who I was and seeing my identity as an asset to education and the school.

When I arrived at my teaching credential program on a hot June day, my aspirations of being an out lesbian social studies teacher were foremost in my mind. I distinctly remember wandering through this new group of people that I would be with for an entire year and desperately looking for someone who was like me—gay or lesbian. As I navigated through the day, I asked questions to determine if anyone's partner had a pronoun that matched their own. I wanted to find someone else to whom I could relate and who could relate to me about being a gay teacher. Perhaps there was another gay or lesbian who shared my same vision and also wanted to become a teacher in order to change the lives and experiences of queer youth in schools. I desired to meet someone who knew about gay and lesbian history and literature who could work with me to find and develop curriculum and instruction. Finally, it was important to me to have my community represented in the teaching profession.

Yet each person I met was either married or presented as heterosexual. I ended that day with a heavy feeling in my heart: I could not believe that in a class of 60, I might be the only one. This would defy statistics, wouldn't it? Some estimate that 1 in 10 people are gay, so there should be at least 6 of us in this program. Where were they?

As I drove home that night, the words of many of my gay and lesbian friends echoed through my head. Almost everyone had thought that I was crazy for making the choice to go into teaching. They questioned whether I could be out, and if I was going to be out, if it would be worth it. What if other teachers would not support me? What if students did not want to be in my class because they knew that I was gay? What if parents wanted their students pulled out of my classroom or, even worse, wanted me fired? What if administrators would not take a firm stance on stopping such homophobia in the school? When I considered these questions, I began to realize why I might, indeed, be the only gay person in my entire teacher education program.

Over that summer I slowly opened up to some of my peers, discovering who was prejudiced against gay people and who wasn't. Coming from a place in which my circle of support was made up of gays and lesbians, I found it a challenge to explain what I was experiencing to so many people who were entirely unfamiliar with gay and lesbian issues. I knew that I needed to find support, even if it was going to come solely from straight people. In order to implement my educational idealism, I also needed to learn teaching strategies and curriculum that would be supportive of queer youth.

It was not clear to me, however, how my peers and I were going to learn the necessary tools to better serve the needs of gay and lesbian youth. Although teaching for social change and multicultural education was a central part of my program, gay and lesbian issues were not included in our early class discussions or curriculum readings. In a bold moment, I offered to teach my entire class of 60 about the needs of gay and lesbian students. Here was my opportunity to share my ideal vision and attempt to create more teachers who would work toward stopping homophobia in their classrooms.

Shortly after I offered to teach the class, the reality of this task set in. I began to fear that my peers would judge me. I was scared that they would stop thinking of me as "Jen" and start thinking of me as "the lesbian." Although I wanted people to see my sexual orientation as part of who I was, I did not want them to see me only for my sexual orientation. Cumulatively, these fears started breaking down my idealistic visions, and the reality of how difficult it would be to implement my ideal classroom set in. If coming out to my peers was this distressful, it would be even more challenging for me to come out to my students. I had barely begun to teach, and my ideal classroom was swiftly fading away.

Although coming out to my entire class was a scary endeavor, I did it for many reasons. First, I felt that it was important that a lesbian or gay person discuss the issues faced by many queer youth. This teaching experience was also a process for me. I had decided that if I was, in fact, the only gay or lesbian person in the class, I should at least find out who would support me throughout the year. I also realized that there were 59 "straight" people in my teacher education class who were going to teach gay and straight students. It was important to me that my peers were working on being allies to queer youth and teachers and that they had some tools to stop homophobia in their classroom.

In the presentation I stressed the importance of incorporating gay/lesbian studies into curriculum. I explained that when curriculum includes experiences of other minority groups, such as African Americans, Mexican Americans, Asian Americans, the traditional notion of history and literature is expanded to better represent students, the people who live in the United States, and the world. Gay, lesbian, bisexual, and transgendered people have contributed to society in numerous ways and are voices that need to be heard. However, this does not mean that I was encouraging teaching about how to "be" gay to young people. When I include experiences of other minority groups, such as African Americans, Mexican Americans, and Asian Americans, in the curriculum, I am not teaching how to "be" a member of that group. Instead, I am expanding the traditional notion of history and literature to better represent the people who live in the United States and the world. Teaching about targeted groups increases an understanding of all cultures and communities and helps to promote acceptance and respect. In part, homophobia exists because youth and adults do not know about gays and lesbians except for the negative messages seen and/or heard in the media from other aspects of their lives.

Although it was clear to me why it was important that I include gay and lesbian voices in my curriculum, when I began my student teaching, my practice went in another direction. The same curriculum gaps existed in the schools. Although I found that the school and teachers understood that gays and lesbians should not be verbally or physically abused on campus, the question of including gay and lesbian history and literature was an entirely different story. I learned that before I could teach a short story that discussed homophobia and included the word *lesbian*, it needed to be approved by the district. The district considered homosexuality a controversial issue and I was told that, if my story was approved, I would need to teach "both sides" of the issue. This meant that I would have to give the "pro" gay and the "anti" gay viewpoint. Teaching the anti-gay viewpoint was definitely not part of my ideal classroom vision.

Here I was, trying to figure out how I could integrate gay and lesbian literature and history into my curriculum and instruction, rather than tokenize it, and I was slammed against another large roadblock. The emotional weight of trying to practice what I believe in and encountering obstacle after obstacle began to take its toll. The stress and isolation that I suffered snowballed. I felt alone and wondered if I could ever make my ideal classroom a reality.

Experiences in my teaching program escalated this frustration and hurt. As the year went on, I found myself becoming what I had feared: the token lesbian. My peers constantly asked me for advice regarding how to talk to gay students or what literature to include in a course. Sometimes I was excited by this communication with other prospective teachers. At a time in which I saw few people even recognizing the existence of gays and lesbians, it was novel and pleasing to hear that some teachers do care and want to act. Yet with time I became frustrated because I didn't have all of the answers. Moreover, I got the feeling that many of my peers, however well intentioned, wanted me to show or tell them how to relate to their GLBT students. This situation heightened my anger and isolation. I could not do the work of learning and understanding about gay and lesbian curriculum and issues for both me and my peers. Straight people need to be proactive by becoming involved in undoing homophobia in society and our schools. But, unfortunately, like other minority groups, gays and lesbians often find themselves working against discrimination alone.

Great teachers recognize that they have a responsibility to address all of their students, including teaching GLBT issues in their classroom. This means stopping class when someone says "That's so gay" as a negative remark. Other times, it may mean creating more positive associations. For example, a math word problem might include a gay couple. Science teachers can discuss the ways in which science has been used to both defend and attack gays and lesbians. English teachers can use and discuss gay and lesbian authors in their curriculum. Social studies teachers can incorporate gay and lesbian history throughout their course. Diverse identity perspectives—race, gender, class, and sexual orientation—not only represent society as a whole but, more important, they represent our classrooms and our students. We do not serve our students if we fail to weave multiculturalism through our curriculum and instruction. When we do not teach to all of our students, inequality prevails.

Experiencing and witnessing these inequalities inspired me to be a teacher in the first place. I now realize my ideal classroom of a year ago cannot be fully implemented, but as I look back over the year, I can see how it has started to take a different form. Although I am not completely out in my student-teaching classroom, I have talked about gay and lesbian issues on numerous occasions. I have put energy into working with the Gay/Straight Alliance on campus, where I am out. I have talked to the other gay teachers at my school and have begun to listen to, rather than criticize, their reasons for choosing not to be out. I have realized that the lack of out teachers is more a reflection on school systems and society than on the teachers themselves.

A homophobic educational system still prevents me from practicing two important things: being honest about who I am within the classroom and school and consistently integrating GLBT issues into the curriculum. There are many aspects of gay culture and lifestyle that are kept hidden because schools do not provide a safe place for teachers and students to discuss their same-sex partners and culture. I often feel as if I am in a bind: I want to talk about who I am and not pretend that I am heterosexual, but I do not feel supported or, in some instances, safe in discussing my sexuality.

I strongly believe in the importance of having adult gay and lesbian role models for both queer and straight youth in schools. This is particularly important when gay and lesbian studies are incorporated into the curriculum. When students know someone who belongs to the group that is being discussed, the effect of the lesson is greater. Yet, in practice, I still find myself questioning whether the risks of administrative, parental, and student backlash against me warrant keeping me silent.

If I cannot have my ideal classroom, what can I have? At the end of the school year, I taught a civil rights unit and was able to answer this question, at least in part. I included gay and lesbian history and literature in this unit in three different ways. First, gays and lesbians were one of eight minority groups on which my students did civil rights research. When the research was presented to the class, I supplemented student answers on the goals and methods of gays and lesbians during the movement, adding historical facts and background. I included additional information about the other groups and, in doing so, felt that I normalized discussing gay and lesbian contributions to history. Finally, I had my students read a short story about a young girl who was grappling with racism and homophobia. After my students read the story, I facilitated a discussion on tolerance and civil rights. This unit worked because respect for all groups and people is a guiding philosophy in my classroom, allowing for students to consider and probe issues of gay and lesbian culture in a mindful manner. My students then engaged in meaningful conversation and discovery of the issues in the civil rights movement that historically have been absent from curriculum.

Implementing my social change philosophies is clearly a slow process, one lesson at a time. For now, my goal is to continue to develop and implement units that are inclusive of gays and lesbians. Building relationships with queer youth through my participation in the Gay/Straight Alliance is also a focus for me. In this alliance, I can be out and a role model to gay and lesbian youth. Although my teaching reality has far from mirrored my idealistic vision, there is still a fire within me that drives me to work to make schools more inclusive and supportive of gay and lesbian students and staff. As I move toward this goal, I believe the gap between my idealism and realities will someday close.

CHAPTER 9

The Big *Lesson*

Ryan Caster

This chapter describes a beginning teacher's confrontation with a student's use of oppressive language that challenges the identity of the teacher. The author examines the broader implications of how to treat teachable moments regarding human relationships as they are framed through language. Readers may want to use this chapter to explore possible immediate and long-term-responses to inappropriate language and consider how they will establish parameters of personal safety in the classroom.

As a recent college graduate who decided to make a career out of teaching English, I am fascinated by *how people use language*. I am interested in language as an observer, but I am also concerned as a participant who lives within the confines and freedom of language. Our progress as social creatures depends on our use of language to create knowledge, to identify our experiences—to communicate. We express ourselves in various ways, and yet *words* remain fundamental. We trip over them as we try to explain, describe, and express. We try to own them, only to find that they are available for the taking; others shape our words with their own, we claim them back with qualifications and augmentation, and the cycle continues ad infinitum.

The complexity of our *language situation* underlies the difficulty of being a language arts teacher. English and language arts teachers must guide students in the use of this slippery stuff, often when we find ourselves (happily, I must note) confused by it all. The conundrums of language generate questions that are at the heart of an instructor's personal philosophy. How do I teach my students to be both careful and bold in their reading, writing, and speaking? How do I convince them that the words they choose have meaningful consequences, consequences that can as easily be unintentional as intentional? Perhaps an earlier exploration of these questions, especially the last one, could have helped me better manage the following situation. Before I decide, I will tell the story.

CAUGHT UNPREPARED

On a chaotic Friday morning, as students were preparing presentations and bouncing around as if the weekend had arrived, a boy broke through the noise by calling for my attention. "Hey, Jew Man!" Danny yelled across the room. My class, a heterogeneous group of rowdy but sensitive 10th graders, began to quiet down, feeling that something was out of place. "What did you call him?" one student asked. "Jew Man," Danny said, half-responding to the student, and half-addressing me. Incredulous, I stared at him a moment, wondering how I should handle this awkward situation. My mind raced as I quickly traced the comment back to its source: Earlier in the year, I had shared that I was Jewish; at the time, I had not considered the possibility that someone might abuse this fact. Now I was stuck. Not only was I unsure of how to act, I didn't know how I felt or how I *should* feel.

Doing what I felt was best in the situation, I asked Danny to stay after class for a few minutes to talk. He seemed to realize that he had done something inappropriate—or perhaps he knew all along. In either case, he didn't stay after class. Whether it was out of shame, pride, or something else, I'm not sure. I sensed his defensiveness as he told me he had to be somewhere and left the room understanding that I would refer him to the administration for leaving. Knowing that I would eventually get the chance to talk to him about what he had said, I went home and thought about what his words meant and how to make this moment instructive—for me and for Danny.

As I thought about Danny's words and actions over the weekend, I had trouble pinning down the problem. Even now, after much thinking and several conversations with friends and colleagues, I still feel the need for a better analysis. I first find it difficult to react to being called "Jew Man" because of the ambiguity of the language and the context. What intentions and consequences surround this choice of words? If I give Danny the benefit of the doubt, I assume his statement was a clumsy attempt at being chummy; he probably felt that we could call each other such names, just as friends have nicknames for each other that might be viewed as offensive in a different context. As much as I want to think that Danny did not want to offend me, I believe that his words reveal, whether he realized it or not, a power struggle that manifests itself in language.

By calling me "Jew Man," he categorized me by my minority status in front of the rest of the class. To do so, if not blatantly racist, is at least covertly oppressive. Most likely, Danny wanted to assert himself as my equal. His actions throughout the year suggested that he was uncomfortable with the power relationship between teacher and student. I, too, am often uncomfortable with this power relationship, and I concede certain marks of it; for example, I allow students to call me by my first name, last name alone, or the traditional "Mr. Caster"—whichever makes them comfortable. I think that I need to be viewed as an authority in the classroom, but I don't insist on my superiority. Danny crossed the line at just this point: Just as I would never call my students something that would oppress them, I expect them not to use oppressive language with each other or me. "Jew Man" is oppressive; though not as overt as a racial epithet, because of the context, Danny had no good reason to casually call me out by my minority status.

More than anything else, this incident makes me think about what I believe is the Big Lesson of English Class: People must be thoughtful and careful in their use of language. I think Danny was more thoughtless than malicious, so my concern with his case and others like it is in figuring out how to teach the Big Lesson. In addition to the life lessons it offers students, teaching the Big Lesson makes the classroom safer. One of the consequences of allowing oppressive language in the classroom is the silencing of certain people or groups. Although the speaker's intent may be low, the impact of certain words is high. Therefore, students and teachers must not ignore these utterances. If classroom members address language that oppresses or unfairly discriminates, they can become sensitive to its effects. Although this point may seem obvious, too many educators ignore it.

Perhaps making it more of a priority to explore the consequences of oppressive language would have helped Danny think twice before calling me "Jew Man." In any case, we discussed his statement on Monday when he called me over to his desk to apologize. I accepted his apology, making sure he understood what he was apologizing for. He admitted he hadn't thought about what he said. I realized that I needed to have my class consider what it means to think about what you say.

I don't know if Danny or the other students in that first class of mine learned much from the "Jew Man" incident. Danny and I had our short, private discussion when he apologized; beyond that, I let the incident go. My lack of self-confidence and uncertainty about how to gracefully revisit the incident kept me from addressing it further with the rest of the class. Making difficult pedagogical moves that are not part of your routine—such as addressing an incident you failed to address immediately—is especially hard to do for the first time. I didn't take the risk with this incident. Since then, I've learned that it is okay to address things that might appear like ancient history to a teenager. (Sometimes addressing an incident a few days after it occurs communicates just how important it is.) To survive in the profession, first-year teachers must forgive themselves for leaving some situations less than perfectly resolved. Yet it would be wrong to make a habit out of ignoring teachable moments. New teachers must begin to take risks in order to progress, for what would be the use of reflection if the theoretical never informed one's practice?

TEACHING THE BIG LESSON

Although I haven't had any "Jew Man" incidents in my classroom since that Friday morning, I *have* taken opportunities to teach the Big Lesson. Presently, in the year 2001, the most telling occasion for this lesson may be in the occurrence of homophobic language in classrooms. This example illustrates the contextual relationship between historical moments and the language problems in our classroom. I have not encountered overtly racist language in my classes partly because students, regardless of how they feel, recognize the impact of racist statements. This is not the case with homophobic language. Because many students are unaware of the import of these words, educators are in a particularly good place to make these moments instructive. We can start by recognizing what our reactions communicate to our students. By allowing students to call each other or things "gay," we send a message to the class—that it is okay to insult someone or something at the expense of a group of people. The classroom thus becomes unsafe for homosexual students, and students do not learn to examine their prejudices.

One opportunity to teach the Big Lesson occurred as students and I discussed what it means to be a man or a woman in anticipation of related themes in Chinua Achebe's *Things Fall Apart*. A description of a man crying in public prompted giggles from a group of boys in the back of the room. When I asked them what was so funny, one immediately told on his friend: "He said that guy's a *queer*." I knew that I would address this comment; I just had to decide—quickly—*how* I was going to do so. After some clumsiness and embarrassment, the class and I were discussing the impact of using words like *queer*. I made sure my comments expressed no anger, but rather a desire to have the class think about how they choose their words. I had excellent results. The student who made the homophobic statement was able to articulate the problem with his words. Other students were being candid about what they did not understand about homosexuality and homophobia. It was a much-needed question and answer session that illuminated understandings of stereotypes and the language that sustains them.

Before having the discussion, I had almost decided to talk to the student alone. Deciding that the whole class was involved (because the confession was a public one), I began a class discussion. The results convinced me that it was a good idea in that instance. Still, I believe a class discussion might not always be the answer. Because there is no formula for addressing oppressive language, the most we can do as educators is think through what we feel about it beforehand and be ready to address it in a way appropriate to the context in which it occurs. That is, we must be committed to the Big Lesson.

The Big Lesson insists that students think critically and beyond themselves. Part of preparing people to function in the world in positive and meaningful ways is preparing them to communicate with each other, which means they must consider the consequences of their choice of words. Activities that make students aware of the effects of oppressive language proactively address the potential problem; taking advantage of an instance of oppressive language as a teachable moment makes the experience instructive and therefore productive.

I was ultimately able to become more proactive in teaching the Big Lesson. For example, while we read Harper Lee's *To Kill a Mockingbird* and discussed the effects of discriminatory language, I worked with student members of the Gay–Straight Alliance in my school to plan a discussion of discriminatory language in high schools and among teenagers. One result was a student-led discussion of homophobia and homophobic language in my freshman survey of literature class. For almost all of my freshmen, this discussion was the first time they had discussed the use of the term *gay* in a structured environment. Many participants, through their questions and comments, showed a new understanding of how associating *gay* with negativity is oppressive, even if it is unintentionally so. Several, including me, confessed a history of insensitivity to the sometimes-delicate relationship between language and power. I stressed that we should not be paralyzed by guilt but rather admit our mistakes and learn from them. The discussions, which were different in each class, gave me a stronger sense of my commitment to the Big Lesson. By making it a priority in both lesson planning and classroom management, I believe my practice as a language arts teacher is more authentic. And because language is the medium of communication in all classrooms, I think *all* teachers can take an important role in teaching this lesson.

CHAPTER 10

Watching Words and Managing Multiple Identities

Grace MyHyun Bang

Grace Bang discusses her family history as a daughter of immigrant parents and explores the stereotypes she confronts as a Korean American English teacher. She connects her experiences as a learner and a teacher to the lives of her students who must cross cultural boundaries to succeed in school. Readers may consider the ways in which they and their students negotiate generational and cultural differences across home and school contexts. Readers may also want to discuss the connections between literacy, identity, and academic development.

I sat at my desk, still tired from the day's teaching, anticipating another sleepless night. Like most student teachers, I was feeling overwhelmed. Looking at my desk—crowded with essays to grade and my own paper for my teacher education program awaiting revision—I was prompted to ask the same persistent questions: Why was I doing what I was doing? Why teach English?

I leafed through a collection of unopened mail sitting amidst the books and essays and came across a letter from my *ah'pah*. Correspondence from my father usually consisted of brief, administrative notes, but this envelope seemed unusually thick. More surprising, it was addressed "For Grace"—less formal and more personal than I was used to. I opened the letter to find several pages written in careful, tentative strokes, the handwriting reminiscent of that found in my grade school tablets. In broken English phrases, he lovingly tried to communicate that I should "finish my hard diploma." Why was I doing what I was doing? Completing my education was, in part, about honoring my parents and the sacrifices they had made to give me my education. It has been a fulfilling and sometimes challenging journey—one in which I have learned to watch my words and manage multiple identities.

As I sit at my desk wondering how and why I have come to be a teacher of English, I think about the sense of guilt I sometimes feel when I explain subject-verb and pronoun agreement to my high school sophomores; I know that my own parents must attend English classes to learn these very things. When I am with my parents, I sometimes struggle with whether I am honoring them or doing them a disservice as I catch myself watching my words, avoiding the use of advanced vocabulary and discussion of my graduate work or the literature I am teaching; I do not want my well-educated parents to feel subordinate simply because of their limited English and unfamiliarity with America's education system. I know that I cannot use the full expanse of my English to communicate my thoughts and feelings or convey my experiences to my father. Similarly, I know my father's English vocabulary does not afford him the ability to fully articulate his sentiments to me. As we speak to each other in English, we silently recognize together this language-imposed distance: I recognize with gratitude that this distance, albeit bittersweet, is what my Korean parents have afforded me through their immigration and its sacrifices.

I weep with pride over the pages of my father's letter, written in impeccable penmanship; he is practicing how to write in English cursive. And though I should be preparing lessons on *Romeo and Juliet* and correcting dangling participles, I find myself again wondering: Why am I doing what I am doing? What does it mean for me to be becoming a teacher of English, a subject of which my father is a student? What does it mean for me to be a teacher of high school English as the daughter of immigrant parents? How do I manage my identity in these multiple roles and why must I watch my words as I do so?

The roots of these questions originate in my own high school experience. Because the issues surrounding entitlement for African Americans and Asian Americans are different, and I believe the challenges African American students have encountered in the United States are immeasurably greater, it was surprising and somewhat comforting for me to find so much of myself in the pages of Beverly Tatum's (1997) book *"Why Are All the Black Kids Sitting Together in the Cafeteria?"* Her discussion of the racial identity formation of high school adolescents validated some of my own struggles with questions of race and identity that I had tended to devalue and shelve as an Asian youth.

In a recent conversation with a friend who is not a member of a minority group, she casually mentioned that race was not really an issue at her high school; the handful of minority kids all seemed to just "fit in." Although I believe this was a sincere assessment of her high school as she experienced it, this comment caused me to consider the choices I made to "fit in" at my almost entirely White school. It rekindled my memories of "racelessness" and struggles with cultural bifurcation as I tried to decipher the contrasting codes of my school and home contexts. As described by Tatum (1997), some minority groups feel a need to distance themselves from their reference group in order to succeed in White school settings. For instance, Tatum (1997) gives the example of Jon, who "felt he had to distance himself from his Black peers in order to be successful in high school" (p. 67). I began to recall where I sat in my high school cafeteria. I shamefully remembered avoiding the small band of "FOB" (Fresh Off the Boat) Asian students at my high school because I wanted to sustain my status as a member of the mainstream school culture. I suppose I wanted to keep my seat at the high social status, White cafeteria table. Looking back now, I imagine that my father would have agreed with this choice.

Why are all the Black kids sitting together in the cafeteria? Many adolescents seek out a peer group in which they have shared experiences and, therefore, greater ability to understand each other. Tatum argues that for some minority and immigrant students, being with those of the same ethnic background provides a source of support and is a coping strategy to counter the shared negative experiences with discrimination and devaluation. Nonetheless, Tatum's provocative title may overshadow the fact that not all minority and immigrant adolescents are sitting with one another in the cafeteria.

This was the case for me, growing up in a predominantly White community. My disassociation from the other Asian students at my high school caused me to be seen as a "twinkie" by my Asian peers, similar to the way in which Tatum (1997) describes an African American female student who was labeled as an "oreo" because she affiliated with White rather than African American peers at her school (p. 63). Choosing to be one of the kids *not* sitting with the Asian kids at my school could have been an attempt to establish eligibility for what I perceived as success in my school's culture. At home and when visiting Korea, however, I found myself comfortably assuming the very different roles ascribed to me by my native culture. Phelan, Yu, and Davidson (1994) describe situations in which students must negotiate their "multiple worlds"; they may feel a need to hide themselves at times in the effort to "fit in," thereby attempting to overcome feelings of isolation (p. 427). While considering how some adolescents struggle to reconcile their identities across different settings, I realized that much of my own confusion about who I was and could or could not be during junior high and high school stemmed from feelings of self-inconsistency and perhaps an inability to manage my multiple identities across home and school settings. I felt divided about my Asianness and Whiteness; my claim on these identities and the opportunities associated with them often depended on the shifting contexts in which I found myself.

CONFRONTING STEREOTYPES

Asian Americans, especially through successive generations on the West Coast, have accessed opportunities typically dominated by White Americans. While growing up on the East Coast, however, the Asians in my community were all first-generation immigrant families. Because I rarely encountered Asians in professional spheres of influence during my junior high and high school years, I was often doubtful when considering certain achievements as possibilities for me. It seemed reasonable for others to circumscribe my future as well. Tatum's (1997) example of Malcolm X, whose English teacher advised him to reconsider his aspirations to become a lawyer, resonated with my own feelings of discouragement about career choice. In my high school, although I consistently exhibited a growing interest in English over any other subject, teachers and friends assumed that I should pursue studies in math and science and encouraged me to do so. When I received lower math than verbal scores on my SAT, I felt unsure and even guilty about what others saw as an anomaly; Asians are always supposed to have high math scores.

Upon my decision to go into English education, my father cautioned that this was not a viable career goal for me. He still worries that becoming an English teacher is not a wise choice for me because I am Asian. Growing up as one of a very small minority population in Virginia schools, I never encountered an Asian instructor or any literary work by Asians until attending college at UC Berkeley. Now I am attending Stanford for graduate school, and sometimes my father and I pause in reflection and occasionally with tears, amazed and grateful that I have been so privileged to have access to such an education. Nevertheless, as an immigrant parent with internalized preconceptions about what is possible for persons of color in America, my father continues to fear that my legitimacy as an English teacher might be questioned and is concerned that I may not be wholly accepted by some students and teachers. "Don't worry, *Ah'pah*, things are different now," I smoothly enunciate, trying to assuage his concerns in the flawless English pronunciation he has sacrificed for me to attain.

Although I remain committed to my professional life as an English teacher, I also realize that some of my father's fears still seem to be justified by my experiences. Recently while I was grading essays at a café near the Stanford campus, a man approached me and asked if I was a language-learning student. Startled and confused by the interruption, I asked him to repeat the question. He proceeded to ask me in slower, simpler English if I was an international student. After telling him cordially that I was, in fact, a student, but studying how to teach English, he responded with a final surprised remark, "Oh, so you speak English fine?" In this brief comment, he momentarily nullified everything for which my parents and I had struggled and worked. Wasn't my degree from Berkeley enough? Wasn't it enough that I was at Stanford, doing graduate work in English

Education? More recently, while I was grading essays at yet another café, a man sitting next to me noticed the barrage of papers on my tiny table and deduced, "So, I guess you're a teacher. What do you teach?" After I explained that I teach English, he added encouragingly, "Oh, really? That's great! What kind of English do you teach? Do you mean like, ESL?" Perhaps partly because of my not uncommon experiences such as these, I must admit my own occasional insecurities that echo my father's doubts. Although my English is "fine," to some I may always be defined as someone who teaches English pretty well, for an Asian.

FIGHTING MARGINALIZATION

During my year in teacher education, I realized that my own internalized preconceptions about who is eligible to teach English profoundly shape the lens through which I see my students and my experiences as a teacher. Around my colleagues in graduate school as well as in the school at which I teach, I caught myself reexperiencing some of the internal tensions I felt in high school. In my student-teaching year, I taught two courses, World Literature–Multicultural and World Literature–Honors. Multicultural is unique to the school at which I teach because it is the only intentionally heterogeneous World Literature section; its unique, ethnically balanced class composition allows for more students of color than a typical World Literature section. In teaching the different student populations of these two classes, I found myself contemplating adaptive strategies to suit the circumstances. The morning after one of my café encounters, I stood in front of a room full of over 30 White honors students who, for the most part, were from affluent, well-educated families, and found myself trying to locate what seemed to be an appropriate ethos in my cultural calculus. Should I use more academic discourse with these students in order to credential myself? What if I make a grammatical error in my speech? What if I mispronounce a word or use awkward diction? Would these mistakes be attributed to the fact that I am Asian? Would these mistakes be forgiven more easily if I were White? If my students knew that my father is learning English, would this disrupt their confidence in me to teach them adequately? Were these pressures unjustified or pressures borne out of experiences such as the café? Underlying these fears was a familiar, persistent consciousness that begged the questions: What should I divulge about my identity? Should I withhold pieces of my truth in order to maintain my students' trust and confidence in me as a teacher of English?

In the 5 minutes between teaching this class and my multicultural class, however, my racial identity quickly shifted from seeming like a handicap to be managed to an asset to be shared. I told the multicultural class about my experiences of writing letters in English for my parents while growing up; some understood the awkwardness of exceeding the experiences or abilities of their parents. I was grateful that my self-disclosure could perhaps encourage them collectively and individually to strive for higher education despite the difficult borders they might have to cross on the way.

At other times in professional settings, I find that I am not watching my words; I just don't say anything at all. For instance, at a writing articulation, an annual gathering of all English teachers from the district in which I teach, I realized that of the over 40 teachers in the room, I was one of three teachers of color. Though I had ascertained this with only a superficial glance, I began to feel a tinge of the same unease I felt upon entering my graduate education program. Similarly, in my graduate program, of the five subject concentrations, English was the least racially diverse; teachers of color comprised less than a fourth of the subject group. I had conversations early on in the program with a Latina colleague in the English cohort, finding comfort in the fact that we both felt moments of inadequacy and silence when our colleagues talked about their discussions with their parents on Shakespeare, and whatever else we were studying in our coursework. What did it mean for us to have immigrant parents who still struggle with English and were not educated in the United States? How could we relay our experiences? Even though our colleagues never failed to embrace us, and we spent an invaluable year learning with and from one another, oftentimes when we gathered as a group, it was difficult not to experience moments of questioning my belonging and membership. The compositions of both my English Department and my graduate program reinforced the cultural stereotypes my father worried about—stereotypes about English and who should teach it. English was the discipline reserved exclusively for especially articulate and almost always White teachers. The actualization of this notion caused me to realize that once again, I had to legitimize my place at the prestigious cafeteria table.

CROSSING BORDERS: BECOMING A TEACHER OF ENGLISH

Why is there currently such a lack of racial diversity in English departments? Is there perhaps more diversity in disciplines such as social studies because people of color fortunately are dedicated to and more invested in revising history? I find myself hoping that as an English teacher from Asian immigrant parents, I can bridge the gap of possibility for immigrant students and students of color aspiring to become writers, or even English teachers. Mia Tuan (1995) argues that immigrants of color must manage persistent worries over discrimination and exclusion based on their visible "foreignness" while White immigrants may not because they can pass as members of the majority (p. 109). It is important to consider the difficulty immigrant students of color may experience as they attempt to remain rooted in their native identities and manage perceptions by others of their "foreignness" that such rootedness might entail. If minority and immigrant students do not see members of their own group represented in certain professions, they may not consider such professions as viable for them. As Tatum (1997) suggests, examples or their lack thereof are critical in the shaping of adolescents' confidence in their futures.

So then, how can those of us who have managed multiple identities draw upon our experiences in a way that may ease this journey for those we teach? Moreover, how can all educators appreciate, understand, and assist students from immigrant families as they encounter the complex challenges of crossing cultural and linguistic borders between their home and school lives, when trying to "fit in"? Phelan, Yu, and Davidson (1994) write that "Teachers' perceptions that [some immigrant] students 'fit in' and have little trouble academically and no apparent problems socially can divert their attention from the energy and efforts these youth expend in navigating their daily circumstances" (p. 442). I learned of the inner struggles my students experience when Ruben, a student in my World Literature-Multicultural class this past year, wrote of the difficulty he faces as he aspires to go to college. Because Ruben's family emigrated from Mexico and none have attended college, he feels a strong obligation not to over-step his parents by attending college; he explained that this would be a clear act of disrespect. Another student in my class, Laura, noted that although she hopes to attend college, it is difficult to motivate herself toward this goal. Laura's moth-er, an émigré from El Salvador, often tells her that college is not worthwhile because she will face limited opportunities anyhow as a minority, even with a college degree. The inability of some students to cross borders successfully does not necessarily imply that they are apathetic or opposed to education and its purposes. It is important to recognize the emotional supports found in students' home and community cultures, and how students may feel that these links must be devalued or even severed in the pursuit of higher education (Phelan, Yu, & Davidson, 1994).

As educators encounter students such as Ruben and Laura, it is important to realize the difficult choices and delicate tensions children of immigrant fam-ilies may face because they must constantly shift and sometimes choose between the expectations and norms of their school and home contexts. Likewise, it is crucial to be aware of parents who may not know how to navigate or even feel comfortable in an American high school. As more students from immigrant families fill classrooms, it is also vital to provide them with support and information about tending to processes such as choosing colleges and fill-ing out college applications. Too many students may see certain options as exclusive and unavailable to them because of who they are, where they come from, or simply because they have never seen it done. Identity is such a complex tapestry, woven from the threads of an individual's volition and imposed by the suppositions of institutions. I have come to realize that as an educator it is essential for me to communicate who I am; my awareness and self-disclosure may invite more students from marginalized groups to understand that they have a legitimate place at any cafeteria table.

Students from immigrant families need to negotiate complex realities in their pursuit of education. I think of Juanita, currently a student in my World Literature class, who shared with me that her mother does not have a formal education beyond the third grade. What does it mean for Juanita to read *A Yellow Raft in Blue Water*? I wonder, does the nightly act of taking out this 400-page book create any discomfort at home? As I try to understand Juanita's experience with this novel, I remember my father and the laundry basket full of children's books he is reading. He bashfully showed me this basket during my single visit home while I was in graduate school. He handed me an easy-reader version of *Treasure Island,* asking, "Have you read this?" I remember accepting it, filled with appreciation; my father was sharing with me his pursuit of mastering English, a language and literary repertoire I had long since acquired. Condensed in that moment of reversed roles between father and daughter, student and teacher, I see the difficult yet sometimes beautiful paradoxes that define my life as the daughter of immigrant parents, and as a teacher of English for immigrant and nonimmigrant high school students, a life in which I have learned to watch my words and manage multiple identities.

The crossing of borders requires courage from both students and teachers, especially those who have large distances to travel. As a teacher, I hope to provide a bridge that connects those worlds and enables my students to walk the path to a new future without leaving their homeland behind. And so, my father reads abridged versions of classics while I teach Juanita *A Yellow Raft in Blue Water.*

CHAPTER 11

Whose Rally Comes First?

Silvia Paloma Garcia-Lopez

The author describes how her experiences as a Latina student and teacher have motivated her to work to bridge the gap caused by cultural and educational discrimination experienced by minority students. Readers may want to consider what expectations and assumptions about students of color seem to be reflected in the academic and extracurricular programs of schools they have experienced, and assess how teachers can support students from traditionally underserved communities in closing the achievement gap.

My desire to work with underprivileged youth brought me to the teaching profession. For years I mentored Latino youth through summer volunteer work with Future Leaders of America (FLA), a Latino youth leadership organization. This program had motivated me through my own high school experience, but I realized that too few of the students I encountered each summer actually maintained the self-esteem we sought to instill in them. I wanted more kids to be able to uncover the opportunities college had to offer. The low expectations for achievement and the daily wear and tear that they faced in their school environment were robbing them of the excitement, motivation, and goals we worked so hard to make a reality. I had to do more.

I wanted to become a teacher so that I could do for my students what FLA had done for me. In my own classroom I wanted to have high expectations for all my students, build their self-esteem, and make each of them feel valued as a member of a community of learners. The participation of all students would be an important component of my teaching as I led students to the paths of opportunity rarely accessed by those excluded from the high-performing track.

"YOU DON'T KNOW WHERE YOU ARE GOING, UNLESS YOU KNOW WHERE YOU'VE BEEN"

Another reason I wanted to be a teacher originated from my own high school experience in southern California. I could tell my students about how I was involved in a plethora of activities: basketball, student government, leading the French club, and a lifelong member of the California Scholarship Federation. However, there was another side of my high school experience that I remembered vividly but did not talk about. Among those memories were the times that my high school basketball team would walk through the doors of another school's gym to be faced by a group of Caucasian teenagers complaining to their coaches that our team, which was half Mexican American, should be searched for knives and warned not to be too aggressive. Or the times I was brushed off when I attempted to schedule an appointment to see my counselor until I mentioned I was an "honors" student applying to college. And then there were the times the discipline system did not overlook me, even if I was the shy type. I was immediately assigned "Saturday school" for being in the hallway, even when others were in the hall without passes at the same time. Was it the way I dressed? What is the way I looked? Was it the low expectations of the "Mexicans" in my school, who made up at least 60% of the student population?

What stood out the most in my memories of San Pablo High was an incident that occurred just weeks before graduation. My friend Estrella and I had been selected by a panel of peers in a speech contest to speak at the graduation ceremony. We had decided to compete when we realized that no Mexican American students would be in the ceremony program aside from those accepting diplomas. Estrella and I were among the four Mexican American students still "swimming against the current" in the honors track by senior year. I met Estrella when I moved into this district in the eighth grade, when at least 50% of the students in the honors track were Mexican American. The growing achievement gap was evidence of the divide the school had created and students had come to accept.

As I prepared my speech for the graduation ceremony, I focused on the fire in my belly, driven by all the things I had seen and experienced that seemed blatantly unjust. I could not understand why my school was not making an effort to make sure that at least part of the ceremony would be culturally or linguistically relevant to the majority Spanish-speaking audience. I showed up with my speech along with six other students who tried out. The selection panel was made up of one teacher and five seniors, each representing a variety of clubs and the student government. When I went up to recite my speech, the panel members' jaws dropped: My speech was entirely in Spanish. This was my political statement at age 18—a way to fill in the gap. I felt a little uneasy about what I had done because it was unexpected, but felt proud that I had followed through and given a well-organized, powerful speech. Half an hour later, Estrella and I were announced as the student speakers for graduation, each of us having earned the highest number of votes.

My glory did not last long. As I walked the halls of the school with enthusiasm, rumors spread across campus. Two other students at the tryouts claimed reverse discrimination had kept them from winning the speech contest. They argued that Estrella and I had been selected because of our Spanish-speaking skills, not for the quality of our presentations. The two students' parents called the school and put pressure on the principal to include their daughters to represent the school at graduation. Otherwise, they threatened to press discrimination charges on the school. I was outraged, and so were my parents. How dare they? I felt *we* should be the ones pressing discrimination charges for all those not benefiting from our system of education. Although I was willing to fight it, I couldn't do it without my parents. Unfortunately, like many Latinos, my parents were hesitant to intervene. They believed fairness would prevail. They encouraged me to talk to the principal and request another speech contest at which he would be present.

I was not able to get an appointment to see the principal. However, days later, the second speech contest was set up at my school with no formal conversation between the administration and the two of us affected by this situation. Estrella and I presented our speeches again. The other two girls did not show up. The principal walked in halfway through my speech and at the end commented that he would like me to add an introduction in English (something I had already done). He missed Estrella's speech entirely. Just before he left, he announced that all four of us would be speaking at graduation with a 2-minute time limit, instead of the original 4 minutes. This second tryout was merely a formality.

The message we received from the administration was loud and clear. The other two girls' complaints would be addressed, and they would be on the graduation stage regardless of the merit of their presentations or their absence at the second tryouts. Estrella and I were expendable, like most of the Mexican American students and parents. After much urging on my part, my father called to ask for clarification on the situation. His call was never returned.

Perhaps it was my parents' work for social justice through the United Farm Workers union that gave me courage as I marched through the halls of my high school determined to show the world that I could break out of little San Pablo and prove them ALL wrong. This dream carried me to beat the odds and prove to my school and society that I was indeed capable of achieving my goals in college and beyond.

REENCOUNTERING THE STATUS QUO

When I finally reached my teacher education program, I hoped to be surrounded by people who, like myself, were driven to change the system in order to open opportunities for more students, allowing them to achieve and feel that they belong in our schools. Yet I found that in STEP, as in my high school and my undergraduate years at Stanford, there is no escaping the "nopal," or cactus, as Chicanos say, located on your forehead. The first thing others see is your race, and many make assumptions about your abilities, your intentions, and the legitimacy of your views. Just as I experienced this as a high school and college student, I encountered it again among fellow student teachers.

When issues of school inequities surfaced in class discussions, I was stunned to hear those who are privileged deny that prejudice and low expectations exist in society today. Many of my classmates did not want to engage in long conversations about racial matters; some explained it was because they were "color blind." Others challenged me and other minority students to back up our claims with evidence. When we read articles like Michelle Fine's (1993) "On Equal Educational Opportunities and Unequal Educational Outcomes," these peers viewed the evidence about dropping out as though it were relevant only to the school portrayed in the article, rather than existing as a system-wide problem. Because Fine's article was not proof enough, our evidence became personal experience. Opening ourselves up to share personal experience was emotionally trying and difficult to sustain.

I kept asking myself how it could be that my colleagues and I had come into teaching with such very different versions of reality. For months, the conversations with my closest peers and my husband in the evenings turned into disillusionment and tears. Did we not come into teaching with a vision of social justice for *all* students? The answer to my question was "no"; no, we did not come into teaching for the same reasons. What hurt most was the realization that without a common view of the inequities in our schools and society, how could we change them? That is what I came into teaching to do: to give all students equal access *and* equal outcomes. In my teacher education program, I wanted to learn firsthand what a teacher can do to change the status quo. I felt betrayed to learn that others did not initially share this view.

My colleagues who shared my "minority" views would ask similar questions. Why must I justify my passion to close the achievement gap between minorities and Whites in schools? Why must I be challenged every time I share my own experiences and observations of this system of education? Why do I find myself repeating the statement that ALL teachers should care for ALL students, even the sole Latino, gay, or Black kid in the back of the class? Do you think those who were channeled through the honors tracks chose to be there and those who did not benefit from the honors track CHOSE to fail or fill the blue-collar positions in our society? I became frustrated with those who would not act simply because they had never "seen" the inequities or who were apathetic in addressing the social issues we confronted.

Once I began to speak up and write about my experiences in my masters' program, I did not want to remain silent. I thought of how many others might be out there who have been silenced since their youth and who were not able to demonstrate their abilities to the satisfaction of those who control the status quo. I was not able to put a label on this experience until I encountered the work of Claude Steele (1992) toward the end of the year. Finally, I could explain the implications of "stereotype threat" in the performance of Latinos, women, Asian Americans, African Americans, gays, lesbians, and other groups with a history of oppression. Steele's work points out the effect that expectations have on the performance of specific groups in our schools, on standardized tests, and in society. His research demonstrates that students will achieve poorly in an environment where low expectations exist and where the threat of being stereotyped is triggered. My high school experience and the experience of my students in my classroom were examples of this negative conditioning I came into teaching to fight. How many youth can step outside of themselves and understand the social construction of "stereotype threat"? The majority of people are not able to identify how this affects their performance.

As I looked for the tools that would give my students skills to overcome obstacles in the system of education, it did not at first occur to me that I would encounter STEP faculty members who would be so invested in those of us who had made it "out" of the place we call "at risk." The director of the program and the faculty sponsor recognized our drive and took an interest in students like me outside of the classroom. The did not just talk the talk of "diversity in the classroom" but went beyond their duties of class lecture, grading papers, and small talk about the theoretical framework we had just covered. They provided not only support, but also researched, published, and continued to take action toward social justice in our public schools and in higher education. Key members of the faculty involved in training teachers for the future made my success at STEP possible because I began to feel validated. I was not alone in this battle. Others with more experience and understanding of the "big picture" of society's social ills supported my vision for teaching. Without these people advocating for their graduate students of color, I would not have found an ear, or a shoulder to lean on, as I embarked on my hopes to bring about broader social change as an educator.

LEARNING TO FIGHT THE SYSTEM

In my quest to make a difference as a teacher and properly channel the "fire in my belly" I had felt in high school and college, I began to focus more closely on the issues in my placement school. I wanted to become that advocate for my students who would provide the listening, support, and hope that my professors gave me. Just as I was feeling undervalued for my point of view, I focused on similar feelings faced by my students in their school context. It was almost the middle of the first semester in my student teaching at Santa Ines High School before I realized just how extensive the feelings of "lack of care" or "being expendable" were in that environment.

My first exposure to how students felt in this environment came from the case-study student I was following for an assignment from my Adolescent Development and Learning course at Stanford. Niki was a student in my second-period U.S. history class. She was attentive and pleasant to have in class but did not stand out from her peers until I started looking for patterns in the participation of my students. In my Group Work for Heterogeneous Classrooms course, race and socioeconomic status are discussed among the factors that affect students' peer status and participation levels (Cohen & Lotan, 1997). I began to wonder if these factors might contribute to Niki's low level of participation, as she was at that time one of only two African American students in my second period classroom. Both she and the other African American student were very quiet in the classroom. They tried to blend into the class on opposite sides of the room and not to draw attention to themselves.

I found their behavior similar to my own as an adolescent in a classroom with very few faces like my own. I wondered if they, too, felt isolated or invisible. Later I learned that Niki was an active member of the Black student group on campus and had experienced a constant wall every time she tried to plan events for her fellow students. There was always a problem among club advisors and in the administration office when it came to taking time out of a regular school day for Black History month or multicultural week. These events were the highlight of the year for students like Niki, and the fact that administrators and teachers were not supportive of them was discouraging to her. "Why does the school care more about a 'stupid sports rally' than a cultural or educational rally?" she would ask. "What are we here for?" My heart ached when she asked me these things. And it continued to ache as I asked myself the same things.

My own history helped me identify the unwelcome feeling that students like Niki were experiencing. As I grew closer to Niki through interviews and observations in class and group meetings, I listened closely for similar feelings from Latino students. When a mural painting project was proposed in a Latino club meeting, Pancho, one of the freshmen in the group, huffed, "Oh you know how much they care about *Mexicans* here. They're not gonna let us put up a mural on the school grounds." No one argued with his comment. It was accepted as common knowledge. I was struck by the honesty involved in his comment. Somehow teachers feel better when they think that students do not recognize inequities. But Pancho recognized the school's low expectations of his peers and the club's potential.

Could it be that 10 years after I began my high school experience, nothing had changed? In this very diverse school, I was determined that teachers and administrators should take responsibility for making the school a better place for ALL students, not just the athletes, student government representatives, and others active in mainstream activities. What about the students who are making an effort to participate in other "nontraditional" clubs and events? What about those sinking in the abyss of the SDAIE (Segregated Specially Designed Academic Instruction in English) "ghetto" and the substandard English as a Second Language Department? The gap between culturally diverse children and their schools (Valdés, 1996) seemed to be growing here. Even though I was only a part-time student teacher at the school, I had to find a way to make a difference, to be part of the solution instead of accepting the situation.

For Niki and the Latino club students, the least I could do was provide support. I could also do my own research into the school's operations. Through my course work, I was learning that teachers occupy a significant role in the lives of adolescents. In order to be an effective educator, I knew I must build an understanding of their worlds. I knew it was important to evaluate whether the needs of adolescents "fit" with the opportunities afforded them by their social environments (Eccles et al., 1993). For these reasons, I spoke to my cooperating teacher and one of the vice principals at the school to find out the history of minority involvement in the school. I found out that the multicultural rally might not happen because administrators were not willing to take time out of the school schedule for rallies other than sports. I also found that very few minorities were represented in traditional school activities, and few were enrolled in advanced placement courses and upper levels of math. This year, the first African American student at the school had made it into trigonometry, as far as the teacher could remember.

A "diversity task force" was in the planning but could not get off its feet without support from more administrators willing to take action. The lip service from the superintendent was not enough to get things moving, one teacher told me. No demographic data had been disaggregated to expose the achievement gap for girls in science or minorities in honors courses, an essential step when developing an organization's cultural proficiency (Lindsay, Robins, & Terrell, 1999). The school newspaper showed that the entire homecoming court was made up of White students except for one Asian student who made class princess. The student government was dominated by Caucasian and Filipino students, with only one student reflecting the Latino population and few reflecting other racial groups on campus. There was something seriously wrong with this picture.

Ultimately, the action I took not only provided support for students like Niki but also for others through club involvement and the social studies curriculum. I became a Latino club advisor, joining a teacher's aide from the ESL

Department. Her vision was to provide a safe place for students to feel welcome and to celebrate Latino culture. I agreed with her goals, but my vision also included building their self-esteem, academic performance, and skills necessary to be leaders in a group. I felt that the students lacked guidance and structure for their meetings, just as Niki had described was happening in her Black student group meetings. The current trend on campus was that clubs should be "student run only." I agreed with this notion to a certain extent, but I felt that in order for students to meet high expectations, they needed role models and guidance unavailable to lower socioeconomic populations. Sports teams and student body government provide this kind of coaching and guidance. So should cultural organizations.

As multicultural week approached in March, Niki continued to prepare for her club presentation regardless of the fact no announcement had been made by the school regarding a rally time for these presentations. I joined the other Latino club advisor to help the students gather materials, coordinate themselves for specific events, and prepare for the imminent rally. Finally, news came that there would be an all-school assembly for each cultural club to perform and then "optional" rallies in the quad during class time, available for teachers who sign up throughout the week. Cheers broke out across the school. Although this was just an additive approach of displaying song, dance, and food, it was a first step to what might become a more integrative approach to cultural proficiency (Lindsay, Robins, and Terrell, 1999). More of my students became involved in the planning, smiled in class, and sat up straight as the week approached.

The assembly was magical: Over 10 groups performed a cultural practice or dance for all the student body to see. Awe, surprise, cheers, and all around joy marked the faces of students I saw after the assembly was over. This was a first for the school. The planning had paid off. The rest of the week went smoothly as several groups performed and shared their culture in daily rallies or after-school activities. The school had gone out of its way to make the environment acknowledge its multicultural richness.

GOING BEYOND WHOSE RALLY COMES FIRST

Although these experiences were worthwhile, I knew they were not enough to undo the negative conditioning my students had encountered. Issues of social injustice, feelings of exclusion, and low expectations in schools cannot be remedied by simply throwing in a token rally, a cultural food event, or Cesar Chavez and Rosa Parks lessons. Multicultural tokens cannot substitute for a much more integrated and culturally meaningful curriculum (Banks, 1994).

During the second semester of my student teaching, I began to teach a SDAIE U.S. history class for English language learners at the intermediate level.

I was exposed to a whole new side of education for a large population of students whose needs are often ignored. In this classroom, the students had been living in this country for an average of 4 years, sometimes more. Yet their writing and oral communication skills were far behind what I would consider "intermediate." Like most SDAIE or ELL teachers, I was advised to water down the curriculum, beef up the use of vocabulary lists and worksheets, and show videos. I discovered that you can sing and dance all of the material to make the ELL students understand, but that matters little if they are not able to read, write, and have meaningful conversations about it. A curriculum that is simplified to worksheets and videos cannot develop the skills necessary to make it up and out of the SDAIE ghetto and into mainstream classes that provide equal access to opportunities after high school.

There is an injustice in the fact that my U.S. history SDAIE students could not write an essay at the 11th-grade level, even when most had been in the country in the bilingual education department for over 4 years. Immediately, I began to take the advice of my ELL methods instructors at Stanford: Don't "water down" the curriculum. I had come to realize how harmful that terminology and practice could become firsthand.

Although Santa Ines High allows ELL students to adjust their schedules and move up at the semester, this rarely occurs. I found that most ELLs follow the bilingual education track throughout high school. Upon graduation, they find it difficult to pass the competency exams, and many leave without a diploma. In my attempt to address these issues, I embarked on a 4-week World War II unit, primarily focused on controversial topics such as the interment of Japanese Americans and the dropping of the atomic bomb. I chose these issues because my goal was to teach my students how to write an essay and engage in meaningful discussion or debate by taking sides and developing opinions. Each student turned in an outline, two written drafts, and a typed final copy by the end of 3 weeks of scaffolding. The unit was challenging and drawn out, but the hard work paid off for both my students and me. The students' essays ultimately surpassed my expectations, and I posted their papers on the wall.

Some of my students who originally reacted negatively to the higher expectations came to realize that I believed they were capable of more than other teachers traditionally expected. Victor began to ask, "So what are you going to teach us today, Ms. Garcia-Lopez?" with a smile on his face rather than the look of sarcasm he had had the first few days of the semester. The students began to realize that I cared about them. My concern for their futures was the reason that I set the expectations so high. This class no longer offered worksheets, videos, and mindless group work that required only one student to finish the project for everyone to get credit for it. It was about meaningful writing, class discussions, and developing skills they, too, knew were necessary for achievement. They were not ignorant; they had noticed they occupied the bottom of the list in school priorities, teachers, and treatment.

As my student teaching year came to an end, I realized that there is something to be cherished about maintaining the hope for social justice. As a teacher, one needs to have a philosophy, to be clear about it, and to stick to it in the face of apathy and adversity. The means by which this philosophy goes into practice may evolve, but the philosophy stays essentially the same. Mine is that all students should feel valued on their campuses. As the California Standards for the Teaching Profession state, teachers must be prepared to meet the needs of "all students" in the system or the system doesn't work.

Now that I have taken a teaching job at Santa Ines High School, all is not miraculously cured. Many students are still failing, and there are obstacles to change. However, the Latino club has become stronger as the ESL aide and I organize officer trainings and introduce cultural activities. More and more students of color are poking their heads in my room to acknowledge the displays celebrating Latino Heritage Month in the glass cases in front of the library. The teachers in my department are collaborating to teach a more integrated and culturally diverse U.S. history curriculum to our students. I am getting to know the teachers who have tried to create social change and who have hit brick walls, yet keep on going. People who believe in social justice do not give up. It is an uphill battle, but one that is worth all the small kernels of progress to make this place a better and more equitable one in which to live and become educated. My story, the story of my students, and the story of my peers in the teacher education program have taught me that we must keep the avenues of communication open and carve out roles for ourselves in the process of social change leading to equal educational opportunity for all students.

Part III

WHO ARE OUR STUDENTS AND WHAT DO THEY NEED?

Linda Darling-Hammond

Who are the students we teach? What have they experienced? What matters to them? How can we reach them? How do we bring the subject matter to them while we bring them to the subject matter? Good teachers are effective because they understand their learners as well as they understand their content, and they are able to bridge the divide between what students already know and care about and what they need to learn. Figuring out how to do this is a particular challenge when our students have had experiences substantially different from our own—something that is bound to be the case in any heterogeneous classroom. To be empathic and effective with all of our students, we as educators need to develop a sense of ourselves as social beings and to develop a sense of our students' experiences and concerns as well.

Teaching in ways that are responsive to students requires that teachers be able to learn from their specific teaching contexts as well as from more general theories about teaching and learning. Without an understanding of how culture, experience, readiness, and context influence how people grow, learn, and develop, it is difficult for teachers to make good judgments about how to deal with the specific events they encounter in the classroom. At the same time, without an understanding of *particular* students, it is difficult for teachers to know how these lessons might apply. Like many other teacher education programs, STEP tries to help students develop this understanding through readings, discussions, reflections, and research about their own students and teaching practices. Cases are one strategy for helping students inquire into teaching and learning in the contexts of different content and culture.

Students write two different kinds of cases during their year in STEP, both of which are represented in this section. The adolescent case study asks student teachers to interview, shadow, and observe an adolescent for a full semester in order to understand his or her social, emotional, moral, cognitive, and physical development in both school and nonschool contexts. Students are asked to choose a student who poses a puzzle or questions for them, not someone with whom they closely identify. They are encouraged to select a student from a different cultural, language, racial, ethnic group, and/or gender background from their own so that they can learn to see and interpret the world from another's perspective. While the student teachers are reading about adolescent development in social and cultural contexts, they are asked to examine how a developing adolescent thinks and reasons, interacts with others, and views himself or herself as a maturing person and part of a social group. How does he or she learn? What motivates him or her? What are his or her concerns, attitudes, aspirations, and beliefs, as well as behaviors?

A second kind of case is the curriculum case students write as part of a course on Principles of Learning for Teaching. While reading and discussing learning theories in relation to teaching strategies, students write a case about a teaching event in which they have encountered particularly knotty dilemmas in achieving their curricular goals with their students. As the case undergoes multiple reviews by peers and colleagues who raise different considerations and possible hypotheses, the revision process helps the student teacher think more deeply about his or her experience from multiple perspectives and to evaluate a number of potential sources of as well as solutions for the teaching dilemma in question. As students share their case-study findings from both of these assignments, they develop a greater appreciation for who their students are and what they need in order to learn effectively. They begin to see school from the students' eyeview, and they take steps along the long path of becoming a learner-centered teacher who can move beyond the initial concerns for self to concerns about students and their learning.

In this section, all five of the chapters are excerpted from such cases: Susan Park's chapter, "Depending on Success," describes the author's experience as a student teacher in a ninth-grade academic literacy classroom where issues of race, class, skills, and standards collided in unexpected ways and produced new insights about students' emotional and academic needs. The chapter questions the meaning of success for the author and for her diverse group of students. Leah Anderson's chapter, "I Ain't Doin' That," describes one African American student's experience negotiating the shoals of a large, depersonalized urban high school with an unaddressed learning disability. The case illustrates what happened when the student moved from a school program that met her needs to one that did not. Roman Garcia's chapter, "Navigating a New World," describes the experience of a newly immigrated English language learner at an urban middle school, once again exploring the ways in which the school sought to meet his needs and evaluating the ways in which it succeeded and failed. Sandra Navarro's chapter, "Drop Out or Push Out?" tells a powerful story about an immigrant student's dropout experience and the ways in which community organizations were able to address her needs and guide her into higher education. Claudia Narez's chapter, "Beyond Cultural Relevance," brings us full circle to what classroom teachers can do to better address student needs by incorporating students' identities into the curriculum and connecting their experiences to the classroom.

These chapters suggest how critically important it is for teachers to understand their students' lives as well as their learning, and they provide examples of strategies to help teachers find out how their students think and what they need. Some questions for discussion in this section might include the following:

How do students' home, family, and cultural contexts influence their experience of school (e.g., their connections to the curriculum, connections to teachers, relationships with peers, and feelings of belonging)?

How might students' home and cultural contexts as well as their school experiences influence their sense of themselves as learners?

How can teachers translate their knowledge of child development into their teaching?

What do we as teachers know about our students' home and family contexts? Their communities? Their prior experiences? How can we find out more?

How can we come to understand the needs of the communities in which we teach?

How well are different school environments constructed to enable success on the part of different individuals and groups of students? What can teachers do to facilitate change?

How can teachers explicitly affirm students' identities and develop their capacities in the ways they select materials, organize their work, and develop relationships among students and between teacher and students?

CHAPTER 12

Depending on Success

Susan Park

This chapter describes the author's experience in a ninth-grade academic literacy classroom where issues of race, class, skills, and standards collided with her own definition of success. Susan Park stresses the need to understand students' emotional and academic needs while looking at what success can mean to students from diverse backgrounds. Readers may consider what "success" may mean for students with different starting points and life experiences and discuss the teacher's role in balancing student-appropriate goals with curriculum expectations.

While teaching a small group of teens in a center for high school dropouts, I opened a class by asking the question, "What does 'success' mean to you?" I was an undergraduate full of ideals and very eager to help those amazing young people as they attempted to get their lives together. We were sitting in a community center in South Central Los Angeles, surrounded by armed security guards and high, barbed-wire fencing—one designed for youth who had been referred as "at risk" but who were viewed as potentially able to make a positive change. In this building marked with signs prohibiting racism and murals showing people of color holding hands, within a neighborhood of abundant liquor stores and languishing drifters, I learned some new meanings for the word *success*.

I had asked my group of teens to think silently and personally about what success means. When the time came for each person in our circle of eight to share, Darnell took my idealistic breath away with this statement, "Success is reaching my twenty-fifth birthday." He paused. "'Cause I don't know too many Black males that get there. You know what I'm sayin'?" With all of my conceptions of the meaning of success, I had little understanding of what Darnell meant. As I blinked back an unexpected shot of warm tears, I took a deep breath of his reality.

WHAT DOES IT MEAN TO SUCCEED?

Darnell's haunting notion of "success" still challenges me as I enter public high school teaching. The small group of teens with one-on-one tutoring has been replaced with a large class in a huge school of by-the-masses teaching. The intimate circle of shared reflections is now two huge U-shaped rows of desks. My agenda of handwritten post-it notes is now a typed overhead projection. Those undergraduate ideals of what can be have become buried under the student-teaching realities of what is required. As I face my group of freshmen in a small, often forgotten city near Oakland, California, I continue to wrestle with what success means to me, to my teaching, and, most important, to my students.

The district of my student-teaching placement was purposefully "my" district. Teaching there was part of a personal full-circle as I remembered the neighborhood that reared me from preschool to junior high. My two older sisters and two cousins graduated from the high school where I now teach freshmen English. For better and worse, my family had saved enough to move up to a suburb with a prestigious high school. My parents are still not sure how to react to their youngest daughter's choosing to teach in a place they had worked so long and so hard to leave—a place that my family's work toward success was intended to escape.

Jefferson High School houses 1,200 students with a racial breakdown of about a third African American/Black, a third Caucasian/White, and a third Latino/Latina, along with small handfuls of various Asian/Pacific Islanders and Middle Easterners. This city of working-class families has little industry. Although the teachers at this high school commute from at least three different counties, all of them can boast of a reverse traffic route. Jefferson is a kind of "no-man's land," to hear my mentor teacher describe it. This city is rarely mentioned, even on local weather reports. Although some students take the train here to get away from Oakland schools, others simultaneously take buses to private schools in Hayward. When one of my students heard me describe how I lived in the same housing project where her family currently lives, she looked me up and down and said, "*You* really lived *there*?"

I really lived and I now teach here, an irony since one of the meanings of success for my parents was to get away. I received a bachelor's degree in English from UCLA to work on my graduate studies in education at Stanford University. I felt successful in my academic achievements and believed teaching would allow me to show others how they could successfully earn those elusive keys to the educational gatekeeper. During my student teaching, I wore college sweatshirts to support emblematically my hopes that my students' success would take a shape similar to my own. My representation of academia was one of many at this high school because there were so many other university researchers on campus. A frame within a frame exists at Jefferson High as researchers from Mills College, Stanford University, and UC Berkeley are each a constant, observing presence—lab rats watching lab rats.

OUR EFFORTS TO PRODUCE SUCCESS

My mentor teacher, Mr. Peterson, and I were part of a group of six teachers piloting a new course called Academic Literacy for freshman English. For this class, there were no traditional texts, such as whole novels. Instead, excerpts from novels, newspapers, magazines, and video clips formed most of the texts. The main goal of this course was to teach explicitly the reading strategies necessary to make sense of a text. As Mr. Peterson says, "Academic Literacy is a course designed to help ninth graders in heterogeneous classrooms become better readers." We hoped that direct instruction and dialogue on what it means "to think about what you're thinking about in reading," or a kind of metacognition, would help empower students by sharing the understanding of how the "what" and the "why" in academic endeavors connect. Getting freshmen to consider their academic strategies early on had huge potential. In my head, all of this translated into teaching success—success in reading, success in academia, and success in choosing from more opportunities for life.

Gloria Ladson-Billings (1994) writes, "Whether they exercise it or not, classroom teachers, particularly in [low-income] communities, have great power in determining the official curriculum" (p. 80). I felt my collaborative efforts with the other five teachers were an exercise of that power as we worked to find texts that were relevant to our students. We chose excerpts from authors of color, such as Malcolm X, Maxine Hong Kingston, and Luis Rodriguez. We centered our units around issues such as the media's bias for and against gay consumers and Black consumers, following Ladson-Billings's observation that "Culturally relevant teaching attempts to help students understand and participate in knowledge-building" (p. 81).

With a mix of African American, Latino/a, and Asian American students, combined with a generation of intense consumer culture and the increasing awareness of gender/sexuality issues, I saw this pilot course in Academic Literacy as a prime site for culturally relevant teaching. For most of my education I had swallowed the words of mostly dead, White, male writers. When I finally reached college, the chance to take Asian American or African American literature courses felt like dessert after a hard-won meal. In my teaching, I wanted to bring these fruits to students as soon as I could.

The numbers: My class of 20 students, thanks to California's recent 20:1 cap on freshman English courses, housed 12 girls and 8 boys. The racial composition mirrored that of the school with 7 African American students, 6 Latino, 5 Caucasian students, one Persian student, and one Filipina. There was one junior who was repeating the course for the third time. There was one student who was open about his homosexuality to certain members of our class. My mentor teacher began and led a Gay/Straight Alliance club during the course of this semester.

One of the major goals of our pilot course was to teach explicitly the reading strategies that get the select few through the precious gate of "academic literacy." When I was first briefed on this goal, I warmed to the idea of enacting the ideas I had read in Lisa Delpit's (1995) *Other People's Children*. I saw this pilot course as a chance to practice what she preaches regarding the need for explicit teaching that helps students of color gain access to the too-often tacit rules of academic success. Before the course began, I thought a lot about what Delpit might sound like and teach like. I looked in the mirror and acknowledged that I am a Korean American woman of petite size entering an arena of mostly Latino and African American students. As much as I was, once upon a time, "from there," I was also one who had left. Researcher Lee Shulman describes teachers as "members of a scholarly community" (Ladson-Billings, 1994, p. 95). I wanted to demystify the loftiness of this community so that my students could access it, but I also wanted to "recogniz[e] the need for students to experience excellence without deceiving them about their own academic achievement" (Ladson-Billings, 1994, p. 100).

Many of my students were not part of the community of scholars. According to survery information, they were coming from homes with few, if any, books. With the exception of one female student, the 19 members of our class made it clear that they found reading tedious and tiresome. I had a not uncommon range of ability levels in this untracked system. One of my students had been in the United States for less than a year, but she had been studying English since she was in elementary school. In our class, her writing was above average. One of our students chose to read *The Great Gatsby*, whereas some of her classmates struggled to read at all.

So far, we had asked the class to consider the types of reading people do in their daily activities. Students interviewed three adults of their choice to see how much and what kinds of reading are required. We were reading excerpts from Claude Brown and Frederick Douglass, as these men described their own struggles to access literacy. On the whole students wrote and spoke about the importance of education; however, they also wrote and spoke about their dislike for having to read school texts.

I wanted all of my students to succeed, but there were many incidents of and reasons for failure. Attendance (many of my students missed at least one day a week), stability (some of my students were being swapped from a single parent to an aunt to a grandparent), and role models (few of my students expected to be expected to attend college) were just some of the reasons. I do not mean to suggest that my class was not capable. On the contrary, my class was amazingly aware of their world and their goals; these just rarely involved academic literacy. I felt lucky to hear the insights and ideas of such a bright group of individuals.

CONFRONTING THE REALITIES OF STUDENT SUCCESS

One of the strategies I wanted to help my students acquire was to be able to understand how grammar is used in text, even if the formal rules were not present. Except in a few English classes, formal grammar rules are rarely present for the progressing reader. I wanted to show my students they might infer or get a sense of certain rules of grammar by seeing authentic text rather than being drilled through a set of meaningless exercises.

Hoping to draw my student into seeing themselves and each other as resources, I put together a groupwork activity. Each group, given a sheet of dialogue and a sheet with four numbered spaces, was asked to examine the piece of text as a piece of grammatical evidence. Without any formal lecturing, I asked the group to articulate at least four rules of dialogue usage based on the text before them. For example, one rule might be, "Use quotation marks before and after what the speaker says," or "Indent every time a different person begins speaking." There were hints to look at where commas were absent and present, to notice how speakers were used, and so on. Instead of handing down what always felt to me as the arbitrary ways in which dialogues are written, I intended to give my students the chance to discover, in a sense, and articulate the grammar in real text. I was thinking ahead to the reflective essay we would begin the following week where students would be required to use some dialogue.

Because this was our first groupwork activity, I expected some amount of settling in to the possibly unfamiliar way of learning. We were only a few weeks into the course, and it was the first time I was teaching independently without my mentor teacher, Mr. Peterson, who was absent. In an effort to get the students to know each other more and to enjoy the activity, I determined the roles for each member, such as the role of writing the rules, by who had the biggest shoe size or the earliest birthday. Deciding how to start can be the awkward part of any group task, and I hoped these roles would help groups get moving. Getting every member to talk was the objective, and a prerequisite of saying one's shoe size and birth date seemed a safe way to get initial contributions.

As I roamed the room to aid groups with suggestions and hints, I realized how I could have aided the whole class before they broke off into clusters. I was repeating myself to each group in one area that could have been addressed to the whole class. Students were struggling with a way to phrase the grammatical "rules" they were seeing. I could have given—or better yet, as a class we could have brainstormed—a few sentence beginnings such as, "When the person speaking…" or "If there is a question mark…" to jumpstart the way groups could talk about the text. As a student teacher it was typical for me to note mentally these kinds of adjustments, and I consoled myself with the idea that my learning about my teaching was important, too.

My plan following the group task was to come together as a whole class to share what the students wrote and, with the teacher's help, to determine the set of rules for dialogue usage based on their findings. I wanted grammar to be what they saw already happening in real text rather than what I mandated from a lofty book of English rules. I wanted the wording of the rules to be their own, not those of a committee of textbook writers whom they had never met. I was hoping to have the "reporter" of each group put the group's rules up as I directed a discussion about which ones we would need to remember to write dialogue in our essays.

We never got to the discussion that I had planned in my agenda. Remembering this day, I realized how the individual agendas each student brings to the classroom table might unexpectedly explode. When I noticed one of the groups was off task (one member was counting money, another was writing a note, and another was doodling on the activity sheet), I approached to inquire about the lack of progress. Although my physical proximity seemed to trigger two of the students to appear back on task, one member kept counting. Remembering all of the theories and strategies from my classroom management class, I squatted to be at eye-level with the student. Quietly, so as not to draw an audience from the rest of the class, I asked the student when he was going to get started. Anthony nodded and counted, nodded and counted. Impatiently, I waited. Then I asked where his pencil was in the hopes of offering a specific way for him to show he would get on task. No answer. "Anthony?" I ventured, once more.

The next words out of Anthony's mouth left me speechless. He looked up and replied, loud enough to draw the audience that I had been avoiding, "Why you always discriminating against me?" My brain raced for a way to find a line back to what I was teaching, how I was facilitating, and where it all went red. I felt immediately hot as the class turned their eyes to me for attention that I had not scheduled into the lesson plan. I had approached Anthony with the assumption that he was a student who could complete the task but was choosing not to and with the intention of prompting, coaching, helping. His comment suggested that I was approaching him in some prejudiced way. What had happened? Was he avoiding the task because he lacked the skills, confidence, or desire? How many seconds passed is not as relevant as how many thoughts went through my head and pumping heart. By this time Anthony had stood up, so I too stood and told him that I did not mean to make him feel discriminated against. I apologized and felt unable to say more.

The agenda on the board—to come back together as a class—had not happened as I had planned. Two of the groups had finished with the four rules, and they were reading silently. One of the groups was having trouble coming up with a fourth rule. It was time to move on to the discussion of the class rules we would use to write our own dialogue, having seen the version from Amy Tan's novel. But with Anthony's comment, my plan stood on its head, and the game of power in the classroom demanded I take my turn as the teacher. In that moment of waiting, the bell rang and Anthony was the first to leave. It was a Friday, and the assigned substitute (even though I taught the class, I did not have a credential yet and was required to have an official stand-in) had to teach another class.

By the time I spoke to my mentor teacher, the red had drained from my head and I could see more clearly some of the difficulties I had set myself up for in my planning. I realized that I was trying to teach academic literacy to some students who did not yet have basic literacy—the ability to decode text—and some who may have had unidentified learning disabilities. I later saw that Anthony could not consistently write from left to right, but used a system of text and margins that was almost hieroglyphic. I started to understand Anthony's outburst as partly a way of diverting attention from what he could not do rather than what he would not do.

I had wanted to find success in how much my students already knew, especially about their culture and experience. I did not want to add myself to the list of failing teachers that had made education painful. I did not know how to define success in a way that would bring the student and the subject together rather than set them in opposition. I had a sense that, for some students, years of academic neglect of their literacy demanded a redefinition of what success might look like. My frame of what constituted success was still academically narrow.

EXAMINING THE MEANING OF ACADEMIC SUCCESS

In our class of 20 students, the rates of success in terms of passing grades were discouraging. By the numbers, a third of the students failed the course, which meant they had received a 59% or lower. One student had returned to special education classes when his trial run through the mainstream level failed to produce what his parents and resource teachers had hoped. One student was expelled for enacting an unprovoked act of violence with racial undertones that ended with the victim's arm being broken. Two students, including Anthony, received a "D minus" that left me very uncomfortable in sending them on to the sophomore English level. Was I setting him up to fail by passing him on?

I think the wall I hit on the day of Anthony's comment came from the huge cracks between what I had envisioned as success and what my students cared about and needed to succeed. The concept of success, academic and otherwise, became frighteningly, frustratingly convoluted as the course ran its four-and-a-half month term. What does success mean for the student and for the teacher with 90 school days to learn English to a ninth-grade level? Many students are multiple grade levels behind. What does success mean for the student who comes to the classroom unable to read? Ninth-grade-level mastery for an illiterate student seems about as reasonable as demanding that a person with broken legs run a marathon. It takes time to learn what has been unlearned for years.

By the fourth month, Anthony *wanted* to read Sandra Cisneros's *The House on Mango Street* during silent sustained reading (SSR) time. He enjoyed this self-selected reading so much that he made a point of letting my mentor teacher and me know that he was unhappy when those 20 minutes were dropped on special-schedule days. My occasional attempts to check Anthony's comprehension on this novel of vignettes involved walking on ice in order to avoid the heated exchange of before. I felt defeated in not being able to encourage in a more meaningful way Anthony's interest with a text that he found worthwhile. There was a potentially teachable moment in his enjoyment of that text that I felt unable to tap.

There was also the important moment when Anthony shared his pride in finishing the Cisneros text, his first book. Anthony chose this book. Anthony read at his own pace during SSR and was not accountable to the usual activities that would accompany the text in a whole-class unit. Cisneros's book is about a neighborhood that mirrored many of my students' daily lives. Relevance, self-regulated pace, and choice seemed to be key themes in Anthony's success in being able to complete this book.

My questions continue as I wonder how much I should compromise or accommodate my curriculum when some of the students come to the classroom unable to read while others come unable to stay interested. Prior knowledge, and the lack of it, opens a huge divide between students and, too often, between races. Delpit (1995) argues that "schools must provide these children the content that other families from a different cultural orientation provide at home. This does not mean separating children according to family background, but instead, ensuring that each classroom incorporates strategies appropriate for all children" (p. 286). I knew I needed to find ways to acknowledge the different abilities each student brings to make the "all" part of Delpit's statement happen. Although I admired the elementary school teachers that Ladson-Billings (1994) described as seeking coaches and other members of the community to highlight students' achievements, I felt unconfident about my ability to parallel this endeavor with the larger population of secondary students. I started to wonder if it is a "success" when a student who can barely read makes the attempt to write an essay because he is interested in the text? Is it a failure because the attempt does not meet grade-level or classmate-level standards? How successful is it to mandate standards that are assigned by age level rather than skill level?

I stepped back from my memories of teaching this class, and I counted. Twenty students, two teachers, and one teaching assistant with a 90-minute block period, and still six students failed. Even our marginal successes—while important—were not complete. Anthony's experience in Academic Literacy left him far from the ninth-grade standards. How many teachers and how much time does it take to ensure the success of "all children"?

REDEFINING EDUCATIONAL SUCCESS

I want to be a successful teacher. And I have come face-to-face with the understanding that my efforts to teach successfully are dependent on my students' ability to learn and keep learning. Having a good essential question to structure a unit is not the same as having a successful one that reaches the students' understanding. There are many valid interpretations for why so many of the students did not succeed in this course. In his essay, "I Won't Learn From You," Herbert Kohl (1994) identifies one reason that students may not learn in a classroom: "To agree to learn from a stranger that does not respect your integrity causes a major loss of self. The only alternative is to not learn and reject their world" (p. 134). In my unintended confrontation with Anthony, I was still a stranger who had not earned his respect. Teaching students who have faced teachers who have not respected them or who have not found ways of reaching them makes the exchange of education less automatic.

I want to be a teacher of successful students. In her book, "*Why Are All the Black Kids Sitting Together in the Cafeteria?*", Tatum (1994) reminds us that "in a situation of unequal power, a subordinate group has to focus on survival. It becomes very important for the subordinates to become highly attuned to the dominants as a way of protecting themselves from them" (p. 25). I must remember that as the teacher, I am automatically part of a culture of power that places me as a gatekeeper of information I can make accessible for all or understandable to few. In some ways, Anthony's outburst may have been a way to avoid the unwanted attention to his skill level. It is less dangerous to refuse to engage in a task than to admit that one is incapable of doing it.

I want to be a teacher of successful curriculum. Does this mean every student succeeds in some way or in the same way? Jerome Bruner (1977) wrote that "good teaching that emphasizes the structure of a subject is probably more valuable for the less able student than for the gifted one, for it is the former rather than the latter who is most easily thrown off track by poor teaching" (p. 9). In the group task I had assigned, I was hoping to show my students how the subject of English works rather than simply tell them. I thought students would benefit from finding the rules of dialogue usage in actual text to emphasize what these rules look like in real writing. I was attempting to reproduce my own experience of figuring out how to use language by looking at language. This was how I succeeded academically. My assumption that my experience would serve as template for my students' learning may have helped the students who came to the table already able to read. Finding alternate routes to success for those who came with less literacy training gives new meaning to teaching "academic literacy."

In my reflections on what succeeded and what failed, I must admit that hindsight only works in the frame of a vision. By hindsight I refer to the ability to realize and analyze what has happened. By vision, I refer to the necessity of aiming for what can happen. When I think about the experience of teaching this course, teaching my students, and teaching Anthony, I try to think about what success will mean in the next classroom. Which standardized tests will my students need to jump over? Who will write the standards my students will have to meet? How can I define and organize my teaching for student success in a accessible way? In hindsight, I can see how I may have violated Anthony's strategy to survive by evasion. I can see how I may have planned curriculum for a class that I assumed was homogeneously literate rather than heterogeneously learning. As I continue to formulate my vision, I want to remember the successes that did happen. I want to remember the notes I took about how to change the group task for next time. I want to remember how Anthony wanted to read a book that he chose. I want to remember that success must be framed in light of what may have been a past failure.

I have found that looking at the meaning of success means taking routes I was not expecting. For students like Darnell who have left the school system altogether and who understand a definition that leaves me speechless, and for students like Anthony who hang on to their precarious position in the school culture of power, to be successful is to survive. The current system of grade-level standards that too often does not reflect reasonable learning goals for all students is failing the ones who begin the school year already too far behind.

As I get closer to completing my teaching credential and graduate degree in education, I wonder what success will mean—for me and for my students. Learning to teach, I have asked my mentors and professors a myriad of questions. What do I do if —, what do I say when —, and so on. I used to get frustrated by the answer "It depends." On what? I wanted a solution. I wanted a success. The more experiences I gather in the classroom, the more I realize that it *can* depend on *me*. Realizing this can be surprising, scary, and then purposeful.

I cannot stop with this understanding and believe it is enough. I expect that the more I learn from the students I teach, the more I will understand what it means to succeed.

CHAPTER 13

"I Ain't Doin' That":
Why "Doing Good in School"
Can Be So Hard

Leah Anderson

The author describes the experience of a student with a learning disability and "minority" racial status in a district with limited resources. Readers can use this minicase to consider classroom strategies for meeting the needs of students with learning differences and to examine school models that better attend to students' needs. Readers may also wish to discuss the broader implications of educational systems that continue to allow large discrepancies in meeting student needs across classrooms and schools.

By the second week of school, almost every time Mr. Roth handed out worksheets to be completed or issued instructions for the next activity, Apryl would fold her arms across her chest and call out, "I ain't doin' that." By the third week, she stopped saying much of anything in class. She would set her large backpack on the table in front of her and keep her puffy jacket and mittens on throughout the class period. She seemed to be erecting a barrier between herself and whatever was happening at the front of the class. I was the student teacher in Mr. Roth's Spanish 1 class. Mr. Roth would complain to me on an almost daily basis about Apryl's behavior. I was developing some of my own hypotheses about why Apryl might be acting the way she was, but I was interested in talking to her and hearing what she had to say about her life. Thus began my case-study work with Apryl.

MEET APRYL AND HER HAIR

Apryl is a 15-year-old African American female. She is an attractive 4 feet, 11 inches tall. She usually wears platform shoes, jeans, a tight top with stripes or a simple logo, and some sort of baggy jacket or sweatshirt to school. She has a small stud in her left nostril and many large earrings hanging from her ears. Apryl wears her hair in highly elaborate styles, and often, particularly the first day or two that she has a new style, she will bring her hand mirror to school to check and fix up her current style. Her hair styles this year have included extensions of various lengths and colors, carefully ironed curls, and various numbers of braids.

On a few days this year, Apryl has come to school without a hairdo. The day I shadowed Apryl was one such day. That day she brought her mirror, and fixing her hair was an ongoing project throughout the day. During some classes, Apryl worked alone on this project, checking in her mirror as she moved the headband up and down on her head and brushed and re-brushed the tips of her hair hanging below the headband. During other classes she recruited the aid of friends as stylists and involved an audience of fashion advisors. The project consumed most of her in-school time throughout the day, and Apryl made it a very public process, making sure everyone knew that as it stood, this style was not complete. She seemed to be asking peers to suspend judgment until she was able to present a final product.

Erikson (1968) explains that adolescent identity formation is based on four processes: how adolescents judge others, how others judge them, how they judge the judgment process, and how they assess their culture's social categories. All of these elements are present in Apryl's careful assembly of her look. She actively judges how her peers present themselves, and she actively solicits feedback and approval from her peers. She studies society's categories for what constitutes good looking and what does not.

Apryl's careful attention to her hair can also serve to distract her from classes that can be difficult or boring. It serves as a realm in which Apryl can be successful in a school day that can otherwise be filled with failures. On the day that I shadowed her, the time Apryl spent on her hair in any given class seemed directly proportional to how difficult it was for her to participate in whatever else was going on in the classroom.

MEET APRYL'S FAMILY

Apryl lives with her dad and grandmother, close to school. She has lots of cleaning responsibilities in the household, and she prepares her own meals. With everyone's work schedule, the family does not get to eat together.

Nonetheless, Apryl says that every once in a while they do something like see a movie together.

Apryl explained, "With my dad, it's cool. Sometimes we get along, but, see, we're different. I'm a Gemini, and he's a Scorpio. We have our moments, and then we start arguing, but then most of the time me and my dad is cool." I imagine that some of Apryl's differences with her father regard attitudes toward fighting. Apryl told me about one time when her father had to accompany her to school after she was sent home for nearly getting in her second fight in eighth grade. She tried to prepare him by explaining her side of the story before they got to school so that he did not buy the school's side, but apparently he was still mad at her for fighting. She exclaimed, "Ooooohh, I got in trouble by my dad."

By the looks of Apryl's cumulative folder, Apryl's dad has been to many school conferences regarding his daughter. He has talked to the learning specialists who have tested Apryl for learning difficulties. He has signed off on all of Apryl's individualized educational plans. In fact, other than one letter from Apryl's mother dated 1990 regarding Apryl's allergies, Apryl's father is the only parent mentioned in Apryl's cumulative file.

When Apryl was talking about how hard math was for her, she explained why her father was unable to help. Clearly the two of them had looked at her textbooks together and discussed them in relation to the different texts he had used in school. It sounds as if he tried to help her with the material. Apryl made a point of telling me that her father was an honors student, and he thinks that school is important. Diane Scott-Jones (1995) defines four kinds of parent involvement—valuing, monitoring, helping, and doing—the first three of which support high-performing students. Apryl's father shows clear signs of valuing education. He seems very much to want to help her with her work, but he does not know exactly how to do so.

MEET APRYL'S SCHOOL

Columbus High School is best known for its diversity, low test scores, and high numbers of truants and dropouts. About a third of Columbus's students are Black. It also has significant Filipino, Samoan, Latino, Chinese, and Vietnamese populations. The school is housed in an old, regal building in a somewhat run-down, urban neighborhood.

A 12-foot black iron gate surrounds the school. There is one 3-foot-wide opening in this gate, monitored at all times by a security guard. Inside, all bathrooms and spaces like the theater and gymnasium are locked, opened only on an as-needed basis by guards and faculty. There is one security guard patrolling each of the five hallways at all times. Students are not allowed in the building until 7 minutes before their first class starts. During class, no student is allowed to be anywhere but classrooms without a pass. During lunchtime, students are confined to the outdoor quadrangle, the outdoor area in front of the school, and the cafeteria (capacity 100). The 5-minute passing periods between classes are the only times in the day when students can move freely throughout the building.

Fights in the hallways come and go. In September, two small bombs were set off in our hallway, but I have heard of no other incidents since then. Although the omnipresence of locks and guards may help keep violence to a minimum, they also communicate a general lack of trust for students. The adults and the students often seem to be competing to see whose agenda will dominate. The adults are armed with consequences. In cases where students fear the consequences, the adults are able to maintain the upper hand and thus maintain order. This is usually the case with Apryl. She is afraid of consequences. She makes every effort to schedule her fights for after school, off school premises, as she does not want to get suspended or expelled. There are some students who do not care as much about the consequences. The school has a long process by which it can eventually get students transferred to an alternative school, but at any given time there are some who actively disrupt classrooms and hallways.

There are pockets on campus where trust is plentiful, where adults and students seem to be working together rather than against each other. One of the ESL teachers lets a group of Latina girls eat lunch in her room. They have a place on campus where they are trusted to monitor their own behavior, where they are allowed to speak their language and be themselves. There is one Samoan security guard who has developed special relationships with all of the Samoan students. They call her "Auntie," and she seems to know all of their names. When she stands at the gate at the beginning of the day, she welcomes them to school with a hug and a kiss. When she has to discipline them in the hallway, she addresses them by name and talks to them about what is going on in their lives.

Last year Apryl was a member of a special ninth-grade academy. In this academy a team of teachers collectively takes responsibility for a small group of students. The teachers structure their curricula to build off each other's classes; they follow how the students are doing in all of their classes and collaborate on strategies for reaching the students. In this academy, Apryl had some trusting relationships with adults. She reports that she felt comfortable asking her teachers for help. As a result she was highly successful with her academics her freshman year. She was on honor roll all year. She has now "graduated" from the academy into tenth grade, and as an anonymous member of the school at large, Apryl is not faring well academically. She has mostly D's. This year Apryl does not seem to have established any trusting relationship with an adult on campus.

Apryl's experience seems a direct illustration of the research of Jacquelyne Eccles and her colleagues (1993) on "stage-environment" fit, that is, how well a school environment meets the developmental needs of the students it serves.

Part of their research focuses on the ability of a school to cultivate positive student-teacher relationships. Although there are pockets of such relationships at Columbus, they are not the norm, and Apryl has not been able to forge any this year. Such relationships could play a vital role in guiding students through the decisions they are ready to begin making and counseling them about how to act responsibly.

Eccles and colleagues (1993) suggest that students need opportunities to make decisions for themselves and to practice higher order thinking. These opportunities may have been more readily available in Apryl's freshman academy than they are in the chaos of the school at large where security guards, administrators, and teachers herd students through the hallways between classes and create rules for them during class. Columbus has school-wide rules about hats, colors, food, drink, bathroom passes, and more. The school is also in the process of trying to refine its tardiness policy. Any student who arrives more than 15 minutes late to school has to get a pass to enter class. This means standing in the late student line so long that many students get tired of waiting and just leave school altogether. The result is that many students who arrive at school 20 minutes late do not get to class until more than an hour after class has started. Apryl does not credit the new system with encouraging her to be in school on time.

MEET APRYL AND WHAT SHE HAS TO SAY ABOUT SCHOOL

Apryl is very explicit about her desire to "do good in school." I never asked her about her grades, but she talked repeatedly about them. She told me that she has to get her two Ds up. In fact, her overall assessment of every class was directly linked to the grade she had most recently gotten. She had thought her fourth-period class was a good class, but then grades came out and she had a D, which made her feel it was a bad class. She has no respect for those who do not take school seriously. When one of her classmates thought Apryl was interested in a particular boy, Apryl commented, "Him?...I'm not sayin' I'm all that, but I could do much better than him. He ain't got nothin'. He ain't goin' to school."

To Apryl, "doing good in school" means pleasing the adults in charge and filling in the blanks. It has little to do with learning and even less to do with enjoying the learning process. She explained that she was learning nothing at school, except maybe in her music class, and that she has not found a subject that interests her. "I have never found a subject that I like yet. That's a shame. I've been in school heck-a long, and I don't even know what subject I like."

Apryl is eager to follow instructions if she understands them and eager to have something to turn in. She does not seem to make connections between different assignments or to extrapolate easily from examples or models. She showed me a chart she had to fill in for social studies. She had forgotten how the chart worked, so, in order to complete the assignment, she just wrote something related to social studies in each square. In Spanish class, she will readily transcribe page numbers and samples off the board, but she cannot continue without individualized help.

The teachers who worked with Apryl in the freshman academy confirmed that she had earned good grades as a freshman and that she took pride in displaying the habits of a good student: complete work, neat binder, perfect attendance. This year Apryl had little occasion to display pride either in learning or in the habits of being a student. Overall, her classes are dull, and her day is full of worksheets. At best, Apryl completes the worksheets in front of her, without understanding the blanks she fills in. At worst, Apryl avoids the work altogether. She enters the room, leaves her big puffy jacket off, and puts her large backpack on the table in front of her. She no longer has to announce, "I ain't doin' that." Her body language and actions make this statement clear. Instead of working, Apryl engages in conversations with her friends, fixes her hair, feeds herself, and organizes her papers. Observing Apryl, one finds it hard to imagine that she ever was on honor roll. Her performance in class rarely represents her stated desire to "do good in school." In the following section I hope to explore some of the reasons for this.

APRYL IN SPANISH 1 ON A DIFFICULT DAY

Apryl walks into class 15 minutes late. Mr. Roth informs her that she cannot sit with her friends. Apryl proceeds to seat herself in the corner with her friends. Mr. Roth declares that he is going to call Apryl's counselor to come to class and talk to Apryl, and that he will give Apryl none of the worksheets the class is required to complete until Apryl moves her seat. As Mr. Roth circulates the room, he makes no eye contact with Apryl. Apryl freezes any time Mr. Roth comes within earshot of her desk. Otherwise, she leans back in her chair, engages in conversation with the boys around her, and rearranges the papers in her backpack.

Apryl raises her hand to ask me for the worksheets about 30 minutes into class. Mr. Roth instructs me not to give her the worksheets, explaining that she will get no work until she moves. Apryl's conversation with the boys around her gets louder and more animated. She pulls food and drink out of her bag and starts eating and drinking. She gets out of her seat every 5 or 10 minutes to stand at the window to see what is going on outside. She starts a couple of exchanges with students across the room. Every once in a while, Mr. Roth shouts at Apryl, "You cannot talk in class." Apryl replies either that she "ain't talking, give me the work" or that she is "waiting for her counselor," and Mr. Roth starts ignoring Apryl again.

Fifty minutes into the 110-minute class, a boy near Apryl gets so disruptive that Mr. Roth starts filling out the paperwork to have security remove him from the classroom. Apryl starts packing her backpack. When security shows up at the door 10 minutes later, Apryl runs toward the door and begs the guard to remove her from the classroom. The guard cannot remove Apryl without a teacher request. Mr. Roth finally tells the guard to take both of them.

APRYL IN SPANISH 1 ON A LESS CONFRONTATIONAL DAY

Mr. Roth is showing the class *Casper, The Friendly Ghost* with voice-over in Spanish and no subtitles. Students are supposed to watch the movie and write down any words they understand. Apryl is seated between two boys. She starts measuring the size of her hand against the hands of the boys around her. Mr. Roth comes by once to ask the threesome about paper. One boy takes out paper. Apryl and the other boy ignore him. They spend the rest of class taking naps on the backpacks in front of them and talking quietly to each other between these naps. They are not disruptive, but they never engage in the activity prescribed for the class.

Some Possible Explanations

My initial hypothesis was that Apryl was rejecting her work because the classroom environment threatened her pride, that to maintain her image she had to reject academics. After talking to her and observing more of her classes, I came to realize that this was only part of the issue. Often Apryl was really unable to do the assignments given her. Furthermore, the social world around her was so seductive that academics often seemed secondary. Apryl's image and pride, the nature of the academic world in which she finds herself, and the influence of social forces all conspire to produce her current situation in school.

Apryl's Pride and Image

Apryl is very clear that pride and image are important issues in her life. She never mentioned them in relation to the classroom, but she spoke extensively about how she deals with issues of pride with her peers. If anyone says anything untrue about Apryl or makes her look stupid, she fights that person, especially if any of this is said in public, in front of other peers.

Apryl's pride seemed to emerge as a particularly salient issue in Mr. Roth's class. Mr. Roth's interactions with Apryl were highly confrontational. He wanted Apryl to comply with his rules, but he never took the time to explain how these rules could work for her or work for the class as a whole. They seemed to be mere extensions of his authority over her. In addition, the rules were sporadic and not universally applied. Therefore, when Mr. Roth attempted to enforce them with Apryl, it often seemed a personal assault instead of an enforcement of stated rules. For example, after the first few weeks of school, Mr. Roth would periodically decide that Apryl should not sit with her friends. He had good reasons for deciding this. Apryl was often highly distracted by her friends. But Mr. Roth never discussed his reasons with Apryl; he never gave Apryl any sort of warning, and he never had a specific plan for where Apryl should sit. On what seemed to be random days, Mr. Roth started class by yelling to Apryl and at most one other student, "You don't want to sit in your regular seat today" in front of the entire class. Apryl had usually taken a seat by this time, and she had the attention of the whole class. Everyone watched to see if she did as the teacher told her or if she did as she wanted. She almost never moved.

When Apryl did not comply with Mr. Roth's requests, Mr. Roth often voiced his frustration aloud to me in Spanish. In this Spanish 1 class, most students cannot understand regular conversation, and Mr. Roth was careful not to use Apryl's name. Nevertheless, I suspect that Apryl can usually tell when she is being talked about, and that the rest of the class can tell when Mr. Roth is talking about her. Once, a Samoan boy sitting near the front of the room blurted out, "Why don't you just say it to her face?" This only made complying with the rules more risky for Apryl's pride and image.

The degree to which teachers degraded Apryl as they issued instructions seemed to have visible effects on her willingness to adhere to such instructions. The day I shadowed Apryl, she had brought a gallon jug of Sunny Delight Orange Drink to school. In every class, she put her gallon of Sunny Delight on the desktop in front of her and drank from it sporadically throughout the lesson. Officially there is a school-wide policy against drinking and eating in class. Almost every teacher responded in some way to Apryl's Sunny Delight. A few made nervous jokes about the large container, acknowledging that Apryl had the drink but never asking that she put it away or refrain from drinking it in class. Mr. Roth yelled, "No drinking," at Apryl. Apryl said, "I ain't drinking," which, officially, she was not doing at the very moment she and Mr. Roth had the interchange. Apryl defiantly kept the jug in front of her and continued to drink from it sporadically, banging it back on the desk after each sip. In physical education, Apryl had the jug in her hand on the gym floor. Her teacher approached her privately:

> *Teacher* (playful tone of voice): How much of this stuff are you gonna drink in one day?
> *Apryl:* The whole thing.

Teacher (serious tone of voice): Don't spill it on my gym floor. If you want to drink it, drink it over there. (Points to fringe of gym, beyond lines painted on floor) I don't want any on the floor.

Apryl came over to where I was seated (at the periphery of the gym) and asked if she could leave her juice at my side. The teacher had approached Apryl privately and spoken to her rationally, explaining why he was asking her to keep the drink aside. He had also already established a positive rapport with the students in the room. Complying did not threaten Apryl's image the way complying with many of the instructions issued in Spanish class seemed to.

The Academic Material Itself

Many of the assignments Apryl gets in school come out of context, with minimal instruction, rationale, or support. Watching a full-length feature film in Spanish is extremely challenging for a Spanish 1 student. Most do not have the language skills to understand what is going on. When Mr. Roth had the class watch *Casper the Friendly Ghost* and asked them to write down words they understood, he never introduced the movie: He did not teach students how to accomplish the task he wanted them to accomplish, alert them as to what to look for in the movie, provide any rationale as to why they were watching the movie, or pause the movie to check for comprehension. He just put the movie in and let it run. As an observer, I interpreted the purpose as a relaxing, nonconfrontational way to wind down a week on a Friday. I was not surprised that students slept through it. There was no reason to want to watch it.

Requiring 110 minutes worth of worksheets is equally inappropriate. Although the material on the worksheets may be more relevant to the Spanish 1 curriculum, no group of students should have to sit still for nearly 2 hours to fill in blanks. Tharp and Gallimore (1988) insist that teachers "must develop ways of balancing 'automatic,' didactic teaching with teaching that assists learning" (p.16). The worksheets Apryl has at school almost always ask her to regurgitate information from another source. They do not represent opportunities for assisted learning, and they do not challenge her to think critically or uncover deeper levels of understanding. These assignments were not unique to the Spanish classroom. In fact, all of Apryl's academic teachers focused on seatwork the day I observed.

Finally, many of Apryl's assignments come with very meager instructions. Mr. Roth usually explains activities orally at the front of the classroom, but his explanations are short and vague and he rarely offers examples or models. Furthermore, he never posts any sort of written reminders to accompany his oral instructions. After issuing instructions, he writes a page number from the book on the board and tells students to start. In such cases, Apryl almost always opens her book to the right page and glances at it. Sometimes she even takes out a piece of paper and writes a heading on the blank page. Sometimes she also raises her hand to ask for further instructions. Usually she just sits at her desk and waits, open book in front of her. If I pass her while circulating the room, she asks for aid. She completes the assignments that have been made clear, but most assignments are not clear to her.

I asked Apryl to bring all of her binders to a meeting in which I planned to assess her cognitive development. Most of Apryl's binders were empty. She explained that she gets worksheets when she gets to class, completes them, and turns them in. Apryl's biology binder was an exception. She had copied down a daily agenda, had notes, and activities and labs. Biology was the only class Apryl had anything good to say about. "We do fun things. We do projects and stuff. Like 3 weeks ago we dissected a worm. And then comin' up we got to look at some intestines and stuff." This class seems highly organized and well prepared. Each day there is an agenda on the board to copy down. Notes are presented clearly with overhead projectors. Labs all have handouts with clear instructions. The activities are relevant and fun. I believe this explains why Apryl completes such a high percentage of the work in her biology class. She responds to more interesting, more organized, and better-explained work.

The problems inherent in vague instructions and poorly organized assignments are confounded by Apryl's learning disability. In sixth grade Apryl was given a battery of tests to check for learning disabilities. In seventh and eighth grades Apryl had Individualized Education Plans, which required that she spend two periods a day with a learning specialist. When she got to high school, she was assigned to the counselor who specializes in learning disabilities, but each counselor at Columbus has close to 500 students. Apryl does not seem to receive extra services in high school. It seems highly likely that Apryl truly needs individualized help with her work. However, Apryl's teachers do not offer assistance and asking for help is not always easy for Apryl. She will ask me only if she does not have to yell across the room to get my attention, and she will almost never ask certain teachers. This seems part of her attempt to protect her image.

When she has access to individualized help, Apryl is able to perform. In Spanish class, if I get her started on a set of worksheets, she continues to complete them after I move away. She was very successful with her work in the freshman academy. I asked her what it was about the academy that helped her. Access to individualized help was the crux of her answer:

> 'Cause the teachers, they would help you. It's like now, some teachers, you gotta keep callin' them over and over, and it's like you get tired of sittin' there and callin' them. See, like, in the Academy, they'll come right to you. They'll help you. They'll sit down with you until you get it. They'll break it down for you. They'll do that with every single individual....And that's

what made me do better. See, now, you gotta depend on yourself more than the teacher. Because you getting' older, you gotta figure out how to do it yourself.

Vygotsky (1978) defines teaching as assisting learning within a learner's zone of proximal development. This is a highly individualized process where support varies depending on the strengths and weaknesses of each learner. It involves a stage where teacher and student complete the task jointly, teacher modeling for student, until the student has the skills to perform the task independently. This is what Apryl needs. Unfortunately she does not have access to such teaching in large classes with no specialists and instructional aides, and with teachers who are not trained to teach to multiple modalities for learning-disabled students.

We are at an impasse in terms of Apryl's success in Spanish class. Denial of individual help is the first consequence Mr. Roth likes to apply for students he feels are not respecting him or listening to his instructions. Apryl is one of the first students to talk to her friends during class and/or put her head down on the desk. Thus Mr. Roth has decided that Apryl is not trying to listen to instructions and therefore does not deserve individualized help. Mr. Roth has forbidden me from talking to Apryl or helping her with her work. He feels that this is necessary to train Apryl to listen closely to directions and respect the teacher. Since Mr. Roth has begun applying this consequence more regularly, Apryl has been decidedly off task.

Mr. Roth hands out lots of low grades, and he points out every mistake that students make, even on points they have not yet been taught. For example, Mr. Roth gave students vocabulary lists for articles of clothing and colors. He reviewed these individual vocabulary words in class, then he asked students to write sentences with the vocabulary. He never mentioned or modeled that in Spanish, adjectives generally follow nouns or that adjectives agree in number and gender with nouns. When he corrected student sentences, he took off points for both of these kinds of errors. He explained to me that he could not let such grave errors go unmarked: You COULD NOT say such things in Spanish. But he did not explain to the students why these sentences were marked, and he did not give students an opportunity to rewrite their sentences. Papers covered in red marks with poor grades recorded at the top were the final product, not one step in the learning process. Furthermore, Mr. Roth does not offer positive feedback on papers; only the errors are marked. It is easy for students to believe that they are personal failures and that they will never be able to succeed.

Almost all of the feedback Apryl receives for the work she completes is negative. She often does not understand what her grades are based on or what she can do to improve them. She interprets them as a sign that she is just not good at school. Although her testing from middle school suggests that math is her strongest area, and Apryl reported that when she was younger she enjoyed math, she emphatically informed me, " I do not like math. I cannot do math."

> When I was little, I liked pluses and stuff. You know, that's easy. I'd be like, "Mom, write me some problems." So I could do them at home. Just have her write them down; I just do them quick. Now, math? I can not, I do not.... Oooh, I hate math. That's just something I do not do.

Given that Apryl enjoyed math when she was younger and given that her test scores were higher in math than in any other area, I imagine that Apryl's distaste for math has far more to do with how math has been presented to her than with her innate capabilities. I imagine that she believes herself to be similarly incapable in most academic arenas. This would explain why she normally aims for completing instead of understanding in her work. It is likely that Apryl does not believe that she is capable of understanding.

It seems that Apryl subscribes to an entity theory of intelligence. This means that to Apryl intelligence is fixed, something that each learner has or does not have. It is not a malleable trait, developed through the learning process. According to Henderson and Dweck (1990), learners who have entity theories of intelligence tend to be far less motivated. They give up readily because, instead of believing that they can develop capabilities, they are convinced by the slightest challenge that they are permanently incapable.

CONCLUSIONS

Working with Apryl has helped me understand the many reasons she might announce "I ain't doin' that" the second week of Spanish class. First, like most adolescents, Apryl cares deeply about image. For the sake of maintaining and protecting her image and self-esteem, Apryl can spend half a day doing and redoing her hair. For the sake of maintaining and protecting her image, Apryl can drop her jacket and backpack in a split second to engage in a physical fight. For the sake of maintaining and protecting her image, Apryl can reject all activities and instruction presented in a classroom.

Second, Apryl is not receiving the structured, individualized aid that she needs to be successful in school. As a result she rejects and avoids many school tasks, and thus she does not perform at very high levels. In classes, Apryl has had very little opportunity to practice formal reasoning. Tasks that require these skills are rarely present in Apryl's classrooms, and when they are, Apryl rarely gets the support she would need to complete them successfully. She is accustomed to not understanding, accustomed to failure, and accustomed to giving up.

Apryl is not a happy case study. Immediately after she offered her one hopeful description of a better world where "people can get along with other people," she told herself to shut up because she did not believe in the world she was describing. Just before completing this case study, I left Apryl's school. I will not have the opportunity to take part in helping Apryl make her dreams of a better world a reality. I hope that others will. Nonetheless, my work with her has opened my eyes to some issues that face adolescents so that I can be respectful of image, provide meaningful assignments with ample instructions, individualized help and constructive feedback, and respond sensitively to social needs for the Apryls I encounter later in my career.

CHAPTER 14

Navigating a New World: The Development of an Immigrant Student in an American Middle School

Roman H. Garcia

Roman Garcia describes one student's experience as a newly immigrated English language learner in an urban middle school that could not effectively meet his needs. The piece illuminates how a newcomer encounters the social and academic complexities of a new school that encompasses many cultures and expectations. Readers may want to consider how students experience such a dramatic change and how schools might ease their social, emotional, and academic transitions.

The point from which newcomer students observe, learn about, and begin to interact with "America" is always from the sidelines.
　　　　　　　　　　　　　　　—Laurie Olsen, *Made in America*

　　For some, adolescence is a positive time where challenges are met with fervor and unending energy; for others, it is a perplexing and difficult time filled with struggle and strife posed by new changes in all aspects of one's older but still young life. Teenagers' new social environments call for new social relationships, and new relationships call for new behaviors. It can be a tumultuous time when a youth is caught between being a child and becoming an adult.

All of these changes are compounded in the lives of immigrant students, who are trying to figure out the answers to essential questions of being in a new place. Language, culture, custom, practice, racial identity, national identity, and social relations are just some of the realms through which a newcomer must navigate. "What does it mean to be American?" (Olsen, 1997, p. 20) is the over-arching question guiding newcomers' efforts to adapt and fit in. Through my experience as a student teacher, I was able to profile these changes in the life of one immigrant student, a newcomer who was living and experiencing adolescence in what was for him a very different and new social context.

As a future teacher in California, I will be expected to teach a multitude of students from very diverse backgrounds. Many will be very similar to Jose, the focus of this case study. Examining the life of this one adolescent gave me a deeper understanding and greater confidence in my ability to reach and engage this type of student in my own classroom.

INTRODUCING JOSE

Jose is a 13-year-old male Salvadorean student attending James Moore Middle School in San Francisco, California. He arrived in the United States only 4 months before this school year began and enrolled in James Moore with his younger brother, who is an 11-year-old seventh grader.

Other than the light mustache on his upper lip, Jose has a kind of "baby face" that shows the potential for growing into a stereotypically handsome appearance. However, he loses status because of his dress: He is growing out of his pants, and thus they are tight and short—what adolescents refer to as "high waters." He wears a stained New Orleans Saints (National Football League) jacket every day, and he wears name-brand tennis shoes, but they are an older style of shoe rather than the "popular" style the higher income students wear. Jose walks with a waddling motion, which appears to be a slight limp or stagger, leaning his weight to one side of his body over the other. This may be because a car hit him when he was younger in El Salvador. His knees appear to be slightly bowed. His dress and physical appearance influence how he is accepted by peers of his age. Nonetheless, he carries himself in a confident manner, despite how his American peers might be viewing him.

The first contact I had with Jose occurred during the second week of school. My cooperating teachers and I were informed that Jose was a very recent immigrant who did not speak any English. This drew my attention to him because I knew he would add a different dynamic to our classroom. In our Spanish immersion classroom, Jose would be in a class with diverse students, all of whom speak Spanish, but not many of whom are recent arrivals like he is.

As Jose took a seat on the first day of class, I could see that the reality of being in an American classroom was hitting him. He uncomfortably examined his unfamiliar surroundings, taking in the classroom and his new peers. He had a look of concern on his face, and he said very little during the class. After class he asked me to help him find where he needed to go. I helped him and sent him on his way. That was the last I saw him for a couple of days. The next day he was moved out of my classroom and placed in another. After a few days, I was approached by a colleague who expressed concern about her experience working with a boy who spoke no English and was struggling from the first few moments of stepping into her ESL classroom. Over the first few weeks of the quarter I learned from his teachers that Jose was not adjusting well socially, and he was not doing well academically.

Jose's Family World

Jose and his family are originally from a rural community in El Salvador. Jose described his home as a "canton," a place that is a small and tightly knit community. He described the roads connecting his town to the "city" as small and unkempt. Jose attended a parochial school in his small town for 7 years before moving to the United States. He studied some of same subjects that he is studying at James Moore. He also studied some English, but he did not retain any of it. Jose used a computer in his El Salvador home for entertainment and for homework, yet it was a model different from computers commonly found in the United States.

Jose's family's move to the United States fragmented his home life. For about 4 years Jose and his siblings were separated from their parents. While his parents lived illegally in the United States, Jose and his siblings lived with their grandmother and with uncles and aunts. Today he lives with his immediate family in the city of San Francisco, reunited with his mother, father, one younger brother, and a younger sister. Jose's father is in charge of monitoring the progress of Jose and his siblings. He has attended various events at the school and has consulted frequently with Jose's teachers over his progress. Jose's father is present at home more than his mother, who works in a clothes factory from 6 a.m. to 8 p.m. I assume that Jose's family is living close to the poverty level, because his parents work so much.

Jose has been strongly influenced by the drastic change he has experienced moving from a small town in El Salvador with a close, tightly knit community to a major metropolitan city that does not have the same sense of community. Jose stays indoors most afternoons. His unfamiliarity with San Francisco street names and different parts of the city illustrates his discomfort in exploring his new environment.

Jose's School World

James Moore Middle School serves approximately 460 students across grades 6–8. The school's population includes 46% Latino students, 27% African American students, 7% Filipino, Chinese, or Native American students, 8% other non-White students, and 12% White students. The student population could be characterized as consisting mostly of students from low social economic status backgrounds. The staff at James Moore has made a commitment to urban school children in the best way they can. Nonetheless, the school was recently tagged as a "low-achieving school," based on SAT-9 test scores used by California to rate the public schools across the state.

Despite the low achievement of its students on standardized tests, James Moore is seen as a leader in urban school reform because of its efforts to redesign the school to better meet the needs of its students. The Spanish Immersion Program in which I student teach is part of James Moore's effort to meet the needs of English language learners. Students like Jose who participate in the Spanish Immersion Program receive approximately half of their academic content in their native language and the other half in English. English as Second Language (ESL) classrooms serve as supplements to instruction received in English. Jose's schedule consists of an eighth-grade social studies/language arts Spanish immersion core, a seventh-grade science/math Spanish immersion core, physical education (PE), and an ESL course.

The faculty decided to place Jose into a seventh-grade Spanish immersion classroom for science/math because he had no English proficiency when he arrived, and he had made no progress in the eighth-grade math/science class in the first few days. James Moore's inability to provide focused instruction for the very beginning learner of English is a constraint on Jose's English-language development. Jose's only exposure to English occurs in his ESL classroom and in physical education. Jose has also been attending an after-school English club that provides tutoring in English and help with homework.

Jose's Social World

Jose's interaction with friends and peers throughout the day is very minimal. He has relatively low status among the adolescents in his classes as well as outside the classroom. Jose mainly interacts with Latino students, who represent the majority of students in his classes. Within this group, Jose interacts mostly with the monolingual and newly immigrated Spanish-speaking students. He interacts less frequently with bilingual students who are native speakers of Spanish but who have gained higher proficiencies in English. He interacts minimally with monolingual English-speaking students and non-Latino students.

It is understandable that in adapting to a new environment, Jose is gravitating to students who are the most like him and are having similar experiences (Olsen, 1997, pp. 41–43). Although Jose has some interaction with second-generation and bilingual students in the academic setting, not much can be interpreted as friendly social talk. Even though students in this group acknowledge Jose in the classroom setting, it is as if Jose is "invisible" to them in any other contexts. In *Made in America*, Laurie Olsen (1997) makes mention of the way more English-proficient or "Americanized" students choose to put down newcomer students for using Spanish, and they themselves begin to reject the use of Spanish (p. 104).

The bilingual students do not treat Jose badly, but they do not strive to help him when they easily could. Early on in the semester, Jose relied heavily on his peers for help in understanding directions and instructions. As the year progressed, many of the students who used to help Jose have distanced themselves from him. He now relies more heavily on his teachers. Although it is good that he is interacting with his teachers, it is possible that his teachers feel overburdened helping him. His style of asking for help can pose other challenges. He often blurts out loudly the moment he doesn't understand something; this causes a disruption and interrupts the teacher's flow. He has yet to learn more appropriate ways of asking for help.

In my shadowing of Jose, I saw some peer interactions that were very detrimental to his well-being. In the course of approximately 1 hour, Jose was verbally threatened on three occasions; he was punched twice, kicked once, and elbowed repeatedly by three of his peers. Much of this was done outside of the sight of his teachers. Jose told me that this has been occurring since the start of the school year. I advised his teacher, and the tensions were dealt with for the day. I noticed Jose was agitated in later classes from the occurrences of the day. The same day, Jose asked me to help him with this problem. Luckily this treatment has diminished because his father consulted with administration and the teachers I notified have helped. I believe Jose's learning is greatly impacted when he has to deal with the stress created by such incidents.

Jose's closest friends, not surprisingly, are two students who are English Language Learners and newly arrived immigrants like himself. Jose spends most of his free time at school with these students. One of his friends, whose name is Salvador, is someone Jose previously knew in his home country, which was a surprise to Jose when he got to James Moore. Jose and Salvador depend on each other and help each other out with homework both inside and outside of school. His other friend, Hector, is a student with whom Jose interacts at school but not outside of the school environment. Hector and Salvador are a year younger than Jose. Jose counts on them in the seventh-grade science/math classroom they share, but he remains without close friends in his other courses.

Jose's closest relationships and attachments lie within his family circle. Jose's family is a large part of his life. He relies on them for emotional and social support. After school he spends a lot of time in the home, caring for his brother and sister. He is strongly attached to his parents. During the weekends he often plays softball or baseball with his uncles and other extended family members. He also gets encouragement from his family, especially his family back in El Salvador. He occasionally calls back to El Salvador to talk to his grandmother and his cousins and tells them about the different things he is learning. He voices gratefulness for their encouragement because he sometimes gets homesick and their kind words make him feel better when he misses the world he left. Jose's experiences illustrate Tatum's (1997) findings on the importance of "familism" found within Latin American communities. Friends and peers outside the family, although close, very commonly remain second in terms of personal importance in one's life.

THE SOCIALIZATION PROCESS AT JAMES MOORE

At James Moore there is a climate of ethnic conflict characterized by daily scuffles and fights between African Americans and Latinos, especially in the halls and on the schoolyard during lunchtime. At the heart of this ethnic conflict is a clashing of cultures that is exacerbated by language divisions. Students' miscommunications with one another have started many conflicts, often because they can't understand each other. Many of the fights start over simple things like someone accidentally bumping into another in the hallways or misinterpreting what one person is saying in reference to another. There is less conflict between bilingual and English-speaking Latinos and African Americans, who are able to avoid potential fights with a few apologetic or tension-calming words, than there is between those who do not share a common language.

Over time, I have seen Jose progressively develop many of the feelings and opinions expressed by Spanish-speaking Latinos toward African Americans. Jose's experience illustrates Olsen's (1997) findings that, in seeking to become American, immigrants place themselves and others on the "racial map" and social hierarchy of American society. Recently, I was surprised at Jose's verbal attacks when speaking about African American students. Early on in the school year, I asked him if he was having any problems with any of the students in his classes or at the school. He said he had no personal problems, but he noted that he knew of conflict existing between Latinos and African Americans. I asked him how he felt about it. He told me he didn't care because they were not his problems and he avoided that kind of stuff.

On another occasion, we witnessed a fight between a Mexican student and an African American student from afar. He shook his head and said, "There it goes again." Jose said this was the second fight he had seen or heard of during the same day. On a third occasion, I was waiting for him to get through the lunch line. When an African American student tried cutting in line in front of him, Jose reacted in a confrontational manner, telling him in Spanish to go to the end of the line. They stared each other down before a cafeteria worker and I intervened. Jose later referred to this student using a derogatory term. He apologized for his language use, but he phrased it as though he was apologizing for disrespecting me by using a bad word rather than apologizing for talking that way about African Americans. He seemed to expect me, as a Mexican or Latino, to hold the same opinion about this ethnic group.

The most recent reference occurred in early November. I picked him up from his classroom before lunch to conduct an interview. He thanked me for picking him up that day, even though it was an unexpected visit. He said, "You saved me today; there is going to be a rumble today at lunch between the Black students and the Latinos, they have been squabbling for the last couple of days, and they were both threatening to bring weapons to school." Again he referred to the African American students in a derogatory way. He didn't apologize this time.

I believe Jose is developing prejudice. I think this attitude came in part from incidents he experienced and in part from hearing these kinds of messages from his Hispanic peers. The word he used to refer to African American students was the word *mayate*, which is a derogatory term used by some Mexicans toward African Americans. Jose may also be picking up some of these attitudes from the actions of some staff and faculty at James Moore. It is not uncommon to go by the office and see it full of African Americans sitting in there for disciplinary reasons. Out of the 691 referrals written over a 6-month period at James Moore, 44% went to African American students even though they account for 27% of the total student population. The staff is confronting this trend, but I think that there are messages sent when African American students are being disciplined around every corner. A student like Jose could be deducing that something is wrong with these students, rather than questioning the attitudes at the school.

JOSE'S DEVELOPMENT IN THE SCHOOL CONTEXT

Supports for Jose's Social and Emotional Development

The picture I have painted of Jose's social development and his efforts to fit in provide a grim picture of his everyday struggles. One might think that Jose is an emotional mess. I don't think this is the case. However, Jose is definitely going through a roller coaster of emotions every day as he moves through different contexts throughout his day.

Observing Jose in different contexts suggests that he is more comfortable in some contexts than in others. It is clear than at James Moore he is most comfortable in his Spanish Immersion classrooms. In these classrooms he can ask questions of his teachers and peers and can expect to hear answers to those questions in Spanish. In these classrooms Jose has enough "functional literacy" to interact. From my observations, it appears that Jose has the ability to "understand regular instruction, to read texts [and manipulate materials], and follow directions, as well as to generate correct, meaningful, and appropriate text in the areas of instruction" (Trueba, 1989, p. 119). This literacy makes social participation in the classroom more accessible. In these classes, even though he may not interact with peers about nonacademics, Jose can and does interact with peers. He says that he has "more" friends in these classes and he is learning the most from these classes. It is also in these classes where he has been able to maintain average grades and have some semblance of success.

The happiest moments of the day for Jose at James Moore come when he is hanging with his closest peers, Salvador and Hector. Jose smiles when he talks about his friends. It is these friends who provide him with the little social/peer support he receives at James Moore.

Jose's Academic Development

Jose's emotional development is tightly linked to the effort and success he is having at school. Jose's idea of success in the United States is based on the idea that learning English is the key. From the onset of the school year, Jose has been more and more disappointed at his lack of learning English. Although he is not wrong, I believe he puts too much emphasis on this. I think because he is not being taught English, the most important thing to him, he does not value succeeding in the classes where he is learning in Spanish.

Jose is undergoing what Olsen (1997) describes as "language shock." Success for Jose has become synonymous with becoming "American." As Olsen says of new immigrant students, "They need to learn English, they want to learn English, but there are also limits on the opportunities to learn and practice English." This frustration with language leads him to "devalue" his abilities in other areas of study (Harter, 1990; Henderson & Dweck, 1990, p. 313). Students who believe that their intelligence is fixed or is dependent on something like learning English begin to "avoid challenges" (Harter, 1990, p. 356). Jose appears to distance himself emotionally from the academic work he is receiving in Spanish and thus not to engage it fully. Most of Jose's academic problems result from the fact that he does not turn in assignments and he gives up easily, even when it seems that he understands enough to complete them.

Jose pays attention in class, and he asks a lot of questions. He tells the teacher that he doesn't understand, but then he can't tell her what part of the directions he doesn't understand. I observed that, in one class, when an aide explained an assignment to him individually he seemed to understand it better.

I am wondering if instruction in El Salvador was more individually focused, or if he is used to getting individual help and attention. His frequent requests may also be because the teacher and the aide are the only people he can really count on to help him without being put off, because his peers do not make any effort to help him. I feel it is because of this frequent lack of understanding that Jose, like many English language learners, is constantly playing catch-up in the classroom and not completing his work.

In my investigation, I analyzed a copy of a spelling test he took in his ESL class. I could see why Jose is not doing well in this class as the words are far too advanced for a student at his level of English proficiency. Observing him in this class, I found Jose very disengaged and his anxiety level high, because success in this class is so distant. This problem is compounded by the inability of the ESL teacher to individualize more effective instruction for him. This is just one of the ways that some of the instruction at James Moore has failed Jose and probably other students in his situation.

There are other signs of disengagement. In physical education, where his grade is based solely on participation, Jose sometimes chooses not to dress even when he does have gym clothes available. It could be that he is modeling the behavior of the students who are viewed as "cool" because they refuse to dress. This may be a means of trying to fit in, or it may be a way of avoiding ridicule from others in response to his awkward gait. Recently, Jose has been missing school more frequently. It could be that he is cutting to avoid being at school altogether, although there could exist more legitimate reasons. The absences occur in a sporadic fashion that would suggest cutting.

On the other hand, I found out that Jose attends after-school English Club regularly. He said he really likes this time because he is learning "useful" English. The English club provides a safer and more comfortable setting where Jose can practice and begin learning English, an important personal goal (Olsen, 1997, p. 98).

The support and encouragement Jose gets from his family and the fact that he is grateful and feels privileged to be in an American school are the only things that keep him going through the motions. He has told me that he is happy at James Moore overall, but it is hard to see how he can say that given his daily experience. Emotionally, I think he has taken on the goal of doing just enough to survive academically.

THE SCHOOL AND THE STUDENT: HOW JAMES MOORE HAS MET JOSE'S DEVELOPMENTAL NEEDS

When Jose arrived, he posed a puzzle for the staff at James Moore. How does the school meet and fulfill the needs of Spanish-speaking newcomers? The majority of James Moore's eighth-grade ELL students are somewhat proficient and function adequately in the bilingual English as a Second Language classroom. Jose's ESL teacher stated his eagerness to help bring him along in his class. He tried to incorporate Jose into his classroom but became frustrated by Jose's lack of success, which resulted from the fact that the language and vocabulary of the class were inappropriate for meeting Jose's more basic language needs. James Moore simply didn't have any structured classrooms or programs that catered to very beginning language learners.

Jose's academic struggles at James Moore Middle School were dismissed early on as simply a case of culture shock. He was placed in Spanish immersion classes, with the expectation that he would begin to perform better. This never happened, and his struggles began to compound. In early October, some teachers voiced concern over Jose's progress. He was beginning to show signs of academic struggle. He was scoring low on assignments and tests, and he was failing to turn in some assignments. At this point his problems were downplayed because the staff felt he was struggling to adapt to his new environment. In his two immersion classes, his teachers did not see any major cognitive problems; he wrote well in Spanish and always showed some level of understanding. He was doing poorly because he was not turning in work. In his ESL class he was struggling because of tardiness and absences. A suggestion was made that Jose be considered for an individual academic plan known as an SAP (Student Assessment Program). By gathering a group of teachers and school staff, recommendations could be made about how to move Jose toward academic and social success. Nothing was done about this suggestion at that time, because students showing disciplinary problems were considered more important for SAP.

Over the next 2 months, Jose continued to struggle. Jose's social studies/language arts teacher suggested that Jose be considered more seriously for SAP because it was clear he was en route to failing his classes. Eventually, when others showed some interest, scheduling conflicts interfered. Finally, an individual plan of action was created for Jose at the end of November. Unfortunately, the people involved did not really know Jose and the meeting was held on a day when neither I nor another real advocate for Jose could attend. The team that met assumed that Jose was scarred by war in his country when in fact he was never directly affected by it. It was assumed that his problems were a result of culture shock. In a short interview conducted by the school nurse, she found out many of the things I already knew about Jose, especially his overwhelming eagerness to learn English.

At this point the school made a plan for Jose. He would be pulled out of ESL to work individually with a counselor, he would be encouraged to attend homework club after school to help him complete his work, and he would be put on a list of students going on a trip to Mexico to help him increase his socialization with peers. At this point it was apparent that James Moore was trying to mobilize its limited resources to help a student like Jose. This action plan was implemented for all of one week.

On December 8, my cooperating teacher and I were called in to the vice principal's office for a meeting about Jose. The vice principal suggested that because Jose would turn 15 years of age on December 20, he would be eligible to attend Newcomer High School. Newcomer High School serves Latino and Asian immigrant students who have been in the Unites States for less than a year. The suggestion was made because it might be a place where Jose's needs would be better met by teachers working with similar students. The Newcomer High School environment might be less threatening because it catered to students in circumstances very similar to Jose's. It could possibly provide a place where Jose could build friendships, interact and participate more easily. An added benefit would be that Jose would receive high school credit toward graduation for work he would do at Newcomer High.

When the idea was proposed to Jose, he seemed somewhat puzzled at first, but as we explained more about the school, he became interested and began to ask questions. The vice principal was very familiar with the services offered at Newcomer and explained them thoroughly. Jose smiled more and more as he heard more information. He seemed glad that we were suggesting something different from James Moore. Jose and his father went to visit the school that same day.

Jose came into my classroom 2 days after the conference to thank my cooperating teacher and me for all the help we provided him during his stay at James Moore. He and his parents had decided that he would attend Newcomer starting the following Monday. Jose smiled broadly, graciously shook our hands, and gave us a thank you hug. He said he was excited to be going to the new school and was looking forward to it. He promised that he would try his best at his new school. He promised to visit and then slowly walked out of the classroom.

That was the last I saw of Jose. As he walked away I felt personally proud of him. I know that Jose is a genuinely good person with a very big heart. Watching him walk out of the classroom, I felt that Jose was going to a good place where maybe he could reach a higher potential as a student and in life. He is a student who, because of his circumstances as an outsider, will be met with further challenges, but with hard work and a continuing resiliency he may very well persevere.

CONCLUSION

Jose's experience provides a good example of the problems encountered by many American adolescents. Jose's adolescent development takes on a different tone because of his experiences as a newcomer to an entirely different social and cultural environment. Jose, like many immigrants to the United States, is experiencing difficulties in the transition. In my opinion, Jose's problems ultimately lie in the difficulties experienced by a person who tries to operate across different worlds (Phelan, Yu, & Davidson, 1994, p. 418). Jose perceives these borders—especially language—as nearly insurmountable obstacles. Jose's lack of English proficiency, his overwhelming desire to learn it, and his lack of opportunity to obtain it impeded Jose's ability to see success as a possibility. This perception, compounded by low socioeconomic status, will continue to pose problems for Jose unless he is in a school that addresses his needs. My hope is that Newcomer will provide better supports for Jose, because further failure will only lead him to a bumpy and obstacle-ridden road of life.

CHAPTER 15

Drop Out or Push Out?
Succeeding in Spite of the System

Sandra Navarro

In this case study, the author describes a student's dropout and gang experiences and the ways in which community youth organizations were able to address the student's needs and guide her to eventual success. Readers may want to consider what schools can do to better meet students' needs for identity development and intellectual challenge and discuss what steps they can take as teachers and school leaders.

In Spanish there's a popular saying: *Cada cabeza es un mundo.* In English this saying essentially means there's a different world inside each head. This case study attempts to understand the world(s) of Karina, a 19-year-old resident of Oakland, California. Karina's is the tale of a late adolescent Chicana who, in the face of adversity, has overcome tremendous obstacles. By exploring these multiple worlds as experienced by Karina, we come closer to grappling with a fundamental question: How is it that some youth who experience multiple stresses in their most formative years learn to cope and become strengthened by those stresses while others do not? As we are bombarded daily by the bleak statistics of "dropout" rates among Chicano/Latino youth, this question becomes an even more crucial one.

I first had the privilege of meeting Karina at a Chicano Moratorium youth organizing meeting a few years back. In the brief interactions we had in the ensuing years, I saw her develop from a streetwise, 49er-starter-jacket-wearing, tough-minded young adolescent to an articulate, vocal, and socially conscious

Chicana working for her community—one who is, as she would say through code switching, "down for her *gente*." Having witnessed this grand transformation, I wanted to come to understand Karina's different worlds

KARINA'S WORLD OF YESTERDAY

Karina immigrated to this country with her mother and sister as she was ready to start seventh grade, at the critical period where most researchers agree that the school transitions coupled with multiple stresses directly affect the self-esteem and academic success of many students, particularly females. Because her family fled from political persecution in El Salvador, she quickly gained political asylum. Before arriving in this country, however, she had already experienced the trauma of a war in which all her male cousins and uncles were assassinated for being part of the FMLN (*Frente de Farabundo Marti para la Liberacion Nacional*). Because her family was constantly under threat, they had to move from El Salvador to Guatemala and Mexico and finally to the United States.

Even though her childhood was in constant turmoil, Karina nonetheless was exposed to a good, stable educational system in which she attended *colegios* or private schools. Through this quality education, she was able to excel and graduate at the top of her sixth-grade class. However, upon her settling in Oakland and attending an inner-city school, much of this changed.

Karina's Neighborhood Through the Eyes of Its Youth

When Karina arrived in the United States, she faced an urban setting with a new and very different language, culture, and educational system. The city of Oakland, a predominantly African American community, is situated in the East Bay near San Francisco. Karina belongs to a neighborhood known as Fruitvale, a community located in East Oakland where an increasing number of immigrants from Mexico and Central America are settling. Perhaps the best picture of this community can be obtained by listening to the voices of its youth. In an *Oakland Blueprint for Youth Development*, teens vividly describe the fragile realities they confront:

On physical safety: "Violence affects everyone; it's not just the person involved ... family members and the community are affected. The community hears the violence... it sounds like a war zone. I've personally lost two friends who were shot and killed."

On suspicions or solutions: "There is a great concern about being arrested for no reason. Even if you dress normal, act normal, don't drink, don't smoke, the police still harass you....They look at you and judge you."

On family bonds and family stability: "People join gangs because they need a family—gangs are like families." "My mom can't tell me not to go to jail because she's been in an' out. Same with smoking weed." "I'm not like my parents. They grew up in Mexico on a ranch ... I know my mom didn't go through what I'm going through."

On financial pressures: "Y'all send somebody to the penitentiary. I was raised on welfare. Had no shoes, no clothes. I said I'm fixing to go get us some clothes. You're wrong for trying to sentence us without even knowing what's going on. People grind because they're trying to take care of their younger brothers and sisters."

On opportunity: "People want to work. Youth are frustrated by the adult population. Respect youth voices; we are losing energy because we are not giving opportunity to youth."

Karina's School

Karina enrolled in Roosevelt Junior High, a large, bureaucratized institution serving a mix of African American, Asian, and Latino adolescents. She coped with these new changes by developing a network of friends who, like herself, spoke Spanish. Karina said that she came ready to learn with the encouragement of her mom, who expected her to go to school every day and to do well. As a new student Karina was put in English as a Second Language classes and for the first semester, she recalls with pride, "I was even on the honor roll."

Soon, however, the misfit between the school and Karina's needs pushed her off the honor roll path. She began cutting some classes, because they were "boring and the teachers didn't know how to teach." When I asked her to explain what was boring, she said, "everything was easy. All we did was work out of the book and on dittos and stuff." Gradually Karina cut more classes, until she wasn't attending any even when she remained on the school premises. Karina's experience mirrored the research that has found that "classwork during the first year of junior high school requires lower level cognitive skills than does classwork at the elementary level" (Eccles et al., 1993, p. 94). This unfortunate emphasis on lower level cognitive strategies is insensitive to adolescents' psychological development. As they become more able to deal with abstract cognitive demands, students like Karina become bored if they are not academically challenged.

The adolescent need to question, to develop a self-identity, and to examine the world from multiple perspectives was also unaddressed. Karina noted that, "Whenever I would question the curriculum and/or ask about my culture, [the teachers] simply ignored me, never taking into consideration what I wanted to learn." She further explained that there were a lot of "fights and stuff," and the school "seemed to be on a power trip, so much that one time I got suspended for questioning a teacher." As Noar indicates, "Teachers who do not fully understand the need for independence are prone to bemoan the seeming loss of respect for their authority.... Instead of encouraging growth in these directions, the school too often makes rules and regulations that deprive the pupils of independence of thought and action" (cited in Takanishi, 1993).

Although Karina felt that she was "cool" with most of the students, she would on occasion get into fights with those "who looked at [her] wrong." Coincidentally, this period of time was when gangs were starting up in Oakland. Soon after that first year, Karina began to hang out with LN (Las Norteñas), an all girl crew that was an extension of the male *norteño* gang. When asked why she joined, she responded by saying, "At first my home girls didn't want me to jump in, but after a while I just bothered them enough and they let me in. I mean I was already hanging out with them anyways. The only difference was now I claimed LN."

That Karina would seek out LN membership is not surprising, since group affiliation is one of the central preoccupations of early adolescence (Takanishi, 1993, p. 11). In Karina's situation, group affiliation manifested itself around gang membership. When asked why the gang had formed, she explained the "gang" was formed primarily because there was a lot of racial tension between Blacks and Mexicans during that time. By being part of a gang, Karina explained, "my home girls had my back and they had mine." Diego-Vigil (1988) notes that "relying on one's peers to manage fear is generally helpful. But to receive such support requires reciprocity; thus, behavior is shaped in a mutually reinforcing way to benefit the self and the others" (p. 155). As a result, this type of relationship grounded in street culture creates an "adjunct to self-image" (p. 156). This fear-centered behavior required Karina to put herself in undesirable situations for the benefit of others in order to gain the same benefits in return. Reciprocity bound the gang together.

Academically, things got progressively worse. Even though she still remained at school, Karina and her "home girls" never went to class. By her report, they "hung out in the gym." This behavior continued for almost 3 years, until Karina was finally socially promoted to the 10th grade and enrolled at Fremont High School. Unfortunately, because the issues Karina faced were never dealt with, she remained in the 10th grade for almost 3 years. Karina continued cutting classes, but now, because it was open campus, she "cut out" to students' houses or parks to "party, drink, smoke weed, you know." Being on the streets largely unsupervised became her pastime.

Eventually, when Karina reached an age at which the counselors figured there was no way she could accumulate enough credits to graduate, they forcibly referred her out to Edward Shands Adult School. This method of "cleaning house" is something I have seen routinely done in order to manipulate the "dropout" rate to appear lower than it really it is. Most of the students who are referred out don't attend the Adult School or get their high school diploma. The referral process is a token attempt to salvage an adolescent's possibilities for attaining a high school diploma. Karina was no different from most others in this position. She "dropped" out.

KARINA'S WORLD OF TODAY

Today, Karina is an expressive, bright, brown-eyed, dedicated, healthy young woman who stands tall (5 feet, 6 inches, to be exact) with confidence of who she is and who she is striving to become against all odds. She demonstrates this in nearly all settings, ranging from when she's hanging out with her "home girls" to when she facilitates weekly youth organizing meetings aimed at raising social consciousness among Chicano youth from all over the East Bay. At times her sporty demeanor and spontaneity can mislead one to think of her as a typical adolescent absorbed by mainstream mass culture. However, as one begins to travel in the path that connects her worlds, the journey reveals that these perceptions are mere façades.

Karina's Development

Karina's appearance can vary from day to day, depending on what she is involved in. If she is intensely involved in a political event, you can see a natural glow emanate from her beautiful brown skin. Most of the time she can be seen with her shoulder-length red-streaked brown hair pulled up in a ponytail. When her schedule is not as intense, she can be seen with her hair worn down and wearing just enough makeup to enhance her already beautiful features. A unique touch is how Karina makes herself a walking bulletin board. She often wears a T-shirt announcing an event she is involved with or a political statement, such as: "I didn't cross the border...the border crossed me!"

Karina has an unshakable sense of self-confidence in her abilities. All of the facets of Karina's life—her school, work, friends, and family—seem to affirm and reinforce her bilingual/bicultural being. The theme of identity is the common thread that runs throughout adolescent development. Karina has clearly achieved an integrated identity. Presently, her identity transcends that of her national origin and defies borders. As a self-identified Xicana with an "X," she identifies with the political definition of the word, and she takes it to a spiritual level based on an indigenous belief system and worldview. Karina writes "Xicana" in this way as a social-political statement that adopts the Nahautl pronunciation of X and rejects the Hispanicized form.

I had the opportunity to witness Karina's spirituality within the context of one of the weekly *Olin* (Nahautl word for movement) meetings in which she has been involved for the past 6 years. First, the whole group, mostly although not exclusively Chicanos, gathered in a circle led by someone with burning sage who acknowledged the four directions—North, South, East, West—and then passed the sage for everyone to smoke. This tradition is grounded in Native (North) American spirituality. The sage, an indigenous plant of North America, is significant because when it is burned, it releases a smoke that guides the bad energy away and into the sky. Although it has many uses, in this particular situation it was used for spiritual cleansing, recognizing the interconnectedness of the body, heart, spirit, and their relation with nature. This ritual illustrated how hope, renewal, and decolonization are integrated into the work of community organizing.

Karina's Friends

As an adolescent who had been pushed out of the formal educational system, Karina has surrounded herself with a peer group that has heightened her awareness and raised her consciousness. She gives credit to a group of Chicanos who have embraced her as no school system ever has. This alternative form of support and guidance has allowed her to evolve from being a "gang" member to lead organizer and role model in her community. Her leadership abilities that once were grounded in the "gang" culture have been channeled and converted to serve as an example and a means of self-liberation. As she points out herself, "When I first became involved in organizing I thought it was bootsy. I would just show up to kick it, you know meet people. I would be wearing my colors proud, until people who talked like me, looked like me and actually went to U.C. BERKELEY started to break it down. They didn't tell me that what I was a part of was wrong, but they questioned it: 'why?'"

Later, through Karina's affiliation with Barrios Unidos, a gang unity organization, she became aware of how gangs were a form of oppression that could divide and conquer young people, preventing them from creating a more powerful and united presence for transforming the community. The role of mentors who served as friends, not teachers or preachers, was instrumental in supporting Karina's positive efforts without explicitly trying to change her behavior or character. These mentors are mostly youth like herself who "walk the talk" and don't just "talk the walk." She first became connected with them when they started organizing at her school. Because they were people deeply committed to working actively toward the betterment of their community, their Raza, Karina became interested. Among the mentors, Karina has a tight circle of friends who have been involved in organizing. Because they are somewhat older than she is, they, like her other mentors, serve as role models.

Among the many things her mentors support her with is advice about school. Karina mentions that they serve as her guidance counselors. Whenever she has questions about papers, grades, or other school matters, she seeks their advice. I observed how their uplifting tone and their confident stance was reassuring and personally empowering for Karina. From these observations and in speaking to Karina it is very clear that both Karina's friends and mentors help provide her with the motivation, confidence, and hope she needs to continue on with her endeavors.

Work

Whereas most young people her age are still dependent on their families for economic support, Karina is entirely self-sufficient. Growing up in a single-parent household, always living from pay check to pay check, and never having the luxuries most adolescents take for granted have perhaps made this transition, although not an easy one, a more manageable one. Currently, she lives in a flat that she shares with friends whom she met while organizing. Although she admits to being "broke" most of the time, it doesn't dissuade her from being an activist while at the same time having to juggle working and taking community college courses.

Karina currently works at the YMCA where she is a youth group leader and facilitator. There, she is able to influence directly the lives of young children in elementary school who are considered at risk for getting involved in gangs. She facilitates meetings where they discuss topics of interest to children ranging in age from 7 to 13. Karina talks enthusiastically about the children she works with: "The kids are so cute! I mean I know I'm ghetto, but they are hella ghetto." When asked to explain, she offers this anecdote. "One day we asked the kids what they wanted to be when they grew up. One kid raised his hand and says, 'policeman,' another student raises her hand and says, 'a cashier at Payless,' then another says, 'a doctor,' and then finally another answers, 'I wanna be a pimp!' Of course all the students burst out laughing. Even I couldn't help it but laugh."

Karina later explained that even though the students might have been playing around, it was a great moment to talk about what the word meant to them, as she mentions most of the students are influenced by the rap songs and the lifestyles they project and that's where they pick it up. Karina's background and good rapport with the students enable her to make such responses into teachable moments to raise consciousness about issues of power even with students as young as 7.

Karina's Unspoken Worlds

Many times I learned not from what Karina said but from what she didn't say or whom she didn't mention. Throughout my quest to understand her family situation in relation to her school experiences, I was faced with the eternal question: "Where's your mom in all this?" As I attempted to question her about her mother's role in her adolescence, Karina seemed to avoid answering. When she reflected upon her "gang" involvement, I inferred that her mother, maybe because of having to work and sustain a household, didn't participate fully as a parent, thus limiting her ability to establish a close and involved relationship with her at this critical stage.

Research suggests that "adolescents are more influenced by friends when their parents are neglecting or rejecting" (Berndt, 1996). After speaking with her friends who had known Karina and her mom, I got the sense that her mother had issues that she might have been grappling with herself. This was later confirmed from an interview Karina conducted with her mom for her class in "Latinas in the United States," in which Karina's mom openly admitted to past and current use of marijuana. Perhaps the traumatic loss of her brothers also affected her mother's ability to deal with the tremendous responsibility of being a single mother in an new and alienating environment. At the same time, the interview illuminated Karina's mother's inner strength and ability to survive and persevere. There is no doubt that Karina's strength has come from her mother, whose personal experience growing up as a revolucionaria enabled her to see women's roles beyond those traditionally held.

Stepping Into Karina's Private World

Karina's room provides a visual representation of the things that influence her. The decor reflects the dichotomy of the worlds in which she is simultaneously immersed. One world is represented above her bed by red (the color representing the norteño gang) hanging T-shirts that carry her nickname, "Wina," and "R.I.P Albertito," demonstrating the self-destructiveness of the gang life. Her present world is represented by certificates of recognition beside the door for her involvement in the Chicano/Latino community, perhaps hung here as a daily reminder of her purpose before she exits out into the world. Posters illustrating the rich Aztec and Mayan history that now defines her identity as a Xicana as she follows the "red road" in her journey toward liberation also are strategically placed on her walls.

Alongside her bed on top of her nightstand is a carefully placed bundle of sage. Karina explains that she burns this as a means of purifying the mind, body, and soul. It also seems to serve as a means to ground her, connecting her to madre tierra. She further explains how through her involvement in organizing she has not only been politicized but has also found a spiritual path that recognizes "[her] indigenous ancestors and their world views."

The small rectangular room is adorned with pictures ranging from family members and close friends to her beloved three nephews. Among the pictures that wallpaper her bedroom, the one that is located symbolically at the center is her boyfriend of 5 years, Pedro, also known as Cabezon, literally meaning "big head" in English. As Diego-Vigil (1988) notes, "The use of nicknames, while it affirms group membership, also grants personal anonymity" (p. 113).

Unfortunately, *el amor de su vida* Cabezon is currently serving a 7-year sentence for gang related homicide. According to Karina, Cabezon was unjustly accused and prosecuted for a crime he didn't commit. She believes that he was set up by the police and coerced to give false incriminating evidence. Although he is incarcerated, it seems that their love and respect for each other have been able to permeate past the cell block walls and withstand the test of time. Along with his family, Karina visits him whenever possible.

Karina's World of Language

Throughout the time that I observed Karina, she was able to navigate eloquently through Spanish and English. She demonstrated her command of both languages by her ease of code switching without hesitation at the word, phrase, and sentence levels. She was able to appropriate meaning by using a Spanish word within the context of an English sentence and/or vice-versa. For example, when she described how sensitive she is, Karina remarked, "I do a lot for people. I expect people to be appreciative. Oh, yeah, *con una palabra* [with a word] you can kill me." This demonstrated her ability to use a popular Spanish expression within the context of English.

Researchers find that there are positive cognitive consequences to being bilingual. As Reynolds (1991) notes, "The picture that emerges of the...bilingual...is that of a youngster whose wider experiences in two cultures have given [her] an advantage which a monolingual does not enjoy. Intellectually [her] experience with two languages systems seems to have left [her] with the mental flexibility, a superiority in concept formation, and a more diversified set of mental abilities" (p.169). From my observations of Karina's language use, it was clear that she was able to demonstrate this "mental flexibility" to get her points across. This is especially crucial as being a leader also involves effective and at times motivational methods of communication. Although she usually uses English as her base language, her ability to code switch adds to her effectiveness in engaging youth who strongly identify with the two worlds across which she speaks.

Karina as a Thinker and Learner

Karina openly admits that she is most engaged in learning when she is not inside a book or in a class but when she herself has to teach. "When I teach I have to know it and so I really get into it." For example, within the organization she is in, she is able to do this through KBLs (Kick Back and Learn). KBLs are informal sessions where youth get together and learn something they are not taught at their schools. Topics range from "Columbus: Hero or Invader" to issues of machismo. Most of the time Karina plans and prepares KBLs with other university students; this makes it almost a social event.

Although most of her learning does take place outside of class, when Karina is in class she demonstrates a high level of cognitive ability. Her most recent English midterm, for example, demonstrates a high degree of metacognition, as Karina's account of her great challenge in learning to be "nice to a man" shows her ability to be self-reflective and self-aware. Throughout her paper she constantly examines and reexamines her feelings and "aggression" toward "guys," using evidence and examples to support her main idea. In her introductory paragraph she strategically links her own behavior to that of her mother and grandmother, offering us evidence about her own insight into the attitudes she has about men. Throughout her paper she offers concrete, vivid examples of her dilemma and how she continues to struggle with it, successfully engaging the reader and revealing her self-reflective thought process. She is conscious that her dilemma has no short-term solution. "For me this is a real and hard challenge that is going to take me years to do something about." Even though her paper ends with uncertainty, knowing Karina as I do, I believe she will struggle with this until she herself comes to realize what is best for her.

Karina as an Actor Upon Her World

Karina never finished high school and, until recently, she has limited her traditional classroom experiences. Today she is doing well in community college, where she has a 3.8 grade point average that she is proud to share. Although at times she is faced with the dilemma of juggling school and political commitments, for example, participating in a rally or protest, she seems to be able to juggle her time efficiently.

When one watches Karina put forth her heart and soul as an activist, it becomes evident that she is fully absorbed in the act of learning by means of acting on her world while actively transforming it. Through her involvement in the organization Olin, she constantly battles social injustices at the local, national, and world level. Being the sensitive person that she admits she is, Karina finds this a moral dilemma with which she struggles daily. She seems to embrace her sensitivity, transforming it into the passion that drives her to face injustices actively. Observing Karina in meetings, walkouts, rallies, I became aware of her deep commitment for change. I saw her participate in the rally against the presence of Urban Warriors in Oakland and at a Bay Area youth walkout protesting many educational issues, among them the passage of proposition 227, eliminating bilingual education. From these observations it became vividly clear how determined this young lady truly is.

Unlike many youth who feel powerless against the dominant structure, Karina is proactive in challenging the status quo. She demonstrates a great deal of moral responsibility to her community, her Raza, which enables her not only to understand multiple perspectives but to argue them as well. This has been learned not within the walls of any classroom but from her daily interactions with social contradictions and her growing understanding that injustice cannot continue because where there is oppression there is resistance!

CONCLUDING THOUGHTS

Karina's story confirms that "there are negative consequences for adolescents who must cope with several transitions at once" (Simmons, Burgeson, Carlton-Ford, & Blyth, 1987, p. 123). The multiple stresses experienced by Karina were intensified during the critical period when she had to adjust to new societal norms, learn a new language, cope with a bureaucratized junior high school, and deal with social alienation and marginalization. This combination of stresses created a crisis situation that was heightened by a school system that failed to offer the developmentally appropriate academic and social supports Karina needed. Given the large impact that stage-environment misfit has on young adolescents, it is vital that we consider not only the consequences of organizing an appropriate school environment, but also a classroom environment that provides adolescents with challenging curriculum that adequately supports their identity development.

KARINA'S WORLD OF TOMORROW

When I asked Karina "What are your future plans?" she answered: "Well, first I want to transfer to Berkeley and double major in sociology and Chicana studies and then go for my Ph.D. at UC Santa Cruz where Angela Davis is." "And then what?" I said. "Basically," Karina responded, "I want to be a counselor, like Diario (a youth advisor and organizer at the Spanish Speaking Citizen's Foundation in Oakland) and work with youth like they did with me."

Karina's plans for the future are buttressed by her passion and her determination to continue her education. Her determination is driven not by individualistic goals but rather by her concern for others: "My mom never saw my sister or me walk on stage in junior high or high school. I want to prove to people that I can do it, that I am capable....*Tambien*, how am I going to promote education when I organize if I'm not going through it myself?" Karina now understands exactly why and for whom she is investing her time and energy, making her journey toward her goals both grounded and realistic.

CHAPTER 16

Beyond Cultural Relevance

Claudia Angelica Narez

Claudia Narez describes both the successes and surprises she encountered in trying to increase student involvement through culturally relevant curriculum connected to students' lives and experiences. Readers may wish to contemplate how
curriculum can be used to create a forum for honest discussion that expands student voice while creating a safe space for all classroom members that translates
into greater accomplishment for students.

My goal is to create an environment in the classroom where students feel
proud of who they are and what they can accomplish. Through my curriculum,
I want my students to find characters and texts they can relate to on a personal
level, so that they "see" themselves in the curriculum and know that school is for
and about them. I believe that teaching culturally relevant curriculum is not
merely throwing a few good "ethnic books" into my Spanish classes; it is also the
cultivation of culturally relevant ideas, conversations, and critical thinking
about the way we live and experience culture in our communities. Thus it is
important to me that my students read about diverse characters who encounter
and overcome barriers similar to those they experience in their own lives.

I believe that students enter the classroom with a great deal of knowledge
and experience; as teachers, we have to build on that knowledge. Cognitive psy-
chologists tell us that students are more likely to remember concepts and theories if they can connect them to their personal experiences. If students find curriculum familiar and relevant to their own lives, it is more likely that they remain
engaged in the subject being discussed. In addressing cultural issues in the
classroom, I feel it is vital to present issues my students experience on a daily
basis. In my Spanish for Native Speakers class, composed primarily of first gen-

eration Mexicans, we address issues that are not always part of a typical foreign language classroom—issues such as immigration, migrant labor, child labor, identity, and socioeconomic status.

According to Ladson-Billings (1994), "Knowledge is continuously recreated, recycling, and shared by teachers and students. It is not static or unchanging" (p. 81). My goal is to "continuously recreate knowledge" in a Heritage Language Classroom. I want to give students a sense of comfort and familiarity they might not find elsewhere.

The high school at which I student taught was an excellent venue for this kind of teaching. Located in San Jose, California, Channel Islands High School's 1190 students were 64% Latino, 19% White, 6% African American, 2% American Indian, and the remainder a combination of Vietnamese, Filipino, and other Asian. Among the 431 English Language Development (ELD) students, there were 301 Spanish speakers, 51 Vietnamese speakers, and 79 speakers of other languages.

Although a Spanish 1 class for native speakers with 38 students of Mexican descent might seem homogeneous, it really is not. Students come from different regions, and they include first- through third-generation immigrants; thus they bring very different experiences to classroom discussion. Some students have just arrived from Mexico and are confronted with an array of unfamiliar situations. Others are familiar with this country, and they are also familiar with the prejudices many of their families have faced.

These differences also influence the manner in which students perceive each other. The students seem to have assigned different labels to their peers in class. At the two extremes are the "new arrival" students, who have difficulty with the language, and the "pocho/a" students, whose parents are of Mexican descent but who do not speak Spanish in their homes and are consequently not fluent in the language themselves. There are students in my class who have had interrupted schooling in their native countries and who now encounter greater difficulties in a new country having to learn a different language and build their reading and writing skills in their native language. These labels in turn affect the participation of individuals in class, because they often feel self-conscious and fear how their peers might react.

In addition to these kinds of diversity, the students in my class cover all secondary grade levels and ages and have very different reading, writing, and communicative skills. There are several students who are enrolled in the Special Education Program, and there are students who are in the Advanced Placement or Honors Program. When planning lessons I always struggle to find activities that will be equally challenging and engaging for all students in my class. My practice is to teach to the top and keep my expectations high for all students as we read through and discuss literature in class. Then, I spend more time working one-on-one to meet the needs of my students and bring them up to a higher level as needed.

In this process I have seen how students who are not native speakers of English experience difficulties while reading texts in my own and other courses, not only because of language but because their cultural knowledge is distinct from what the texts assume as a base. All texts make assumptions about referents, life experiences, and language usages readers are expected to bring to the reading process. As Carol Lee (1995) observes, "The influence of cultural background knowledge on reading comprehension is particularly problematic for students whose home language or language variety differs markedly from the mainstream standard dialect that is taught in most schools in the United States and that is reflected often in the canon of literary texts taught is most secondary schools" (p. 611). Culturally relevant readings that make stronger bridges to my students' life and language experiences have helped me negotiate the challenges I've faced in my development as a student and a teacher.

THE STRUGGLE TO CREATE
CULTURALLY RELEVANT CONNECTIONS

Given all of the diversity present in my Spanish for Native Speakers course, I encountered many different points of view that frequently led to heated class discussions. Students find themselves torn between the identity that has been assigned to them by society and whom they perceive themselves to be. As a teacher, I wanted to address these "labels" by showing my students that as a class, we all face similar experiences as a subculture within mainstream America, and by helping them create a more positive sense of self and community.

These tensions, evident throughout the year, escalated during my unit entitled "Our Life in Community." This unit included an array of literary texts that focused on the relationships within Latino communities. I thought that it would be enriching for the students to address issues they might be experiencing in school or in the community, including experiences with racism and discrimination they had shared in class. I wanted students to see the richness that their culture brings to the community and to confront the negative feelings many had expressed when speaking of their Latino heritage. When we raised discussions of cultural matters, the students would often say that they did not want to talk about "those things" because people would call them "wetbacks." They seemed to believe that the labels given to them by society were reinforced and validated when they talked about cultural issues.

As a Latina teacher who had experienced similar feelings as an adolescent, I wanted my students to understand that our culture should not be hidden or thought of as shameful. In college, I was exposed to texts relevant to my identity for the first time. Being exposed to texts about topics I had encountered in my life and having the opportunity to discuss them led me to increased self-awareness and a feeling of validation, instead of a sense of shame and obscurity. I wanted to share with my students the experiences Latino authors have shared about racism and discrimination through literature. I wanted to let them know that it was acceptable for them to talk about the issues present in their communities.

When discussing controversial subjects such as racism and immigration, I anticipated that students might not be aware of what occurs in their own community. In class discussions prior to this unit, some students had accused their peers of excusing society's oppressive treatment toward people of diverse racial backgrounds and denying the reality that exists in minority communities. I could not figure out how to address this issue until I read a case written by Deborah Juarez (1999), a teacher who found herself in a similar situation. She states, "We in this country have the task of dealing with these issues that are often perceived as threatening; however, the greater threat is denial. More than being ineffective, denial is debilitating, building walls rather than breaking them. Either we deal with issues of race, culture, and class or the issues will deal with us" (p. 125).

I wanted to share my own awareness of these issues and open a dialogue with my students. I saw myself in them as they looked at their school and home communities. Finally, I could see that by ignoring these difficult issues, my students were becoming disempowered as I once had been. As a teacher, I felt it was my responsibility to turn their class experiences into empowering ones through supportive dialogue.

As part of my unit, the students were to read a short story entitled "El Premio" ("The Prize") by Marta Salinas. This story discusses issues of identity and discrimination experienced by a young Latina student. On the basis of my observations of and conversations with the students, I felt that the lesson related to problems present in our classroom as well as the students' lives. I hoped that the background of the students would facilitate comprehension of the text. Like Deborah Juarez (1999, p. 113), my intent was to affirm students' reality through an academic focus and elicit their response in the process. I wanted them to become aware and empowered while learning about social injustices. By analyzing and discussing different issues, they would in turn build analytical skills that would transfer to other subject areas and allow them to assess social issues more critically . But would this be enough to generate empowerment? And how was I to face the challenge of controversy?

CLASSROOM CONTROVERSY AND ITS SURPRISES

I decided to confront the controversy by first helping students more clearly identify their views. As part of my unit, I used eight statements to set the stage for the two short stories. The students were to determine whether they agreed or disagreed, based on their background knowledge and prior experiences. The statements were as follows:

1. Justice always prevails at the end.
2. In the majority of cases, teachers are fair and just with their students.
3. Students should respect teacher decisions even though they might not agree.
4. One must always fight or defend their rights.
5. We should not trust those who do not look at us in the eye.
6. Students of low socio-economic status are not successful academically.
7. Race and ethnicity does not influence the various awards given to students.
8. Advice from parents and grandparents is always valuable.

The students' responses to the eight statements produced a heated discussion. All the students in the class wanted to answer and give reasons for their points of view. Although the responses and reactions varied among students, in many ways, the discussion went very well: It motivated the students to pay close attention to the story they were about to read.

In the discussion, when some students shared their experiences and interpretations, others played the "devil's advocate" and shared alternative interpretations for scenarios. Some students in the class expressed their frustration because they felt that Latinos are treated unfairly by dominant cultures. This led long-suppressed feelings of anger to surface. For example, Francisca, a sophomore in the class, expressed a great deal of resentment toward teachers. In response to the statement that "teachers are always right," Francisca argued, "Students have no rights, you can kick us out. Teachers have the power in their hands and when it comes down to it and a student complains 'cuz they were unfairly kicked out of class—who are they gonna believe? I mean, students have no rights, really." Many students agreed with the examples Francisca provided, although they seemed hesitant when sharing those thoughts. I felt this was partly to do with my being "the teacher" in the class.

That entire class period was dedicated to discussing the various topics that would be addressed in the stories to be read the following day. Although I was inspired to see how many students were affected by the class discussion, I noticed a few students were not participating and seemed simply to listen to the comments made by their peers. I began asking questions to the class in hopes of encouraging others to participate. However, this actually encouraged the students who were already participating to dominate the discussion even further. After class, several students approached me and shared thoughts on the issues addressed in class. I suggested that they share some of those experiences with other students in the class, but they seemed almost offended that I suggest they share such personal experiences with other students. These students felt that they would be labeled "stupid" by their peers for not having better handled the situations they had encountered. Discussing discrimination had a negative connotation to these students because they think it is partly their fault that they are discriminated against.

I was concerned that perhaps the environment created in the classroom had been geared toward certain students in the classroom, and consequently excluded many others. The students participating in the discussion included some who were usually the less vocal. I knew that it was a great achievement, but I still wanted to push other students to participate and feel included in the discussion.

The following day, we began by briefly addressing the issues discussed previously. We continued reading the first story, "El Premio." The story focused on the experience of a young Latina who performed well in school and was offered the honor of being the valedictorian of the school. The protagonist overheard a conversation between two teachers discussing why she should not be given the award because she was of Mexican descent. One of the teachers wanted the award to be given to the daughter of a school board member. The administration staff decided that since they could not turn her away because she had the highest grades in the school, they had to figure out a way to have her decline the honor. The principal of the school offered the protagonist the award but told her it required that she pay a fee she could not afford to pay. When she asked her grandfather for the money, the grandfather simply said "No!" The grandfather thought that it was unfair to charge a student for a prize or an honor she deserved. She then proceeded to go the principal and let him know that she could not pay the money. Ultimately, the principal's conscience would not allow him to deprive her of her prize, and he honored her with the title.

While reading, various students raised their hands and asked clarifying questions. When the class finished reading the story, the students reacted strongly; they were frustrated at how this young Latina was treated at the junior high school she attended. Griselda and Norma both asked whether this was a real story, as they could not believe that something like that could happen in a school in the United States. I directed their question back to them and drew their attention to the eight statements addressed at the beginning of the story. I asked them why they seemed to be so adamant about the racial injustices they felt occurred in schools and how they could now seem to challenge a situation in which those same injustices were played out. Their answer surprised me. As it turned out, they felt as though the story's inauthenticity was not in its portrayal of discrimination but in its conclusion that justice would prevail in the end. Norma was passionately angry that the character in the story received her prize and the title of valedictorian at the end of the story—an outcome she thought was unlikely. She and Griselda discussed the different possibilities, but they reached no agreement. Both felt that while the character received what she deserved, there were hundreds of students who did not.

Listening to the discussion allowed me to sit back and observe the connection students made between the community and context presented in the text and their own. Thirty out of the 38 students in my class contributed to the conversation. Although this pleased me, I was concerned that the way in which some students expressed their views threatened to silence others. While there were several students who expressed a great deal of hostility toward the text's story line, others felt that what was being seen throughout the story was true and that for students in the class to challenge those ideas was "stupid."

Two students in particular seemed to be participating more than usual: Martln and Everaldo. Both students are labeled at Channel Islands High School as "at-risk " students. As I came to know them, I felt that because they were labeled as "at-risk" students throughout their academic careers, these students made it a self-fulfilling prophecy to live up to those low expectations. Time and time again I had attempted to talk to both Martln and Everaldo about their attitude in class, yet they continued to express their frustration in the classroom. They often directed their frustration at me as well as their peers.

After speaking to both students, I found that they wanted to succeed academically, but the different barriers placed in their path denied them that opportunity. Speaking to Everaldo made me realize how students feel disrespected when he said to me, "Why should I care if teachers don't care about me either? They always say that I am going to fail anyways...whatever I do!" Everaldo's comment made me look at teaching in a different light. He made me realize that what we give students goes beyond teaching; we have the opportunity to provide them with the tools to succeed not only as a student but also as a human being.

THE COMPLEXITIES OF ENABLING STUDENT VOICE

It seemed as though the theme of this unit gave both Martln and Everaldo an incentive to come to class everyday and on time. During the initial days of the unit, they would come to class prepared with all necessary materials (i.e. books, paper, pencils, notebook). They allowed students in the class to see ideas through a different lens. With their rich experiences and explanations they allowed us to see who they really were. Slowly these two students began to break out of the protective shell they had created as a defense tactic. They both contributed experiences describing situations involving racism and discrimination they had overcome. I assumed that this increase in participation was a direct result of having culturally relevant curriculum that enabled them to connect with the text. They were able, as Carol Lee (1995) notes, to draw on their prior social knowledge to build interpretations of the text.

However, MartÌn and Everaldo's participation often created disruptions in the class because of their demeanor with the other students. They often insulted their peers under their breath, would talk to each other while others were talking, place their sweatshirt hoods over their heads and place their heads on the desk. Although I acknowledged the disruption in classroom, I felt that their contribution to the conversation was valuable and that forbidding them to sit together would discourage them from coming to class. As our concerns about the effects on other students grew, however, my cooperating teacher and I decided several days into this unit that a new seating chart should be created for the students in the class. Everaldo and MartÌn's behavior in class had escalated and it was time to seat them away from each other. The students, in particular MartÌn and Everaldo, were not very happy about this change.

On one particular day during this unit plan, my university supervisor conducted an observation. As both students walked into the classroom, they decided they wanted to sit where my supervisor was sitting that particular day. Class had not yet started, so I approached them and asked them to sit in their assigned seats. Everaldo looked at me and under his breath said, "I ain't doing that, Bitch!" I was caught completely off guard and hurt by his comment. My cooperating teacher approached him and took him out of the class to the office with one of the counselors. I felt as though I had let Everaldo down as a teacher: He was expecting me to support his behavior in the classroom. Yet I felt that by supporting him in this instance I would be letting down my principles as a teacher.

Reflecting on this particular event enabled me to see the class and the lesson through Everaldo's and MartÌn's eyes. It made me realize that perhaps the student reaction was a combination of emotions reacting to many outside sources. Perhaps my supervisor's presence contributed to a feeling of alienation and invasion of privacy that led to the reaction Everaldo had when confronted. I assumed that the curriculum in the classroom would enable the students to act in a way that would be conducive to class discussion. I found that engaging students not only requires culturally relevant curriculum, but it is also an environment in which students feel *comfortable* and *safe*. I found that curriculum can be irrelevant if the student does not feel he or she can participate in the classroom. Although the lesson itself was enriching, I was still concerned that a number of students, like MartÌn and Everaldo, did not feel part of the class, resulting in negative reactions and behavior. This highlighted for me the need to build opportunities for their safety and success in other ways.

BEYOND CULTURAL RELEVANCE: DEVELOPING OPPORTUNITIES FOR COMPETENCE

After this experience, I continued to include culturally relevant texts in my classroom. Just recently I began a unit on immigration and have incorporated different ways in which the message and interpretation of immigration has been developed. I have integrated music, prose, poetry, art, murals, and films. In this unit, students are given the opportunity to dissect different forms of expression and analyze the different messages and effectiveness of each way for each individual. This addresses their multiple intelligences (Gardner, 1983) and helps me find ways to create bridges to the curriculum to facilitate comprehension by the students.

Both Martĩn and Everaldo seem particularly engaged in the assignments and tasks I have developed. They expressed a great deal of interest when we analyzed different Mexican American muralists and their murals in California. Both have expressed a great deal of interest in art and drawing and have participated in contests and competitions using their artistic talent. This was a great opportunity to use the skills they already had and apply them to another form of classroom task. They became invested in the class and showed a part of themselves that had previously been hidden behind their sweatshirt hoods and bravura.

I was amazed at the incredible work they produced. This assignment gave them the opportunity to display what they perceived as valuable in their lives. Martĩn drew an image of an Aztec god he felt represented the importance of his Mexican heritage. It was interesting for me to witness how this was the first time Martĩn had expressed any type of reference to his roots and he chose his most treasured skill to share it with the class. He also drew an image of a woman that he said depicted both his mother and his sister who are of great importance in his life. Although it took a great deal of effort to find out that both would be engaged and extremely interested in art, it was the most valuable and rewarding experience I had as a teacher. This experience helped me understand what culturally relevant teaching brings out in our students when it enables them to share and develop their competence as well as their concerns.

Part IV

WHAT IS THE PROBLEM AND WHAT CAN WE DO ABOUT IT?

Linda Darling-Hammond

As a teacher, a researcher, and a parent, I spend a lot of time in schools. Over the years, I have had many occasions to look at schools with the question in mind, "Is this a good school for *my* children?" I have learned that what is a good school for one child may not be good for another. In particular, a school that may be "good" for many of its most advantaged students may be positively damaging for many others, including low-income children, students of color, recent immigrants, and gay and lesbian students.

To this day, most schools in the United States do an extraordinarily poor job of educating low-income and minority students. The reasons for these inequalities range from policies governing school funding, curriculum offerings, staffing, and tracking systems to factors that depend much more on teachers' knowledge, skills, and expectations for their students. This section provides a springboard for discussing some of the school practices, presumptions, and pedagogies that make a difference for children, from those that operate on a system level to those that operate within classrooms. These include the school structures that shape students' experiences and sense of themselves as learners and human beings—especially the ways in which students are grouped and tracked for instruction and are allocated resources within these tracks—and the more intimate interactions that occur between teachers and students in classrooms—interactions that either empower or undermine children's development and, in the process, either grant or deny them the right to learn.

Minority students are still largely segregated in American schools: More than two thirds attend schools that are predominantly minority, primarily in central cities. Those who attend integrated schools are often segregated in separate tracks. Not only do funding systems allocate fewer resources to poor urban districts than to their suburban neighbors, but schools with high concentrations of low-income and minority students receive fewer instructional resources than other schools within these districts. And tracking systems exacerbate these inequalities by allocating fewer and lower quality materials, less qualified and experienced teachers, and lower quality curriculum to the many low-income and "minority" students assigned to lower tracks (Darling-Hammond, 1995).

At the same time, a growing body of research illustrates that the vast differences in learning opportunities within and across U.S. schools are the single greatest source of differences in outcomes among students. Studies repeatedly find that students from different groups who take similar courses and have access to equally rich curriculum and equally well-qualified teachers perform similarly (Darling-Hammond, 1997). However that kind of equal access is rare.

Perhaps the most important differences in what happens to children at school depend on who their teachers are: what they understand about children and about learning, what they are able to do to respond to the very different approaches and experiences children bring with them to the learning setting, what they care about and are committed to as teachers. An "equity pedagogy"—one that makes knowledge accessible to all students—can be built by teachers who are able to connect the diverse experiences of their students to challenging curriculum goals, and who can marry a deep understanding of students and their learning to a wide array of strategies for bringing knowledge to life.

The chapters in this section reflect all of these constraints and possibilities. Suzanne Herzman, Erin Hays, and Laura Blythe all confront the issues of tracking in large comprehensive high schools. Herzman compares her own experience growing up in the Regents examination system in New York with the experiences of students in the high school where she student taught, drawing parallels between the "non-Regents" classes she knew existed and the "Skills" class she came to teach. She unveils how the process of tracking occurs in this high school and frames the issues that need to be confronted to redefine students' learning opportunities. Hayes examines the ways in which her high school handled tracking for English language learners and illustrates the dilemmas many schools and teachers face: how to maintain high levels of support and caring while maintaining high standards, as well. Laura Blythe echoes this theme as she compares the differences in the experiences of the under-resourced English language learners in a large, highly tracked urban high school with those of a much better supported group of English language learners in a wealthier, smaller, but still tracked suburban school. Her analysis proposes a school reform that would better serve students' needs for both rigorous content and a caring environment.

Allison Rowland and Ana Ruiz continue this theme by describing their practices in connecting with and empowering their students. Rowland describes how she learned, within two very different teaching settings, how to establish a community in the classroom that values all students. Having taught urban minority students unsuccessfully as an untrained teacher, Rowland describes how what she learned in her teacher education program has enabled her to be much more successful with the diverse group of students she now teaches. Finally, coming full circle to the themes that began this book, Ana Ruiz, a teacher of mathematics, explains how her identity as a Chicana mathematics teacher *con conciencia* informs her work with her students and her efforts to work with colleagues toward social change. Ruiz stresses the need for classrooms that enable students to take charge of their learning and for teaching to become a profession in which teachers are empowered to learn together how they can meet the needs of all students.

Although these stories reveal the obstacles student teachers perceive in schools and classrooms, they also provide examples of strategies that can contribute to social change. As readers read these cases, they may want to think about how the issues raised here play out in the schools they attended as students and in the schools in which they are teaching now; whether there are different manifestations of the problems or different resolutions of these tensions; and whether there are strategies they want to share with others. Questions for discussion in this section might include:

What are your experiences of tracking—as a student and as a teacher?
How do you weigh and balance the benefits and shortcomings of different strategies for grouping students to meet their needs?
In the school at which you work, do different groups of students have equal access to key school resources, such as well-qualified teachers, high-quality curriculum, and instructional materials (computers, texts, supplies)?
What do you think is needed to ensure both high-level standards and high levels of support for different students in your classroom? In your school?
Think back to a classroom you have experienced that had many of the

features of a caring community. What did the teacher do to build that community?

What do you see as the critical components of an equity pedagogy?

What do you personally want to learn more about as you develop your own capacity to meet the needs of all learners in your classroom?

CHAPTER 17

Finding the Right Track

Suzanne Herzman

Suzanne Herzman reflects on the parallels between the tracking systems she observed as a high school student and those she now sees as a teacher and examines how tracks are formed at her school. Readers can use this chapter to explore how tracking systems have operated at the schools they have experienced or, alternatively, how tracking has been avoided or eliminated. Readers may also consider how teachers can work with students, parents, and colleagues to address both school- and self-tracking that prevent students from gaining access to challenging material and to greater academic success.

Before I enrolled in a teacher education program, I don't think I gave tracking in schools the careful thought it deserved. I believed that tracking is a fundamentally undemocratic practice, but without working through why. I had reduced the issue to two simple equations: tracked=bad, heterogeneous=good. Yet like so many of my classmates, I found myself at Stanford as a result of two decades of being in the *right track*. I wish I could say that a year of student teaching has solved the dilemma for me, and that I can now enjoy track-free education in my classroom, and in the school, community, and society beyond. Alas, this is not the case. But a year of student teaching in a multitracked high school has forced me to ask more thoughtful questions as a result of reflecting on how tracking influences me, my students, and *all* students. As it is with so many issues of equity in education, it is easy to become discouraged or even ambivalent. After all, doesn't it feel rewarding to teach an honors class? Isn't it easier not to think about what happens to the students who don't take advanced courses? Isn't it easier to believe that these students have made a conscious decision about their track? Aren't they getting the support they need in lower level classes? Although this past year has not provided me with solutions, it has convinced me of the need to work toward more equitable solutions for bridging achievement gaps.

A PRODUCT OF TRACKING

As much as I felt tracking went against the democratic principles I was trying desperately to develop, it wasn't until I taught a course called Skills that I began to think about how tracking played a part in my own high school education. I attended a rural high school in western New York State. Our school was predominantly White, so at the time, and for years afterwards, I didn't see how tracking could be undemocratic. It is only now, when I reconstruct the class composition of my track—the honors track—and the others that I see how the tracks perpetuated socioeconomic status in our community. My classmates were the children of college professors at the local state university, doctors, lawyers, and other village professionals. The "Regents kids," who also took the state-mandated examinations, formed the middle track. The third track was comprised of students who were not expected to take these examinations, and who would therefore not receive a Regents Diploma. Not only were the classes labeled "non-Regents," the students in them became known as "non-Regents." These students lived in one of the even smaller towns outside the town limits. The higher tracked students were known to use "non-Regents" as the ultimate insult; in our adolescent minds, it was as powerful as—even synonymous with—such epithets as "retard" or "scum." In a graduating class of 75, even if we didn't know much about the backgrounds of students outside our own track, we were certain of exactly which track the others were in, and that no one ever moved up.

I know I benefited from the challenges that honors classes provided me. Or perhaps more accurately, I benefited from the *perks* of honors classes: I was seen as a student who had *what it takes* by teachers and administrators at my high school, and by college admission panels—which leads to a bigger dilemma of a tracked society. Reflecting back on the content of these courses, I now believe that the intellectual challenges I faced in my honors classrooms could also have been presented in a heterogeneous classroom by a skilled teacher, one who knows how to make sure that *all* students are challenged and are equipped with what it takes to succeed.

After I graduated from college, I returned to my high school as a substitute teacher. The unthinkable had happened: Classes had been detracked. I taught 10th-grade English to the children of farmers and the children of university faculty *at the same time*. And I hated it. How could I teach anybody anything? How was I supposed to go fast with the honors kids and slow with the "non-Regents" kids, as my teachers had done? One day, I held up the class by inadvertently assigning a part in *Julius Caesar* to a student who couldn't read, further emphasizing the achievement gap among the students. Within the classroom, it was clear who would have been in what class had the classes been tracked. The new system seemed to be a disservice to all students. In retrospect, I see that detracking a school involves more than simply removing honors and remedial classes. Teachers must be skilled in teaching diverse students. This can only come from a fundamental belief that all students can succeed, supported by knowledge of many strategies to enable this success. But I didn't see that until many years later.

THE SCHOOL

When I began STEP, I wanted to be placed in a school with an ethnically and socioeconomically diverse student population. When I learned I'd be teaching at XHS, I assumed that my request had been disregarded. I was taken in by the stereotype of a wealthy suburban community; I pictured myself teaching in classrooms full of faces as White as my own, belonging to the children of Silicon Valley entrepreneurs. My students would be eager to please in the classroom, but their pushy parents would remind me that they could buy me if I didn't provide their children with the A's they needed to get into the colleges of their choice. I'd let my imagination get the best of me.

I was not prepared for the extremes of wealth I encountered at my new school. Indeed I found an affluent population of students. But there were many other students, from families barely hanging on in an economy that was shutting them out. A number of them qualified for free lunch, and were left behind when their classmates hopped into their cars and drove into town in the middle of the day. At times, these disparities in wealth left me feeling that the only middle class was the faculty. Between class periods, the hallways reflected the ethnic demographics of the school. Just over half the population was White, close to a quarter Latino, over 15% Asian, and 5% African American. Soon I caught on to another disparity; there were very few classrooms with student populations that resembled the racial/ethnic diversity of the school as a whole. This was particularly evident in a class I taught called Skills.

FIFTH-PERIOD SKILLS

It was really by default that I taught Skills this year. My cooperating teacher seemed uncomfortable with the idea from the onset but acknowledged that "another adult in the room" might be a good idea. Almost immediately, I understood her hesitancy; clearly this was not an easy class to teach.

Skills was a backup course for the first in the sequence of college-preparatory classes in English at XHS. Because Skills was designed to serve as a supplement to the college-prep class, Skills students in essence took two English classes. Each of our 20 students was there for a different reason, and the extremes were pronounced. My students ranged in age from 13 to 18. For some, this was their first year at XHS. Others in the class had already participated in English as a Second Language and literacy-building classes in the school. A few students were in the class simply because they didn't do their homework last year. The one characteristic most students had in common was that they came to the class at the recommendation of a counselor or teacher even though the course was listed as an elective in the catalogue. Our goal, according to the course outline, was to give students the support they needed to succeed in mainstream English. As I soon discovered, this mission could be interpreted in many different ways.

What THEY Need

The moment the first bell rang in late August, I was acutely aware of the fact that the only White faces in the classroom were those of my cooperating teacher and myself. At times, I pretended not to notice—after all, I had no control over who was in the class. So we got right to work. We began each novel covered by the college-prep class a couple of weeks early so that by the time the Skills students were asked to participate in discussions in that class, they could be "experts" because of their experience with the novel. Beginning with *Of Mice and Men*, we focused primarily on the plot and characters of each piece of literature. We supplied Skills students with study questions, which we went over together chapter by chapter.

Although we varied the instructional techniques, most classes followed the same basic pattern. We would read aloud together—sometimes the students read, other times it was one of the teachers, and then we worked through the study guide. We posted acceptable correct answers to the questions on the overhead for the students to copy onto their papers. One day I watched two students walk into class, look at the agenda on the board, and groan. I recorded my frustration in my journal: "While I have tried to vary the activities as much as possible, the basic formula of each class has remained the same: read the book, answer questions. The students, I believe, need more. The students should trust that this class is truly supporting them, not simply asking them to do the same work twice."

The culminating activity for most of the literature units in freshman English was a thesis essay. As with the reading, we began work on the essay weeks ahead of the college-prep class. We provided the students with a topic, suggested quotations, and provided workshop time. It was on the workshop days that having two teachers in the room made a world of difference. On these days, I worked one-on-one with students and came to know how capable they were. And these were the days that saved me, for like the students themselves, I sometimes fell under the illusion that they were not capable of doing the work required in college-prep English.

I became aware of how seldom we asked our students to engage in critical thinking. I won't soon forget the day I attempted to solicit students' thoughts on *To Kill a Mockingbird* and Maya said to me, "Aww Miss Herzman, you're trying to make us *think* again." "Just tell us the answers," she and her classmates urged. When Maya reprimanded me for making her and her classmates think, she voiced something that had been on my mind since early in the year. This class was not about thinking. In some ways we excused them from thinking. The idea was that we should support them with basic understanding of the plot line, so that they could do the thinking part in their college-prep class. One day when we were plowing through our study guide for *The Bean Trees*, Ray, a Mexican American student in the class, explained the behavior of one of the characters (a man of Mexican descent) in the novel by declaring that "Mexicans are stupid." When I called him on this, he modified his statement to "Mexicans are lazy." I realized then that laziness had become part of the classroom—not the Mexican—culture. Ray and his classmates didn't have to face being smart or stupid or anywhere in between because they didn't have to put forth effort in the class.

I was never able to build a community of learners in this classroom. Often there were behavior problems. Put-downs became a classroom norm. Students took to calling each other "dumb-ass." What more proof did they require than a spot on the Skills class roster? But because the class was technically an elective, one at a time, the "difficult" students began to disappear. And the "good" students took on the role of difficult. Alfred started the year in my classroom as the personification of the new teacher's dream. He was attentive and eager. He kept up with his homework, participated in class, and encouraged his classmates to do the same. "Come on, guys," he would plead when he noticed he was the only student responding to the recall-based questions my cooperating teacher asked. A few months into the year, however, he realized that academic achievement wasn't the name of the game in Skills. He stopped doing his work, and began to use the time to play.

I began to hold my inexperience as a teacher responsible for the discouraging learning environment in this classroom (and still do, although I'm now willing to share the burden of responsibility with the school culture that created Skills). There I was, desperately trying to incorporate all my new teaching methods from the proverbial bag of tricks. I tried out Reciprocal Teaching, Complex Instruction, and anything else I could take from my education classes, but met with little success in this class. The students were more receptive to my lessons the more teacher-centered they were. At department meetings, we spent a great deal of time talking about what *those kids* need. Those kids need structure, my mentors told me. More structure became the answer when things weren't working right. When we provided them with outlines and boxes to fill in—and told them what to put in them—classes ran smoothly.

This *structure* also infused our classroom management. My colleagues instituted the point board. Students received immediate feedback culminating in a weekly score based on class participation. They received their first point of the day if they were in their seats and had their materials out and ready to go when the bell rang. During class, they might lose a point by calling out of turn, throwing paper, or disregarding the no-food-in-class policy. It took me some time to get used to running back and forth to mark the board during my lessons. In the last months of the school year, when I took on full teaching responsibilities in the classroom, I felt we should revisit the point board. I asked the class to vote by secret ballot as to whether to do away with the board. The students voted overwhelmingly to keep it. I was dismayed: How could I have been a part of a class in which the students need to see their progress in terms of a publicly displayed score?

"They Put Us Here 'Cause They Think We're Dumb"

I became aware of the daily reminders, including the point system, we were giving our students of how they were different from the mainstream at XHS. At least a quarter of the students in my class had been a part of the school's English Language Development Program. They were sophomores, juniors, and one senior placed in freshman English because it was the first in the sequence of college-prep classes. Many of these students were placed in Skills for language support, even though it was clear they were cognitively very capable. Eric, a Brazilian student fluent in three languages, made a comment the first week of school that stuck with me for the entire year. I was chatting with him before class when he revealed why he and other ELD students had been placed in Skills. "They put us here 'cause they think we're dumb," he explained. During our writing workshop, Eric composed one of the most richly detailed narratives I read this year from any class. During our Shakespeare unit, I discovered that Stan had already read *Romeo and Juliet*—in Russian. Nancy's poems about growing up Mexican were truly powerful in their imagery. How could anyone mistake these students for dumb? I do not accuse anyone among the school's faculty of labeling the ESL students or any of the other students in the Skills class dumb. But our school culture labeled them Skills, which was as powerful a label as non-Regents had been in my own high school.

The stigma of being in non-Regents, or Skills, or whatever name the remedial class holds, is problematic in itself. But what is the impact when our students look around the room to find that Skills can mean many things, but not White? What covert—or not so covert—message do we send out when our students of color see themselves in low-ability tracked classes, and White students in honors? Kids know they are in the class because someone along the way felt they needed extra help. But what happens when they see that all the students who are identified as needing help are students of color?

CAN TRACKING BRIDGE THE ACHIEVEMENT GAP?

XHS has identified a population of students who require extra support if they are to succeed in freshman English. Teachers and administrators are very aware that a population of students, primarily Latinos and African Americans, is not succeeding in the current system. Clearly they recognize and want to bridge this achievement gap, and Skills is one of several efforts to do so. The idea behind a class like Skills makes sense to me: If we give students extra support, they will succeed in the mainstream classes. In fact, a number of teachers of freshman English feel the program is successful because many Skills students appear prepared enough for the mainstream class in that they participate in discussions and turn in their essays. However, the following year, the students are faced with an elaborately tracked program for English: non-college-prep, college-prep, and honors—and no support class. Under the current system, there seems to be no bridge from Skills to honors.

Making Tracks

Skills was created in part so that all Freshman English classes at XHS could be heterogeneous. Aside from the ELD or literacy programs, full-fledged tracking in English does not begin until sophomore year, when students might find themselves in an honors, college-prep, or non-college-prep course. In this way, freshman year becomes somewhat of an audition for future English classes at XHS. Students who have not qualified for 10th-grade honors by earning an A or A- in 9th grade may choose to apply to the program by submitting to the English Department a portfolio of what they feel is their best work from the year. These portfolios are reviewed, although the final say is teacher recommendation. I took part in this process at XHS. We collected over 50 portfolios, split them among ourselves for review, and made recommendations. At a subsequent meeting, we discussed the applicants one by one, making a stack for those who went on to one of the two honors classes and one for those who did not. I heard one phrase repeated over and over: "This student does not have *what it takes* to succeed in honors."

As I sat in on this meeting—more an observer than a participant—I wondered why it wasn't our responsibility as their teachers to be sure that *all* of our students are equipped with *what it takes* to succeed. Instead, we went through our rosters and put our students in boxes. In this and other meetings, we found a track for each student in our classes: the honors box, the college-prep box, even the multicultural college-prep box. Not one Skills student made it to the honors track. Despite their abilities, Eric, Stan, Nancy, and the others were dropped right into the college-prep track. There they were left to sink or swim.

As we placed students into their boxes, I thought about a conversation I had had earlier with a colleague. I asked what I had missed at the last department meeting, and she told me it was the same old discussion the department had been having for years: How can we see to it that Blacks and Latinos get into honors classes. She seemed to imply that I hadn't missed much, that there was no solution. I got the strong sense from this and other experiences that many of the school's faculty and administrators believed that students of color weren't in honors classes because they didn't want to be. Fortunately, I had seen evidence to the contrary.

Raymond's Essay

For his last writing assignment of the year, Raymond, a Latino junior in my mainstream class—his first non-ELD English course at XHS—wrote about his participation in a district-wide student focus group. He wrote about how he and his classmates discussed the very same topic as their teachers, namely, why there aren't more students of color in honors and AP classes. His essay reminded me that the issue of accessibility is not the passing fancy of a few idealistic new teachers (and those who teach them) in teacher education programs. Students recognize that the access is not there, and they are willing to work toward changing it. Raymond and his classmates felt that open enrollment into honors classes for any student willing to do the work would be one way to ensure that more Latino students join the ranks of high-achieving students. He also wrote about the difference strong leadership could make, acknowledging that teachers and administrators truly have the power to create access for the students. He was hopeful, and reading his piece made me hopeful because he clearly refuted the misconception that students of color don't want to succeed academically. I was also encouraged by the fact that the district provided a venue in which student voices could be heard. Raymond is working hard at the district- and school-wide levels to reverse the prevailing sentiment that students of color do not belong in classes for high-achieving students.

A Question of Choice

Both Raymond's essay and the honors portfolios led me to question how decisions are made regarding who has access to challenging curriculum. Raymond's idea to open enrollment to honors classes suggests the possibility of student choice. This might create access for some students, yet I wonder if other students might feel that they belonged in these classes. When I imagine what would happen if someone asked my Skills students if they wanted to join honors, many of them would likely decline the offer. They might say they didn't want to do the work, when, in actuality, they might feel they can't do the work—after all, they hardly tasted success in my class. My colleagues pointed out—and I agree—

that it would be unfair to set students up for failure by enrolling them in classes for which they are not prepared. Yet not enrolling students in challenging classes—and not challenging them in the classes in which they are enrolled—perpetuates the cycle of low expectations and low performance I observed in my Skills class. In this way, choices have been made for students long ago.

I think back to why it seems that "these kids need structure." I think it may have something to do with the fact that they've been told what to do until this point. When students do not have opportunities to make decisions—to think for themselves—they learn that they aren't "supposed" to do those things. I tried to incorporate student choice into my methods of instruction without acknowledging that one of the biggest choices had already been made for them: the choice to be Skills students. Because they had already missed out on this fundamental choice, they were hesitant to take ownership of their learning in my class. It is perhaps for this reason that they were most comfortable when my lessons were teacher-centered. Furthermore, as we learned in our teacher education program, structure is most effective when it works like scaffolding, when it provides supports toward ambitious goals and is removed slowly but surely so that the students can succeed as they take ownership of their learning.

Of course, we should never underestimate our power, even when we, particularly new teachers, feel powerless in our schools. After all, it was teachers who had the final say in who was in and who was out of 10th-grade honors English. There seems to be little way around the fact that society is tracked. The dilemma of whether detracking starts from the bottom up in the schools or top down from society becomes the chicken and the egg of creating equity. We must be careful not to make decisions—even unconscious ones—about who will fill what positions in the world beyond high school. True, auto mechanic and cosmetologist are worthy professions that are absolutely necessary in our society. But these positions should not be filled because a 10th-grade English teacher feels her student didn't have what it takes in school. Often these are not intentional choices. In the same way, school personnel did not explicitly place students in classes by the color of their skin. Yet students—and perhaps teachers— learn the color of a class. Students know what tracking looks like. They know that honors classes are White and maybe Asian. They know that a class like Skills will have disproportionate numbers of Black and Latino students. And they may not feel as if they have much choice.

All the Answers Are Right Here

I wish I could write this paragraph. But I don't have the answers. Nor am I ready to take an absolute stand against tracking, thereby supporting the equation I opened with (tracking = bad). As is the case with so many debatable and heavily debated equity issues in our society, like the death penalty or affirmative action, it is often too easy to take an absolute stand without working it through—or at the very least, examining its effects. I am grateful to have had the opportunity to see some of the facets and faces of tracking this past year, and to really think them through.

Instead of answers, I offer more questions. Whenever we find ourselves in a position to make choices regarding ability and other groupings, we must be prepared to deal with the outcomes for students, particularly if they are irreversible or life-altering. If a program is tracked, do all classes—even support classes—provide an environment in which critical thinking is not only encouraged but also required? Second, and for me really the most salient lesson of my Skills experience, does tracking perpetuate existing barriers in terms of race, ethnicity, class, and culture? Only when we examine these issues can we begin to work toward equitable solutions.

But What Can We Do in Our Classrooms?

When asking the big questions is not enough for me, I replay the year and think about what I could have done better—and what I will do next year, when I begin my career as a full-time high school English teacher of all students. I don't know how much I can do to overcome the confidence issues faced by students when they confront the fact that they have been placed in a remedial class. But I can try. Teachers have power to create a positive tone in the classroom. Skills is not the only program that seeks to bridge the achievement gap for minority students. A program springing up in many schools known as AVID (Advancement Via Determination) targets students of color who are able but often considered underachieving by district standards. AVID's message is more productive: You are here not because we think you might fail, but because we know you can succeed. As your teachers, we will do whatever we can to support you. I think I became a better teacher when I realized that I truly believed my students were capable of challenging work.

Members of the community have commented that lower-income and low-achieving students are lucky to be attending as wealthy and academically strong an institution as XHS. But students here do not climb the ranks. In the current system, Skills students do not become honors students any more than non-Regents kids in my high school could be anything else. Often teachers—again, particularly the new ones—must work with the courses they are handed. If overturning tracking is not yet plausible, then we must think about what we can do within our own classrooms to make them places where students will be motivated to achieve. When we enable our students to feel they belong in classes that challenge them and that they have some power in deciding their futures, we take the first steps toward equitable education.

CHAPTER 18

To Track or Not to Track: That Is Still a Question

Erin Hays

The author relays her experiences as a teacher and presents profiles of three students with different backgrounds in an English Language Learner (ELL) Program to describe the dilemmas that arise in supporting ELL students while ensuring that they are prepared for academic challenges. Readers may want to consider how they have balanced the needs for student support and challenge for students in their own classrooms, and explore strategies for creating a safe environment while simultaneously holding high expectations.

When I reflect on my year as a student teacher at La Vista High School (LVHS), I am struck by how different my two classroom experiences were. Both classes were titled World Studies, but one was designed for students learning English as a second language, and the other was designed for all freshmen students. More specifically, one was "tracked" as a part of the ELD programming, and the other was a deliberate shuffling of ninth-grade students to create heterogeneous classes, regardless of students' middle school tracks. This teaching experience complicated my views of tracking, as I came to recognize both positive and negative aspects of the way LVHS groups English language learners together. While I saw how organizing students to meet their academic needs was sometimes more efficient and supportive for them, I also saw how these groupings can reduce student aspirations and their ultimate achievements. The dilemma schools face is how to assure the intimacy and care offered by supportive groupings while preparing students for a larger world in which they must compete. The solutions, I've found, may be very different for large schools and small ones that offer possibilities for individualization beyond tracking.

THE SCHOOL

For my student teaching, I was placed with a "CLAD-certified" teacher in two of her World Studies classes, one that was mainstream and the other designed for students learning English as a second language. CLAD is California's Cultural and Language Acquisition Development certificate issued to teachers who have studied how to teach new English language learners and others in culturally and linguistically diverse classrooms. La Vista High School is a public school located in the San Francisco Bay Area, with a student enrollment of approximately 1700. About 50% of these students are Caucasian, 25% are Latino, 15% are Asian, 6% are African American and 4% are Filipino.

Students' socioeconomic status also varies widely, with four feeder middle schools serving mostly affluent students from one set of neighborhoods, and two serving mostly low-income students from another. Regardless of students' middle school experiences, all freshman classes are heterogeneous. In the subsequent grade levels, however, students are offered AP and honors courses. Some students—my students—are placed in an English Language Development (ELD) track, regardless of grade level.

On the Track to Learn English as a Second Language

At LVHS the ELD program offers students the opportunity to take courses in English and social studies that are designed to advance their English skills. When a student in the process of learning English first enrolls at the school, the ELD office uses tests to place him or her in Beginning ELD I, Beginning II, Intermediate, or Advanced. If a student progresses to Intermediate ELD she or he is eligible to enroll in Specially Designed Academic Instruction in English (SDAIE) courses in social studies, which satisfy California State University or University of California admission requirements. Courses at "lower" ELD levels do not count toward college admissions. At the time of my student teaching at LVHS, SDAIE courses in math and science were not offered.

My world studies SDAIE class was comprised mostly of freshmen, with a few sophomores and juniors, and one senior. Approximately two thirds of the class was Latino, one third was Asian, and there was a single student from Africa. Many of the students were originally from Mexico; other countries represented in the class were El Salvador, Vietnam, China, Taiwan, Japan, The Gambia, and The Philippines. Among the students who were in permanent living situations, attendance was excellent.

Aside from the homogeneity created by all being English Language

Learners, there was substantial heterogeneity with respect to academic skills, educational background, family background, socioeconomic status, and motivation to learn. Students' proficiency in English varied widely, from a fairly "low intermediate" to a "high advanced." As could be expected, the students most proficient in English were the most outspoken, but overall the class was fairly quiet initially. This often made class discussions painful to facilitate. Only four students were willing to speak in whole-class discussions without being called on, and the rest chose to sit as silently as possible. Few would ask for assistance if they did not understand something; most would wait for the teacher to approach them. Because of the tendency toward quiet behavior, I made it my mission to get the class accustomed to academic conversations and presentations. I discovered that with enough scaffolding and support, the students could rise successfully to academic challenges.

Instructional Strategies and Pedagogical Approaches

Given the class makeup, whole class discussions usually worked best after pair- and group-work activities. The students needed to discuss the material with each other to process the information before taking the risk to share their ideas. Using technology in the classroom was also successful, as it seemed that all of my students loved using the computer and viewing historical films. Basic lecturing needed to be kept at a minimum, as I noticed that the students' eyes would glaze over after 10 minutes of listening. It seemed that the students could absorb only a small amount verbally without supporting representations or the opportunity to confer with their neighbor for clarification.

For assessment, we used a combination of projects and testing. Many students were more successful with projects, but tests were necessary to help prepare for the SAT-9 standardized exams deemed very important to LVHS. Writing was also a major focus of our course, and students grew accustomed to writing more than one draft of an essay by the end of the year. No matter what the learning task was, whether a large project or a small homework assignment, we made sure that it was well-scaffolded.

The pedagogical strategies used in an ELD classroom are in large measure simply elements of good teaching. As in any classroom, large concepts need to be broken into smaller ideas; students need to learn how to read, write, and speak well; and a variety of strategies must be used to help everyone learn and succeed. Where more specialization is required of the teacher, it is when deciding how much scaffolding is necessary or how to explain a concept through a variety of methods. It was, perhaps, both the specialized methods and the nurturing environment that made a difference in these students' learning.

Academic Challenge or Emotional Support?

By mid-spring, I felt that my students had grown tremendously. They had experienced some very successful jigsaw reading activities, submitted complicated journal writings as various characters through history, and presented large, individual research projects. But to an outsider, their advances were not as impressive as they were to me. When one of my colleagues visited to conduct a formal observation, she noted that it appeared to her that the students were rather unmotivated. She also noted that I have a "gentle way" of working with my students. At first I thought that this was a compliment, but then I realized that my "gentle way" could really be interpreted as not communicating high expectations for academics. In retrospect, I realize that my empathy for their struggles in learning world history in a second language caused me to push less hard than I otherwise might have. If a student did not want to speak in class, I usually let it slide. My greatest fear was that I might not provide a supportive, understanding environment. I believe I may have in some ways overcompensated in creating a relaxed environment.

My actions as a teacher were consistent with practices in the ELD Department, which offered a most supportive environment for the students and their families. The teachers and support staff were very welcoming, and just as dedicated to the program as to the students enrolled. It was clearly a caring environment that considered the needs of its clientele through a variety of support systems. Students and families have access to a community counselor, translation services in many languages, specific tutoring for students from migrant families, academic counseling, and numerous adults who care about their welfare. In addition, the office arranges an ELD Information Night every autumn and an ELD Awards Night every spring.

The practices of the ELD office also reflect a concern about who the students are and where they are coming from. When a student first enters LVHS as an English Language Learner, the placement form not only assesses English skills but also requests information about literacy in the student's first language. The ELD Department recognizes the significance of the relationship between first-language literacy and additional language learning. This information allows the staff and faculty to evaluate the academic needs of the student. I often overheard and engaged in conversations among the faculty and staff members about what was or was not working for a student's academic and/or emotional growth.

The support extended to cultural literacy as well. In the civics SDAIE course students obtain information about and instructional assistance in the naturalization process. In addition, students in the civics SDAIE and U.S. history SDAIE course may participate in a "close-up" field trip to Washington, D.C. that is designed for students who have immigrated to the United States and are learning English as a second language. Overall, this is a department that has worked very hard to provide quality services that are sensitive to the needs of the students. Unfortunately, high expectations for academic development were not always the norm in this mix of support systems.

EFFECTS ON STUDENTS' ACADEMIC GROWTH

As I learned more about the students and their academic backgrounds, I grew more and more concerned about the ELD track. One student was clearly having difficulties in processing information, demonstrated by his combination of great oral skills and oral reasoning with a low level of writing ability. When I referred him to the Student Assistance Team, nothing was done to help him and his teachers discover some appropriate learning modifications. I suspected that his specific learning needs may have been overlooked, given that he was labeled ELD. When I became aware of the lack of concern over this student's learning needs, I began to reflect on the academic profile of the other students in class. I realized that, for many of my students, their learning was in different ways both supported and impeded by the ELD tracking system.

Rose

Rose is a student I grew to know and understand fairly well, as she offered to be my subject for an adolescent case study I had to complete for my teacher education program. She moved to the United States from Vietnam at age 15. Now, at age 18, Rose is going into her senior year at LVHS and has successfully completed almost all of the classes offered by the ELD Program. She has taken all ELD courses, up through Advanced, as well as U.S. history SDAIE and world studies SDAIE. The last course she is eligible to take is civics/economics SDAIE, which I believe she is scheduled to take.

Rose has loved her experiences at LVHS, specifically within the ELD Department. She often speaks of how important her friends are and how much she loved ELD and SDAIE because her friends were in the same classes. In her junior year, she started to venture out more into the mainstream classes, taking geometry and biology. Rose aspires to become a medical doctor someday, and in the beginning of her junior year she was determined to enroll at UC Berkeley for her undergraduate studies, then apply to medical school. The medical school dreams were bruised—but not shattered—by her experiences in mainstream biology. Unfortunately, her previous experiences with the ELD courses did not prepare her for success in the mainstream courses. The differences in learning cultures, from the supportive community of ELD to the competitive practices of mainstream, reflected in her academic performance. When she was faced with a great challenge, she gave up.

Although many of us in the ELD Department offered her encouragement to remain in biology, Rose did not think that she could succeed. Rather than pushing her to study more and to use the tutoring services, school officials allowed her to drop the course. By the end of her junior year, Rose had decided to attend community college to further develop her English language skills, and then transfer to a 4-year college. I certainly understand the benefits of enrolling at a community college first (I did that myself), but I still question Rose's decision. Judging by how much Rose loved LVHS and the ELD Department, her emotional needs were obviously being met. However, she has dreams of medical school—dreams that are not being fully realized while she is on the track to learning English as a second language. Had she been challenged sooner, had she been expected to make the transition to mainstream classes, and had supports for her been available when she got to those classes, might Rose's future already be securely launched?

Manuel

Manuel was a quiet, ninth-grade student at the beginning of the year. His eyes would always follow the action of the classroom, but they often glazed over in confusion. Manuel did not complete assignments or participate much in class, and I was concerned that the material was too difficult. As is common in an ELD course, I had to approach Manuel to offer assistance, at which time he would let me know that he did not "get it." By November his confidence was growing, and he finally earned a B on an end-of-the-unit exam. That success led to an increase in completed assignments, and he produced one of the best semester-end projects in January.

The successful trend continued for Manuel through the third quarter, when he earned an A+ in our course. As a result, my cooperating teacher and I recognized him at the ELD Awards ceremony in the spring. I noticed that he was also recognized for working hard in his Math A class. My assumption at this point was that Manuel had clicked into a mode of understanding English as he never had before, that he had been living in California long enough to work more flexibly with the language. I was so excited that he was experiencing academic success in such a short time span.

At the end of the year, I was shocked to discover that Manuel had been involved in an ELD program since the second grade. Second grade! I was outraged that the ELD track had not worked for him much sooner, that he was still taking Intermediate ELD—a level that cannot qualify him for admissions in the state university system—even though he had been a resident of California for almost 10 years. Bright, hard-working, and quiet, Manuel had been lost in a schooling system in which people had not expected him to learn and succeed. How much sooner and how much more might he have accomplished if he had encountered higher expectations?

Juan

Juan entered our sheltered world studies course 1 month into the second semester, as a 12th-grade student. Not long after Juan joined the class, he reminded me that I had observed his U.S. history class a couple of weeks before. It was then that I recalled a Latino student walk in with another Latino student an hour into the 90-minute class, without disruption. I had been shocked that the teacher did not comment on what seemed to be tardiness, and I inquired about this teaching decision after class. The teacher explained that the late arrival of the two students was because he sent them to a tutor on the block days. This very experienced and effective teacher decided that the two students needed additional support, so he sought out resources for them.

Although it was impressive to me that LVHS had such resources, I was disturbed that their academic support occurred during class. This caused the students to walk in an hour late every Wednesday, missing the material that was being covered in the class while calling attention to the fact that they were struggling with the material. Once those two students reentered the classroom, they were silent and withdrawn until the bell rang. In stark contrast, the silent, shy, insecure Juan from U.S. history was confident, relaxed, and a willing participant in sheltered world studies.

My cooperating teacher had been Juan's teacher before, and she was worried that he would be an underachieving and disruptive student, as he had been 2 years before. At first she denied him entry into the class, but his counselor enrolled him anyway. For precautionary reasons, my cooperating teacher warned Juan on his first day in the class that his enrollment was not guaranteed, and that he would have to complete assignments to stay in the class. After that discussion we learned Juan's true motivation for taking world studies, SDAIE: It was easy for him. He had been struggling in mainstream courses the first semester, and chose to return to a sheltered course where the work was "easier."

Although Juan was not the most motivated student with respect to homework and projects, he was an active participant in class. He shone during large group discussions because of his strong verbal skills, as he sat with a casual confidence that was not evident when I observed him in a mainstream course. In addition, many of the students knew Juan from other classes, and it appeared to be that he was well-respected among his ELD peers. It became clear to me that Juan was in an SDAIE class because it was comfortable, not necessarily because it was the best academic fit for him.

SUCCESS, YET FAILURE

There are many more stories I could share that all echo the same theme: The ELD track is an emotionally supportive environment, but it is not an academically challenging one. I felt that we were breaking ground in academic confidence, as I assisted in projects and assignments, but as soon as I spoke with the class about the school process of testing into AP courses, I realized that they were without hope of progressing out the ELD track. One student said, "But, Ms. Hays, we are only SDAIE. We cannot do AP," which was followed by student laughter and nodding.

I often wonder what the future holds for that class of students, whether any of them will fulfill their life dreams. Where will they learn that their potential is far greater than they imagine? What will happen to them once their support system is gone? How prepared will they be to succeed in college courses, if the "gentle" teaching they've experienced makes them perceive that mainstream courses are too challenging for them?

At LVHS, the ELD community has certainly made the students supported as people, but not necessarily as future leaders. At the same time, in the mainstream courses where students are shuffled from class to class in a sea of 1700 other students, their individual support is compromised and their confidence is easily shaken. Ideally, I would like to see the high expectations of an AP class combined with the emotional support of the ELD track for *all* students.

I am now working in a small school in an African American and Latino community that is designed to support students academically while upholding high expectations. Each grade has no more than 20 students, and we serve "mainstream" and "ELD" students alike. There are a variety of skill levels represented in each class, but the smaller size and the personalized approach to education allow me to work with each student individually. Furthermore, the smaller size allows for the students to learn each other's talents and not to stereotype each other on the basis of their academic track. I finally feel that I have found a model for education that serves both academic and emotional needs.

Can this work in other high schools, too? I realize that building small schools in every district may not be possible in the near future. However, I believe that it is our responsibility to reform the learning environment in larger institutions so that everyone is a member of a small learning community that supports both the academic and the emotional needs of *each* student. We can no longer prepare ELD students for menial work if their ambitions are greater, and we can no longer place our mainstream students on an assembly line of academics without individual supports. In fact, if these two "types" of students were engaged in small learning communities together, where high standards could be joined with high supports—chances are that all of their needs would be better met.

CHAPTER 19

Unity and Division: Working Through the Issues of Equity in School Reform

Laura Blythe

This chapter explores alternative proposals for meeting the needs of English Language Learners at a large urban high school. Readers can consider their own answers to the important dilemmas the author raises about how to provide support, access, and inclusion for students without isolating or overwhelming them. Readers might also develop and debate their own proposals for equity-oriented school reform.

It was a warm May afternoon when we first met around a table with pencils, paper, some notes, and a few books from our school reform class. We were three novice reformers, and our assignment was clearly laid out for us: Write a proposal for a school reform. We chose Washington High School because it was one of our student-teaching placements and because of its size: 4,400 students! Our colleague who taught at Washington continued to remind our three-person committee of the immense student capacity that the school supported. The three of us had recently completed some research on the programs for English Language Learners (ELL) at our respective teaching placements. The two of us placed at smaller schools both noted that the smaller size of our schools enabled the ELL students to experience access to and intimacy with the teachers and each other in the program. We then asked the obvious question: How does—

indeed, how *can*—a school with 4,400 students create a similar feeling of intimacy and support for its ELL students?

OUR STARTING POINT: COMPARING TWO SYSTEMS

Washington High School's ELL Program

More than 45% of Washington's 4,400 students speak English as a second language. There are at least 46 different home languages, with Tagalog, Vietnamese, and Spanish predominating. Washington's mission statement sets a high ideal for the education of its ELL student population. The school, according to its mission statement, aims "to provide a safe and caring learning environment where students achieve the academic, personal, and social development required to continue learning, pursue post secondary education, compete in a job changing world, and participate in a multicultural, democratic society."

However, there are only eight full-time ELL teachers and 60 teachers in sheltered courses to educate more than 2,000 English Language Learners at Washington, a ratio of more than 30 students for each teacher. Although the school aspires to offer courses in students' first language, limited teacher availability means that there are only three introductory courses offered in Spanish or Vietnamese. Although almost half the population of the school is English language learners, Washington graduates only 150 ELL students in a senior class of 800 students each year. These 150 students must meet all graduation requirements and pass a district exam requiring students to demonstrate minimum competency in reading, writing, and mathematics. If a student begins the ELL program as a freshman, she or he can graduate in 4 years. Students who enter at a later time are allowed a fifth year to complete the graduation requirements. Those who cannot do so do not graduate.

The System Up Close

The teacher from our reform group who was placed at Washington High School felt that although this program did provide the ELL student with some opportunities to succeed in the U.S. school system, many students were prevented from realizing their academic potentials. Some of her frustrations and fears were expressed in this journal entry:

> Reflecting on my classroom, I am surprised by the range of speaking, writing, and reading abilities in my ESL3 classroom. We have a range of students who have been in the US from two months to 14 years, which makes it challenging to meet their different needs. Some of my students

are familiar with colloquial English, but struggle with writing. Other students have exceptional writing skills, but weak oral and listening skills. Often I feel that my students' attention span is limited, and I often observe their loss of interest during instructional times when I am meeting the needs of my students with lower oral skills. My fear is that ESL students will lose focus and motivation as they struggle through a day of mediocre teaching, communication problems, and different cultures and learning styles within their classrooms six times a day, five days a week. Most importantly, I believe that a large part of their academic energy, potential and knowledge is wasted as they progress through an ESL program.

At our last department meeting, teachers confessed to a void in the ESL programs. As teachers, they felt that they did not have the appropriate materials and training/guidance to meet ESL standards. Actually, many teachers do not know what the ESL standards are. Also, the teachers noted the ESL program is a weak link in Washington High School's English department. More specifically, teachers questioned whether their instruction is geared towards the needs of the students; many were frustrated.

Washington High School has a beautifully diverse student body, and a large percentage of the students move through the ESL program or have a connection to it. I feel that the philosophies behind the program that support bilingual education are appropriate. However, I think that the school's program is structurally challenged in meeting the needs of the great number of students.

In assessing the needs of one of her ELL students for a teacher education assignment, she noted:

My ESL3 student has course schedules and opportunities similar to the native speaker. However, I still fear that curriculum may be "watered down" for this student and that his high school career is inhibited by his language abilities. Although he is understanding and experiencing success in our classroom, he still has difficulties finishing homework and mastering the materials presented to him in other classes.

A Response from Another Vantage Point

As I heard about my colleague's experience, I could relate to her frustration that her ESL3 student was experiencing success in the ELL classroom while he was not yet successful in mainstream classes. While working on this project, I taught in the ELL program at Sycamore High School and wondered how students in my sheltered ELL classes would fare in mainstream classes the following year. Although the most successful of my students produced thoughtful work, they still needed to refine their basic language skills. I also worried that a watered-down curriculum was not challenging all of my students to achieve their potentials. In my classroom, I, too, wrestled with finding ways to present challenging, grade-appropriate curriculum through a medium of simpler language.

My colleague's description depicted a dilemma of many schools today. The school's teachers and resources are not prepared to provide effective instruction that meets student needs for which most mainstream classrooms were not designed. Learners with unique needs—whether they are language, curriculum, or behavioral learning needs—are often placed in classrooms together so that a teacher can focus on meeting those specific needs. Even in such segregated classes, however, many ELL students do not receive teachers who are trained to provide them with effective instruction. At the same time, they remain in a class that is without opportunities for them to interact with students who could provide additional language models and support. In many schools, ELL students are trapped in classrooms in which they are not adequately prepared to advance to the next level of language learning, and they are also not provided with models for what that next language level may look like.

Sycamore's ELL Program

Although I could see some similar concerns in my school, my teaching experience in Sycamore's ELL program was also very different. There were just over 1,500 students at Sycamore and fewer than 100 students in the ELL program. A committed staff had created a program in which most students were content, if not proud, to be a part. The ELL teachers at Sycamore also wrestled with the issues of watered-down curriculum and how to create opportunities for ELL students to successfully enter mainstream classes. However, the small student population allowed the staff to get to know each student well. The smaller and more tightly coordinated staff enabled teachers to discuss students individually, to take action from these discussions, and to make progress in supporting students' growth and development.

Sycamore's program for English language learners offers a total of 5 years of instruction in various courses starting with Beginning I courses and ending with sheltered mainstream SDAIE classes in a wide range of academic subjects and electives. The program was begun in an effort to respond to the great number of English language learners who were previously not supported in instruction and who were failing in school. Though there is further progress to be made in the instruction of English language learners at Sycamore, much progress has already been made.

ESL students at Sycamore report having positive experiences in their courses in the ESL program. I enjoyed the positive and personal atmosphere created among the staff and students, which included birthday cakes at teacher meetings and an end-of-the-year ice skating party for the students. I learned new ways to support my students both in and out of the classroom; these ranged from teaching strategies like dramatizing difficult sections of books to support strategies like providing a means for students to contact non-school-related services in the community. I looked forward to using similar ideas in my future years of teaching, and felt that the program could serve as a model for schools seeking to improve upon their own ELL programs.

DEVELOPING A VISION STATEMENT

Our team of three reformers came to the task of designing a school with diverse teaching experiences that led us to develop different visions for what reform would be best and how it could be best implemented. However, we strongly agreed that positive reform needed to take place in Washington's ELL program. Our vision statement included the following: (1) All students develop the academic and social skills they need to live successfully in a mainstream environment; (2) all students have meaningful interactions and relationships with students and teachers; (3) both students and teachers are held to high expectations with *ample support systems* in place for student and teacher success; (4) English language learners are successful, supported members of a freshman class that serves each other and the greater community.

The Details: Caught Between a Rock and a Hard Place

We completed our vision statement within 15 minutes. When we set out to work out the details, we soon found ourselves caught between a rock and a hard place. The reformer who taught at Washington High School stated, "We need to mainstream all the ELL students right away. That is the only way that these students will have the opportunity to have quality teachers, quality and challenging curriculum, learn English from and practice English with their classmates." The other reformer in our group nodded her head in agreement and I found myself nodding my head as well. However, something made me uncomfortable about this idea.

I pictured the students in my sheltered ELL class at Sycamore who were in their fourth year of ELL education. Many of them would be ready for mainstream classes next year, while others were still struggling to stay above water in this class. I tried to picture these students being immediately immersed in mainstream classes and saw that some would have considerable difficulty. It would be an amazing academic feat for a student simultaneously learning English and curriculum content to reach success in a mainstream classroom equal to that achieved by as a mainstream student in a competitive college-preparatory high school class. I questioned whether I myself would be able to do much more than flounder in such a situation.

It was difficult and yet a relief for me to acknowledge this observation. Many of my ELL students were conscientious and driven. If my ELL students were at a school in which their classes were taught in their first language, they would be capable of achieving at least as much academic success as many of my mainstream students at Sycamore. However, I felt that mainstreaming these students would put them right back in the dreadful position that inspired teachers to create Sycamore's ELL program 5 years ago. Continuing to improve Sycamore's ELL program seemed to be a better choice.

The more we progressed in creating our reform proposal, the more mainstreaming students became central to our reform, and the more uncomfortable I became. I continued to tell myself that I was not an actual member of this school's staff, and that this reform was not an actual reform that would take place. Despite the situation being hypothetical, I was not able to turn in the paper for our class without saying something to our group. "I am willing to go along with this, but I just need to express that I truly do not agree with what we are proposing." I explained to my group members why I felt this way. My colleague at Washington High argued that learning content while learning a language is feasible, as she spent a year of high school doing just that in Germany. She explained that almost half the school is in ESL classes, and that most of the classes present watered-down curriculum that does not challenge ELL students who hope to be successful in college one day.

These arguments made me reconsider my views. ELL students *did* need to be around English speakers, and ELL students *did* need challenging, high-quality instruction to provide them with a chance to be successful in college. Once again, I went along with the idea of mainstreaming students, but as we progressed my feelings of great discomfort returned, as I thought about the risks for the students involved and the more supportive environment for English Language Learners I felt I had observed at my school.

The third group member became the mediator in our group. She listened to and seemed to understand both viewpoints. We decided to try to work out some kind of middle ground between our two points of view. Having a mediator in our group made it significantly easier to discuss how we really felt about our proposed reforms. She brought reason to what could have turned into an emotional discourse. It occurred to me that such mediators are key for schools that are engaging in reform processes. In a sense, we were replicating what happens in the process of school reform in many schools, where the experiences of different participants produce ideas that may differ significantly even when they share the same goals.

Looking for a Middle Ground

Our group set out to create a proposal that acknowledged ELL students' need to be challenged by curriculum that is content- and language-level-appropriate and the need to interact with English-language speakers. Although these ideals seemed fairly feasible at Sycamore, they became more difficult to achieve in a much larger school with many more new English language learners. We decided to begin our reform with the freshman class. We felt that there were great gaps in communication and community that often prevented ELL students from receiving the support that they needed for a fruitful education. Thus personalization would be the key to our school reform. During freshman year, the student to teacher ratio would be 20 to 1, with a teacher assistant present in the classroom, an idea made feasible by California's recent funding of class size reduction in grade 9 along with funds for English Language Learning programs. Along with personalization, another equally important goal of our reform proposal was to expose ELL students to educational opportunities equivalent to those experienced by native English speakers and to minimize tracking, that is, to make any level of schooling permeable. We felt that teacher collaboration and strategic scheduling would increase personalization and educational opportunities for ELL students.

The Nuts and Bolts of the ELL Curriculum

The Challenge

As we rediscussed the details of our proposal, our goal remained rather general: to *successfully* mainstream ELL students as soon as possible. Perhaps one of the greatest curricular challenges for teachers in mainstream classrooms today is to develop curriculum that reaches *all* students, as mandated by the California Standards for the Teaching Profession. These standards require teachers to engage *all* students in a curriculum that provides relevant content matter for *all* students and that meets *all* students with appropriate strategies and styles of instruction. This curricular challenge is a difficult one in a mainstream classroom with students who have reached different achievement levels in content. This challenge is compounded when teachers are seeking to reach students in a classroom with diverse English proficiency levels as well. As reformers of Washington High School's ELL program, we questioned how to provide students with the support to enable all students to be successful in a given subject matter, while also enabling students to have equal opportunities and to become proficient in English through meaningful interactions with native English speakers.

Divided Options

While discussing the structure of our school reform, we considered developing a program that would mainstream students as soon as possible. At the other extreme, we considered developing a comprehensive and challenging ELL program that would potentially educate students throughout high school, if needed, and mainstream students in college, or junior college. The first option is based on a philosophy that the best way to learn English is to be surrounded by English speakers and to *need* to learn English to succeed to English taught-classes. The second is based on a philosophy that all students need comprehensive instruction that challenges them to take the next appropriate step in their instruction, rather than needing to take all of those steps at once.

We found that our conversation mirrored the arguments in the field of bilingual education. In a report released in 1993, a panel of bilingual educators and researchers evaluating federal policy for ESL students argued that, "Language-minority students must be provided with an equal opportunity to learn the same challenging content and high-level skills that school reform movements advocate for all students" (Crawford, 1999, p. 234). The current state of affairs at Washington High School reveals a picture all too close to that of the dreaded "ESL ghetto" denounced by many researchers and teachers. In such a program, ESL students are not receiving equal opportunities for a challenging curriculum that offers high-skill instruction and student advocacy. How to address this problem, however, is not at all obvious.

One option we saw was to eliminate ELL classes that are not accomplishing their purposes and to mainstream all students at every ELL level. This option is based on the concern that bilingual and SDAIE classes could be a poor substitute for a well-developed mainstream curriculum and could place students in classes with poor teachers who are unfamiliar with their students, untrained in ESL methods, and who water down curriculum in an attempt to teach language skills. In evaluating this option we acknowledged the reality that exists in many California schools: that the ESL track is often staffed disproportionately by teachers without adequate training for teaching generally, as well as inadequate skills for teaching language learners specifically.

This option resonates with the concerns of some researchers, teachers, and others who have questioned whether ESL programs, even good ones, provide a crutch for students and inhibit language growth. The *New York Times* published a story in the early 1990s that echoed these sentiments. The headlines read, "School Programs Assailed As Bilingual Bureaucracy Throws Away The Crutch of Bilingual Education In U.S. Schools, A War of Words: Bilingual Education Effort Is Flawed, Study Indicates" (Crawford, 1999, p. 225). This article did not cover studies about the positive impact of bilingual education or programs that helped to support language preservation alongside new language learning. Although the study that examined student achievement in bilingual programs did not consider factors such as socioeconomic background or long-term progress in subjects, it nonetheless captured substantial media attention and echoed the concerns of many educators and members of the public.

Another option we saw was to create an ESL program that is not a ghetto. This option is rooted in the idea that students developing their English-language skills need a program in which they will be challenged to comprehend complex content matter, while also using English in meaningful ways to develop their language skills. This program would be staffed by well-trained professionals who understand the content, the language, and their students, and who meet their students' learning needs. Students would be supported with curriculum and relationships that acknowledge and celebrate their diverse backgrounds. The ESL program would be a place where students can be successful, feel proud of who they are and of their accomplishments, and develop meaningful relationships. However, while the ESL program would be a positive experience, it would also be a program that keeps students focused on the road to mainstream curriculum. Students would be heading toward proficiency in English-language skills in order to develop their content skills more effectively and to function with ease in mainstream society.

The vision for this program structure is also inspired by research. For example, research has shown that offering bilingual education for ESL I students affirms students' cultural and linguistic backgrounds. In their study of high schools that successfully promote the achievement of language-minority students, Ruben Donato, Rosemary Henze, and Tamara Lucas (1990) found that "value is placed on the students' languages and cultures by learning students' languages and hiring bilingual staff with similar cultural backgrounds to the students" (p. 324). This study also found that "high expectations are made concrete by providing a special program to prepare language minority students for college and by making it possible for students to exit ESL programs quickly" (p. 324).

This second option aligns with the recommendations of the Stanford Working Group on Federal Education Programs for Limited-English Proficient Students (1993), which argued that, "Proficiency in two or more languages should be promoted for all American students. Bilingualism enhances cognitive and social growth, competitiveness in a global marketplace, national security, and understanding of diverse people and cultures" (Crawford, 1999, p. 234). We concurred that a bilingual education will enhance student comprehension of concepts, encourage their development as growing social beings, and provide bridges for international collaboration for both first- and second-language English speakers.

Our Decision

In our discussions we swayed back and forth. We finally agreed to provide 2 years of ELL instruction for students and then to mainstream students the third year. We built a plan that would personalize education for students and help teachers support each other in planning effective instruction.

ESL1 classes will be bilingual classes taught in Spanish, Vietnamese, and Tagalog. Students' core subjects would assure access to a college preparatory curriculum. The schedule allows for blocked classes that enable interdisciplinary work in math/science and English/history; extra academic and personal supports for students through advisories, special ESL support courses in each subject area, and supported study halls; student engagement in the life of the community through weekly community service; and shared teacher planning time.

Student Supports

According to Henry Trueba, "Acquisition of a second language and culture for linguistic minority students must be gradual and should not jeopardize their self-esteem or overall adjustment to school and society" (Trueba, 1989). Because our program will encourage ELL students to integrate into mainstream classes, we will need to provide a well-developed support system to prevent them from falling through the cracks. In our school, ESL1 students will have additional language support in class through (1) volunteers: student teachers, university/college students, older students, and members of the community who speak the students' native language; (2) technological supports; and (3) encouragement in reading and writing letters. Additional support includes an after-school program that will give students a comfortable place to study and receive help from older peers, community members, and teachers.

ESL2 classes will be SDAIE courses that provide mainstream curriculum instruction and are taught in English using diverse modes of instruction. Finally, students will enter mainstream classes after advancing beyond ESL1 and 2. There will be an additional period each week to provide further language support for students. This class time will allow teachers to equip students with the key language skills needed for the next week's lessons and give students an opportunity to preview a concept and become familiar with it before they learn it in the content class. Each day will be set aside for a different content area. The teacher from that subject will come and offer further guidance for the course material. The ELL support class offered in the afternoons will also provide technological supports, such as access to tapes of the course books in students' first languages and classroom access to the Internet.

Class Placements

To avoid the inappropriate placements that often characterize ELL programs, all student placements in our school will be determined through the aid of annual placement tests that assess skills and knowledge in every subject. These placement tests will be administered in both English and in a student's native language of instruction. Through these tests, teachers will be able to decide on the best placements for a student by separately assessing the student's English-language skills and his or her analytical skills.

Advisories

We recognized that freshman students need a great deal of support to help them adjust to the high school world, particularly a high school with a population of 4,400 students. When the members of a school community see each other as individuals, growth in respectful and meaningful relationships is more possible. Students need to be in relationships in which they treat each other well, and in which they are treated well.

Beginning in freshman year and continuing throughout their senior year, all students will meet in advisory periods each day, modeled after the approach used at Harold Wiggs Middle School in El Paso, Texas, where students report that "the more personal advisory relationship with a teacher made them feel more connected to school; it gave them the opportunity to 'talk to a teacher like a real person'" (Berman, Minnicucci, McGloughlin, Nelson, & Woodwork, 1995, p. 5). Each student wants to feel "like a real person." ESL students, in particular, may feel this deep need as they may feel estranged in a new culture. This personal element is essential to provide students with a "home" in their schools. If students are seen by teachers as real individuals, they in turn will be more likely to see teachers and other students in the same way.

Advisories will provide time for developing supportive relationships with one teacher and with 11 other students. These advisory groups will be composed of ELL and mainstream students, thereby providing a rich and supportive environment for students of diverse language and cultural backgrounds to get to know one another. During advisory time, teachers will develop relationships with students, follow up on student behavior, and work with students on individual problems with teachers, other students, and outside school issues. Advisories should be particularly helpful for ELL students who need further assistance to adjust to a high school in a new culture in which they will speak a new language.

Community Service

ELL students will have further opportunities to develop their language skills by contributing to the community in a service situation. The students will use English to communicate with fellow volunteers on site from their school and from the larger community. Students will also have an opportunity to "try on" different work environments and to begin developing a vision for their future goals. The community service activities will take place while teachers have collaborative meeting time.

Students will also participate in community service projects that are directly connected to themes they are studying in their other school subjects, such as human needs, education, the environment, or public safety. Such community service projects could include building a house with Habitat for Humanity or cleaning up a beach with Youth for Environmental Services. This program can provide students with real opportunities and skills, give students a sense of civic responsibility and a commitment to positive social change, empower students by helping them recognize that they are catalysts for change in their communities, make learning more relevant, and increase students' investment in school.

Parents and Volunteers

Parents and other community members, such as senior citizens, will be encouraged to be a part of the ELL community at Washington High School as tutors and in other ways. The school will seek out parents and community members who can speak the different languages of students in the school. Parents will also be involved in governance of the school through a parent-teacher association. A group of parents will be in charge of contacting other parents about possibilities of involvement, much like the approach used at Inter-American public high school in Chicago, Illinois. There, "the school has two part-time parent volunteer coordinators who have been assigned space at the school and who take responsibility for contacting parents about school activities" (Berman et al., 1995, p. 8). Inter-American School also involves parents as judges at school fairs, visitors to classrooms, and contributors to the curriculum.

Staff

Staff development is central to our reform proposal. Washington's ELL teachers experience the difficulties described by Trueba (1989), "Teachers of linguistic minority students know that their role is plagued by difficulties such as lack of support, materials, training, and general incentives" (p. 107). Our reform group felt that the staff needed to be prepared to meet the challenges of the new programs, including knowledge about how to teach effectively.

The goal of our proposal was to train all ELL *and mainstream* Washington teachers in effective strategies for teaching ELL students. As students enter mainstream classrooms, they will need teachers who are well prepared to identify learning needs and to offer the necessary support for these needs. Our group realized that not all teachers may be enthusiastic about taking on these new challenges. However, teachers could develop enthusiasm as they begin to share ideas, use new tactics and activities, and talk with each other about the success or failure of different approaches. Teacher communication and collaboration are crucial to our reform. During a Wednesday morning block, teachers will serve as resources for one another by working together within and across curriculum areas, discussing concerns, and offering strategic support. Teachers working in teams will be able to plan thematic units. We will place a high priority on "hiring bilingual staff with similar cultural backgrounds to the students" (Donato, Henze, & Lucas, 1990, p. 324), in order to create a resourceful staff that can better understand their students.

We plan to offer incentives for teachers who take advantage of ELL teacher training programs. This ongoing training will include sessions before the beginning of the school year, in the middle of the year, and near the end of the year. The training will provide teachers with effective instructional strategies for teaching ELL students, principles of second language acquisition, and greater knowledge of student cultural backgrounds and experiences.

We also felt that teachers at Washington, like others, needed more time to learn their curriculum in order to teach it more effectively. McDonald (1996) emphasizes that the curriculum is at the heart of meaningful relationships between students and teachers. He states that "teacher-proof curriculum (packaged lessons teachers can receive and teach without investing time in better understanding the content) is not a substitute for a teacher being deeply immersed in and knowledgeable about content and how to teach it." McDonald recognizes that this kind of thinking about curriculum "requires of school that it become a place for teacher learning too. This requires extensive rewiring: introducing opportunities for teachers to meet in learning groups, study privately, gain access to teaching resources, get their minds around what they teach" (p. 104). Thus, our school will have "built in time for learning on the job" (p. 105).

FINAL REFLECTION

The final version of our school reform proposal changed a number of times, and has further room for development. The process of creating this proposal engaged our group of three in much discussion on dilemmas that students, teachers, and administrators face in schools today. I walked away from this situation with a new awareness that even first-year teachers can bring experiences and mental frameworks that promote very different school reform ideas. I feel that I have had a taste of school reform, and I am amazed by how challenging it was for three teachers to create a reform proposal that was only hypothetical. We learned from each other's different perspectives, and we benefited from having a form of mediation in the process. A larger school staff of teachers creating a reform to be instituted may have a more acute need for mediation, as well as a willingness to learn from ideas not envisioned at the beginning of the process and a deep commitment to do what is right for the students—finding a path to greater equity in the reconciliation of competing views about how to get there.

CHAPTER 20

Checking In:
Bridging Differences
by Building Community

Allison Rowland

This chapter describes how a beginning teacher learned to build community in the classroom in order to overcome the student resistance and mistrust that can impede learning. Readers may want to consider what causes students to decide to opt out of or into a classroom, what makes them feel they belong, and how teachers can create relationships that can also sustain their academic agenda with students.

My first year of teaching was an example of a dreadful paradox that engenders inequity in education: I was an untrained, inexperienced teacher working with the students who had been the least successful in the San Francisco Unified School District. On my first day of class at the continuation school (a school for teens who had truancy or behavior problems), I was acutely aware of being a White teacher in a class composed entirely of students of color. While I was attempting to quiet down the chaos, one of my students yelled at me, "You f— ing racist!" The student's words smacked with a vehemence that made me take a step away. My insides wilted at being accused of something I abhor. Speaking into the mayhem, I tried to explain that I understood their distrust of me as a teacher coming into the school after it had already been in session for a month and a half. I told them I knew I would have to earn their respect, but I hoped they would try to stick with me for now. My little speech did not change their impassive stares. At the end of class, the students' faces were pressed against the small square window in the door waiting for the bell to ring. I wanted to race out of the door with them; I was already crying when the bell finally rang.

DETERMINATION IS INSUFFICIENT

As the year scraped along, I planned for my classes more and more intensely with a fear of failure spurring me on. Despite my diligence, my plans were more often than not disrupted by a student yelling because someone had insulted her mother, or something being thrown when I faced the blackboard, or a student adamantly insisting, "I can't do this." The amount of time and effort I spent on a lesson really did not change the outcome. My teacherly zest was squelched day after day. I could see potential in everyone: Tim's snapping quick wit, Stacy's ability to perform caricatures, Rose's persistence at getting to the bottom of gossip. Transferring these skills into academics was my hope and my job. This did not happen. I disappointed and blamed myself daily for not helping the kids change their lives through education.

Lunchtime was my sustenance; the students lounged around the table where I sat monitoring the hallway. Over the pizza slowly adhering to our paper plates, they chatted about their lives. In these seemingly unimportant moments, the kids talked about family, friends, weekends, parole officers, gangs, and school. Their favorite discussions revolved around explaining the nuances of an urban teenager's life to their naive teacher—I appreciated their insights. These interactions were less stressful than the classroom where the world tumbled away from my control. Some of the kids who had made my voice shake with anger 10 minutes before made me laugh about myself. They told me I was just like the woman in the movie *Dangerous Minds*. When I watched the movie for the first time, I prayed that candy and karate moves could turn my class around. When the bell signaled the end of lunch each day, my stomach tightened around the unpredictability of my next class.

The students with whom I spent extra time during lunch and in my advisory were some of those who began to engage in my class. They were the first to begin humoring me in my efforts. At about the same time, I heard a few African American students speaking about a new African American teacher who they thought was "tight." I assumed they felt culturally closer to her; this left me feeling at a loss as to how to bridge the cultural distance between us. It never occurred to me that the bridges we were constructing over pizza during lunch could be built during class. Classes were supposed to be academic; when personal stories were shared, they needed to relate to the curriculum. The academic state of my classroom, however, left me staggering under a heavy backpack of biology curriculum and the weightiest of failures: The students were not learning from me.

After a year at the continuation school, my exhaustion and demoralization forced me to take time away from the classroom. Teaching had become dreadful and unpredictable; it brought me little joy. Although I was proud of the meaningful relationships I had formed with many of the students by the end of the year, I questioned whether I truly wanted this job at which I seemed doomed to fail. Ironically, the desire and fascination with such a seemingly insurmountable challenge led me back. My inner voice wouldn't let me choose any profession other than teaching even though I toyed with many other possibilities. For my next foray into teaching, however, I vowed to be prepared and supported so that I could give pedagogy a fair trial. A credential and a masters' degree were in order.

LEARNING TO TEACH SO THAT STUDENTS CAN LEARN

In my teacher education program I have begun to discover how to liberate myself from the burdens I encountered as an untrained teacher. I have learned about curriculum design and lesson planning, and I use these skills daily. I know much more about how to engage students, organize work so that they are active participants, and scaffold their learning so that they make steady progress. Additionally, I have worked with a cooperating teacher for whom establishing a community in the classroom is as salient as teaching content and skills. In our racially, socioeconomically, and academically diverse class, there is a strong sense of community. We work in a 9th- and 10th-grade program where we plan with other members of our teaching team for the heterogeneous group of students we share for 2 years. This community that borders on being family solves many of the problems I faced at the school in San Francisco: I know the students as individuals and they know me as an individual. The students know and respect one another. Classroom management is about maintenance, not meanness. I enjoy teaching; and I teach my students compassion, respect, open-mindedness, and integrity. Our diversity feels enriching rather than uncomfortable. Undoubtedly, this ease arises both from my increased knowledge and skill and from the sense of community that has been nurtured and guarded daily.

The idea that community draws students into learning is not a new one. Herbert Kohl (1994) writes about student resistance to learning in environments that do not respect their identities and backgrounds. He states:

> Not learning tends to take place when someone has to deal with unavoidable challenges to her or his personal and family loyalties, integrity, and identity. In such situations, there are forced choices and no apparent middle ground. To agree to learn from a stranger who does not respect your integrity causes a major loss of self. The only alternative is to not-learn and reject their world. (pp. 134–135)

Kohl asserts that challenges to student identity lead to a rejection of a class or a teacher. I believe that, for many students, simply not acknowledging students' identities can have the same effect. On the other hand, explicitly embracing the students' identities welcomes them into the learning community. Furthermore, community fosters a sense of trust and belonging, creates a safe space for learning, and helps to overcome divides based on differences among students.

The primary approach my cooperating teacher and I use to build community in our classroom is a concrete and specific strategy: Everyday, for approximately 5 to 10 minutes, the students and I check in about our lives. We hear about such things as parents' divorces, baseball victories, birthday parties, boyfriend trials, sibling rivalry, current event opinions, rapper madness, embarrassing moments, and video game triumphs. These stories weave connections between all members of the classroom so that academic work arises out of this authentic, safe community.

During check-in, I ask the students if they have anything to share that day—and then I see what happens. The other students and I respond to the person who is sharing; side conversations, especially those unrelated to the topic at hand, are discouraged while someone is checking in. Sometimes I will ask quieter students a question if I know they have been involved in an activity or have a certain interest that relates to the topic at hand.

The time devoted to check-in is not fluff. Check-in provides many "teachable moments": how to deal with disappointing a friend, the hurt and injustice of stereotypes and labels, the ramifications of selfish or irresponsible behavior, what it means to be part of a community. It is an opportunity to help students develop as caring, sensitive people. The benefits of check-in time permeate every part of the class by deepening the understanding I have of the students, they have of me, and they have of each other. Academic discussions about sensitive issues such as race, religion, gender roles, and stereotypes become much safer forums for sharing and learning.

Unlike the distrustful atmosphere I experienced in my first year of teaching, our classroom is a productive environment where students understand one another and themselves as learners who can offer opinions, try something new, or step outside their roles as 15-year-old girls and boys. Boys volunteer to share their poetry, and girls are vociferous about their opinions. The "cool" kids participate in class without ruining their reputations, and the quiet kids sometimes speak their minds. Through check-in, the classroom becomes a place where the students garner support and understanding for their lives and their peers' lives, buoying their academic performance in the class. Check-in systematizes the process I discovered while eating pizza with my students in San Francisco. I have learned to foster a community in the classroom.

MEMORABLE CHECK-INS

The class in which I have done my student teaching is about 20% African American, 15% Asian American, 5% Latino and 60% White. The racial tension I encountered in my first teaching experience at the school in San Francisco is nonexistent in my student teaching classroom, although I'm certain inadvertent racial exclusion has sometimes occurred in the curriculum or other aspects of this and other classes. However, because we know each other well, ethnic differences seem only to add a richness to our class. Sexual discrimination has been more problematic; when slurs have been made about gays, lesbians, bisexuals, or women, check-in allows us to address them in the moment.

In some cases, check-in has really changed the learning context for a specific student and the community as a whole. For example, one day a student was sharing about dance practices she was attending in preparation for a school rally when she mentioned that Shatara, a shy, African American student, was a part of the class. I asked them if they would give us a sneak preview of their dance. The girl who was sharing said she had missed so many practices that she didn't actually know the dance, but she said Shatara was one of the best dancers. I was shocked when Shatara walked nonchalantly to the front of the class as I scrambled for a seat in the audience. She performed a step dance with African American cultural roots while the class sat riveted by the scintillating rhythms she conjured with stomps, claps, snaps, and slaps. The cheering at the end was authentic and heartfelt. From that time forward, Shatara became noticeably more vocal during both check-in and class discussions. This experience appeared to raise her own confidence level and her status in the eyes of her peers.

When students are sharing about their experiences outside of the classroom, their language sometimes reflects the way they speak with friends in social situations. Outside of the carefully constructed community of the classroom, their stereotypes and prejudices, both conscious and unconscious, surface. Thus check-in provides opportunities to make students aware of the effects of their thoughtless comments. For example, early on in the year, Chad was displaying his newest model of Nike high tops. Patrick shouted across the room, "Those shoes are gay!"

"You're gay," Chad called back, bending his hand at his wrist in an effeminate mockery. I knew it was important to stop gay slurs immediately, but I had no idea how to deal with the quick comments jabbing across the room. My cooperating teacher stopped the banter: "When you say that something is gay and what you really mean is that it's stupid, ugly, or un-cool, you are making a connection between being gay and being stupid, ugly, or uncool. You would be offended if someone said, 'That's so Chad,' and what they meant was

'That's so stupid.' Being Chad is essential to you, just as being gay is essential to someone who is gay. This classroom is for all students and you are not allowed to put anyone down in here." At first the students tittered and wondered at the seriousness of their teachers. "I will be personally offended if you make judgments about other people's lives," my cooperating teacher continued; the students sensed her gravity. In this situation, we were able to deal explicitly with the common homophobic comments made by our students because check-in brought up real situations and experiences. We revisited homophobia as the issue arose both during check-in and in the curriculum throughout the year.

Check-in often creates invaluable opportunities for addressing status issues in a classroom. For example, Bill, a White student who plays video games with the ardor and discipline of an athlete in training for the Olympics, often related his triumph of beating a particular game or the agony of the electricity going out midplay. Initially other students ridiculed him for his video game passion; my cooperating teacher and I stifled the giggles with the same questions about the video games as we would ask a student telling us about a basketball game. Our enthusiasm caught on, and now the students remember to ask Bill how he fares in video game tournaments. Although it is complicated to determine the roots of change, I believe that as we showed interest in Bill's check-ins, the students began to see him in a new light. Instead of excluding Bill for being different, they have become curious about Bill's passion and appreciative of his individualism.

Through the check-in process, I hear the students' personal stories as they unfold. Staying abreast of their lives in time, rather than after significant events have already occurred, yields a plethora of "teaching moments" and a forum for the discussion of choices. For example, Craig related the events of the previous evening at his water polo practice. The coach had screamed at him for being late to practice while Craig was trying to explain that his mother had not been able to get off work to bring him in time. Craig decided, "I didn't deserve to be screamed at," and walked away from the coach. As a consequence for Craig's "disrespect," the coach banned Craig from the next water polo game. Both my cooperating teacher and I praised Craig for his decision to walk away without becoming embroiled in a senseless yelling match. We applauded his unwillingness to be verbally abused, and then we coached him about ways to have a rational, calm discussion with the coach.

The next day the plot had thickened. The coach wanted Craig to apologize to him before he would allow him to play in the next water polo game. Craig did not feel he needed to apologize; his teammates agreed, deciding to boycott the next game unless the coach himself apologized. The class was enthralled by Craig's story and had lots of advice for him. They drew connections between their own experience and that of Craig to help him make an informed choice. During this week while Craig's saga unfolded, we discussed abuse of power, justice, worthwhile causes, teamwork, peaceful protests, communication tactics, and respect. This time was well-spent for everyone. Ultimately, Craig and his teammates prevailed over the unfair coach who was not asked back to the school to coach for the following season.

Check-in not only helps kids navigate their way to becoming better people outside of the classroom, it also engenders prime moments for tending to the classroom community. A striking example of this occurred in the last months of school this year. The students had come to know each other so well that every adventure shared during check-in inspired 30 related side conversations. I was continuously stopping the class to remind the students that it was rude to the person speaking if others were talking at the same time EVEN if their conversations were relevant.

On this day Kara, who usually shared about her attempts to meet the heroic 'N Sync band, was bursting to describe her trip to New York for a concert. Her story was dripping with details about clothing decisions and cell phone calls to the 'N Sync agent—some of the class lost interest. I quieted them down and she continued to relay the adventure of her pilgrimage. Unfortunately, however, her tales of mobs of screaming girls provoked several conversations among a few boys. She stopped abruptly as her face flushed, "FORGET it, just FORGET it. You guys are being so rude. I was so excited to share about the concert, but you've ruined it for me. You're so unfair." She covered her face and started crying. The class was silent, aghast at what they had done. The gravity was clear to everyone: They knew how much the concert meant to Kara because they had heard about intricate preparations in the weeks leading up to the event. They had heard about all of her other attempts to meet the band members, and rumor had it that this time she finally had met them.

My cooperating teacher spoke into the students' silence: "This is why side conversations are not allowed while someone is talking. You don't think they matter but people can get hurt. Erik, Carl, I know you didn't mean to hurt Kara, but you did. You're not mean people, but your behavior has made Kara feel disrespected." Erik and Carl and some of the other guys were looking at the floor. They said, "Sorry Kara," like they meant it. My cooperating teacher asked Kara if she wanted to go outside for a little bit and she did. Check-in was over and the class went on with a much more subdued tone. After much pleading and cheering with Kara the next day, the class listened carefully to her story of the highlight of her life.

Of course, not everyday produces a powerful lesson, discussion, or change in status. Most of the benefits of sharing occur over time and in more subtle ways as more kids participate, feel comfortable, and take risks.

HOLD ONTO CHECKING IN

In my teacher education program, the goals of knowing students well, personalizing instruction, and teaching habits of heart constantly arose in our discussions. Check-in is an explicit avenue for achieving these goals every day. The temptation for a teacher, in the face of overwhelming amounts of material to cover and lessons to complete, might be to cast aside time for students' personal stories because they do not appear academically relevant. One might think that students sharing about their lives can occur in the 5 minutes between classes when they're scrambling for their seats or in the context of an academic discussion. It does to some extent, but it is not common knowledge for everyone, especially you as the teacher. The community that is built and the learning that occurs make every bit of check-in time worthwhile.

Check-in builds a strong community within which the other tools of good teaching in heterogeneous classrooms are enhanced and become more successful. Complex instruction, project-based learning, multiple-intelligence approaches, and individualized instruction rise to a new level of effectiveness when the students feel safe as individuals and as members of a community. The need to uphold a certain image or to just work with friends relaxes and the classroom environment becomes more conducive to learning. Students become more willing to take risks and to stick with learning even when it's not the most engaging material. When all of the people in the classroom know each other better, the barriers come down and the learning becomes a part of what we do rather than what we're forced to do.

As I think back on my year at the high school in San Francisco, I wonder how different the experience would have been had I been able to connect with my students in this way. I know that honoring each student's individual experiences and cultures would have made a tremendous difference, along with the many other teaching strategies I have since learned. I know, without a doubt, that the students would have more readily engaged in the class had I made a commitment to establishing authentic relationships with them from the beginning. In my next classroom as a full-fledged teacher, I am confident the experience will be much more empowering and enjoyable for me and my students. I will never be from the same culture as all of my students, nor will I have shared all of their experiences; however, an explicit agenda and a well-developed strategy for building community can bridge some of these distances and create a rich foundation for learning.

CHAPTER 21

Wanted: Teachers with Conciencia

Ana Louisa Ruiz

Ana Ruiz describes her drive to be a mathematics teacher "*con conciencia*," with consciousness, in order to reach her goal of increasing student success in mathematics and in life. Readers may want to consider how they define teaching *con conciencia* for themselves, and how this social awareness influences their classrooms and their work in the profession. Readers may also want to discuss examples of curriculum and classroom structures that provide access to diverse learners in their own field.

I became a teacher to make a difference one learner at a time. As I finish my year of student teaching, I now know that I am also committed to becoming a teacher *con conciencia,* one who has the passion and continually develops the skills to teach ALL students. My arena for making a difference is the teaching of mathematics.

TEACHING MATHEMATICS AS A PATH TO SOCIAL JUSTICE

Regularly, my grandmother would ask why I would want to become a math teacher, "Anita, *por qué te gustan los números*?" My answer to her was an extended litany of reasons:

> I am committed to students' success in their individual lives and as citizens. Mathematics is a gatekeeper to higher education and a major obstacle to social equality for many.

I am committed to building strong classroom communities that offer groundbreaking curriculum, thought-provoking projects, and a healthy environment where adolescents can develop physically, emotionally, psychologically, and cognitively.

I am dedicated to help students tackle their "mathphobia." Mathphobia is an irrational and encumbering dread of mathematics. And yet, nearly every important issue of the day—ecology, inflation, poverty, education, defense, and international trade, to name just a few—has a strong mathematical component. Mathematics can be seen daily in almost all phases of human activity. Breaking down this fear requires a school to welcome ALL of its students, challenge them, and inspire them to tackle their fear of mathematics.

I aspire to have students experience and discover mathematics by "getting their hands dirty" and becoming empowered to use mathematics for their own purposes. This requires a focus on in-depth learning of powerful concepts, emphasizing understanding, reasoning, and problem solving rather than memorization of facts, terminology, and algorithms. It requires that students are active in their learning and are applying their knowledge of mathematical ideas every day. Through this process, as self-confidence increases, mathphobia fades. Students become empowered to develop the mathematical literacy necessary to make informed decisions and to function as full participants of society.

I believe that students can develop mental structures for mathematics that are more complex, abstract, and powerful than the ones they currently possess so that they are increasingly capable of solving a wide variety of meaningful problems.

I believe that students can become autonomous and self-motivated in their mathematical activity so that they see their responsibility in the mathematics classroom not so much as completing assigned tasks but as making sense of, and communicating about, mathematics.

Above all, the reason that I want to become a mathematics teacher is that I believe unconditionally that all students have the ability to think.

Like most students, I have taken mathematics classes that did not allow me to "think." Instead, they required "stolen" manipulations of formulas following algorithms given by the lecturer. Maybe the reason that I favor a constructivist approach to teaching mathematics is that it slowly decreases the chances of discrimination against diverse students. It creates access by giving mathematical voice to the "voiceless," regardless of their background or the societal labels they are forced to carry. It provides the means for all students—including students of color and students from lower socioeconomic communities—to be included.

One of my own teachers opened my eyes and gave me sight, expanding my *conciencia.* I was having trouble seeing the use of the Quadratic Formula:

$$x = \frac{-b \pm \sqrt{b^2 - 4ac}}{2a}$$

He then began to tell me a story about two brothers who got into an argument after the squared brother lost four apple computers. As soon as he had concluded this little mnemonic story, my thinking wheels began to turn. I managed to "see" the Quadratic Formula through means that made sense to ME. I knew that the story contained no mathematical content, but I also understood what my teacher was trying to say: that all students learn math differently. Not all students learn math by listening to lectures. Some need stories. Some need hands-on work. All learn mathematics uniquely. Hence it is the teacher's challenge to discover how math makes sense to all students. And it was then that I decided to become a math teacher.

TEACHING FOR EQUITY IN THE MATHEMATICS CLASSROOM

The first time I officially stepped into a classroom, I began to realize the many layers of teaching that must go on in order to achieve these goals. It is not just a matter of communicating content. Although I've had a short teaching career thus far, I can already see that most students thrive in a classroom that fosters autonomy, positive self-esteem, and a willingness to explore and to accept each other. I also realize that obstacles arise unexpectedly where classroom management skills need to be put to work and that certain behaviors on the part of students can be misinterpreted. Equity in a mathematics classroom means giving students choices of ways to learn. It also requires allowing them voice in expressing their frustrations about learning.

For example, regularly, during the first minutes of class, I ask my students for input as to how they were able to use mathematics at home. One Monday morning after a three-day weekend, there was little response; however, one of my students made sure that the whole class listened to her frustration. "Ms. Ruiz, when are you going to start teaching us something?" Here I had in front of me one of those moments that seemed endless on the surface, and that felt even more prolonged beneath the surface as multiple thoughts raced through my mind. However, my *conciencia* as a teacher respected the fact that one of my own students had the courage to voice her honest opinion about how she was feeling about what we were doing in class. It is when my students don't feel the safety to voice their opinion and "frustration" that I worry most. It's a deeper challenge to gain access to a silenced, closed door.

I knew that regardless of what I could express to this student (and now to the whole class because they were focusing on I would say in response), she still was not going to be convinced. I knew that a student like her likes to be shown what I mean, rather than just receiving a verbal explanation. The insights I have gained in teaching my students since the first day of class allowed me to understand that what this student was really saying was, "Ms. Ruiz, you're the teacher, just tell us what the right answer is!" I decided not to treat this as a classroom management problem but as a request for greater understanding of what we were doing together.

I did not respond that day. The next day, taking advantage of the curricular exchanges within our school's math department, I gathered a warm-up from another math teacher to give to my own students. My students took a while to begin to work on figuring out a pile pattern presented in this warm up. They were to come up with a rule to describe the relationship between the pile number and its area. As I worked the classroom, I started to notice that the groups' rules were "different." Because their rules were not the one I had figured out for this particular pattern, I gathered some scratch paper and a pencil to work out each of the group's findings. Out of the six groups of four in my class, there were four "different" rules that came up, plus a fifth, distinctive explanation of one of the rules already found. Disregarding the rest of my lesson plan for the day, I gave all the groups a transparency and colored overhead markers. We had the groups present their "different" rules. After the presentations, students had their chance to give their input, "Cool!" "Hey, that's hella different!" Of course I also took the opportunity to put my two cents in.

I made the decision to address my student from the previous day who had been so courageous in voicing her frustration: I said that I had seen my students putting their heads together to come up with a rule for this warm-up. However, the class had come up with five "different" rules. I told her and the class that if I had given them the rule that only I had thought of, the different rules would never have been discovered. I would have been making the assumption that my students couldn't think for themselves. However, I believe each of my students can think for him- or herself, because they're all smart and intelligent. Then, I told them how some of my former teachers used to tell me that I was "slow" with my math just because I seemed to think differently. Thinking differently, I emphasized, doesn't mean I'm slow or stupid, it just means that I'm actually using my brain to think through my own point of view. The courageous student now saw why we were exploring ideas in the classroom rather than just giving out "right answers."

I could have reacted in many negative ways to the situation that arose within my classroom. However, I knew it took courage for this student to articulate her frustration about math learning. I also know that in order for me to help my students help me, and to help them see the variety of math tools and intelligences that surround us each day, I have to listen to how students are feeling. Part of that is creating a safe space where we can discuss the concerns they may have about publicly displaying wisdom they already possess as well as questions they have. I have learned how important it is to create an environment in which students do not have to fear continuous evaluation, where they can make mistakes and learn from them, and where they do not always need to worry about meeting someone else's standard of excellence.

I was asked recently if I had any discipline problems within my classroom. "What's a discipline problem?" I answered quickly. To me, discipline problems arise when the students are not engaged with the subject or activity currently taking place. The minute that teachers allow teachable moments among students to become "problems," we lose focus. Instead of focusing on attacking the subject, we attack students. This invites more reactions from the students and strays from teaching subject matter, skills, and critical thinking. Instead, the goal is misperceived as emerging victorious in "competition" with one of our own students. When this happens, I have found that greater problems develop.

It is important to me not to go against my students. I know that battles and obstacles can be successfully overcome only if both teachers and students become members of the same team, knowing that together everyone achieves more. Many of our students are carrying a heavy weight. They might be the first students from their family to pursue an education, or they might be the oldest siblings in a large family who are trying to show the path to the rest of their brothers and sisters. I know that as a teacher *con conciencia*, I need to respect my students' different lives.

In respecting my students' lives and minds, I wholeheartedly believe that the role of the teacher is to guide and support students' invention of workable mathematical ideas rather than to transmit "correct" adult ways of doing mathematics. As teachers we must remember that student knowledge is actively created or invented by the students themselves, not passively received from textbooks. Students construct ideas and make them meaningful when they integrate ideas into their existing knowledge structures. Thus learning mathematics should be thought of as a process of organizing one's quantitative world, not discovering preexisting ideas imposed by others. When teachers allow students to think for themselves, they open the floor to what students have to say; when they engage the students, they build on what students have said; and when their evaluation of student responses is positive, they certify new turns in the discussion produced by student thinking.

This does not mean there is no role for the teacher. The teacher must guide the focus of the students' attention by offering appropriate tasks and opportunities for dialogue and thus directing their learning. Teachers should expose students to abstract mathematical concepts, create links to students' own experiences, require them to be active in considering these ideas, sustain student-initiated ideas and responses, and consequently promote articulate thinking. As a teacher, I want to engage students in probing and substantive discussions. When I can "chain" together my questions and the students' responses in a conversation rather than the standard initiation-response-evaluation sequence, we enter into a partnership in which we are committed to working with one another, in terms of each other. In my classroom I want the students to become the "teachers": to discover math on their own. I believe that empowering my students to think mathematically for themselves is part of the path to equity and social justice.

SEIZING THE TEACHING MOMENT

I first discovered how powerful this process could be when I was preparing my students for an upcoming final exam. They were especially apprehensive about taking tests, not because they could not do the material but because they feared the possibility of failure. As a means of preparing them for the final, we did a "warm up" to review problem types they had previously learned so that they could recall the material and I could assess their understanding. I regularly call on students to present their solutions to the whole class and to query one another, so that they can build their self-confidence and their ability to ask and answer their own questions without depending on a teacher.

In this case, Jerry presented the last warm up problem on solving equations, to which he strongly believed the answer was –30. Shamanda questioned his answer, asserting that the answer was actually 24.

I grew concerned when it appeared that Jerry was being influenced to disagree with his (correct) answer; however, I hesitated to suggest he was mistaken in agreeing with Shamanda. I knew that if I asked the class "Does anyone have a question?" not a single hand would go up. So instead, I directed my students to "Ask a question!"

Almost immediately, Dalila provided a solution that agreed with Jerry's first answer. I decided to pursue the exploration of the answers, although that deviated from the day's agenda. So that Dalila would feel validated for her work, I asked her to go up to the overhead and explain her solution. Initially, she removed Jerry's work and set it aside. In order to acknowledge both pieces of work as valid ways of thinking I requested that Dalila place Jerry's work alongside her own. As Dalila explained her thinking, Shamanda took time to review her work, con-

Shamanda's Explanation	*Jerry's Explanation*
$-3x^2+x$	$-3x^2 + x$
$=-3 \cdot -3^2 + -3$	$=-3(-3)^2 + (-3)$
$=-3 \cdot -9 + -3$	$=-3(9) + (-3)$
$=27 + -3$	$=-27 +(-3)$
$=24$	$=-30$

cluding that she had made a mistake and assuring Jerry that he was correct. Others concurred as they evaluated the solutions. The class as a whole, through the students' presentations, was able to realize that people demonstrate their thinking differently. They were also able to recognize a misconception that is constantly made in an algebra class, that $(-3)^2$ does not equal -3^2.

Although I was aware that the warm up was consuming "too much" time, the discourse in the classroom was worth much more than what I had planned to do for the day's lesson. The teachable moment occurred while my students led a mature and sophisticated discussion about mathematics while I stood against the wall. I redefined my goal for the day in order to allow the students to take ownership of their learning and become active participants. As a result of this awareness about my students, I have become a teacher with *conciencia*: a consciousness that allows me to look at my students and know that they are capable of achieving their goals.

BUILDING A COMMUNITY OF TEACHERS OF CONSCIENCE

If we are to learn how to create these kinds of opportunities for all students, the same dynamics that create communities of learners in our classrooms must operate in our professional learning with one another. Like my students, I have had to learn how to achieve voice in communities of other educators. This summer, I experienced two events that have given me more insight into myself as an educator and the challenges in our profession. I attended a summer institute for math teachers. As usual, I faced the typical demographics of teachers in our area: a group of about 50 people, most of them White, in which I was the only Chicana. However, all of us are teaching mathematics to the same diverse student population, and many among the group had much wisdom to contribute to the conversation. After noticing that the workshop format did not allow these experienced educators to share their knowledge with the entire group, I approached the institute instructor to inquire as to when it was that the expertise of the teachers attending the institute would be tapped. In response to my inquiry, the instructor of this course said, "I noticed from the beginning of the class that you have an ATTITUDE."

This cutting statement reached the bottom of my soul. I couldn't manage to think of the right words to seize my accumulating anger. Hearing such words from others does not crush me as much as when they come from another teacher, especially a teacher who is supposed to be teaching a diverse population of students: students who are motivated to learn, but whose potential too often gets crushed by someone's animosity. I questioned whether or not I should be a teacher. How can I think about being a teacher? I'm just *someone* who believes that all children can learn and should have access to an equitable education.

However, my way of thinking sounded too demanding, and so with the stabbing words, I was shut down. I questioned my expertise as a beginning teacher.

It was then that I realized I must go beyond what I want to what is needed. I have a choice: Either I can get filled with anger or I can do something about it by educating my colleagues and myself. So, by the end of this institute, I managed to connect with a handful of teachers who also have an "attitude" like mine, and who are willing to begin building bridges among open-minded individuals in order to serve our students better. It doesn't serve my students when I feel "small"; there aren't many positive outcomes from feeling insecure. It's simple, really: When students ask for clarification, they're not attacking the pedagogical structures already in place; instead, they're just expressing their own worthy personal opinion. My mother always said, "*La verdad no peca pero incomoda.*" (Truth is not a sin, but it's uncomfortable.) Even when it's uncomfortable, teachers, like students, need to express their thinking.

The second event changed my views as a teacher. I attended a retreat that featured the same demographics, but this time the outcome was different. Once again I openly shared my beliefs about how all students can learn mathematics if given the tools. I was not only listened to, but several teachers asked clarifying questions about the insights I had shared with the group. My colleagues at this retreat shared the belief that as teachers with a *conciencia*, we gain by sharing our knowledge so that we can provide the means for ALL students to be successful.

This time, we got down to working on HOW it can be possible. We respected our differences but worked from the roots of our similarities. The work of equity is not work that needs to be done alone or competitively: It must be a collaborative effort. The only way that I will become a better teacher is through an exchange of ideas and resources. It's not about selfishness in wanting ownership of ideas but about pedagogical maturity in sharing what we already know so that our students, all our students, can benefit from it. If our conversations make it seem that everything is working, we're not trying hard enough to make things better by bringing about change for all of our students.

What happens when we do not teach all students? What are the societal consequences? There are students who fall through the cracks in our educational system. Perhaps this is because they are too busy helping their families with their corn crops. Or, perhaps they don't have the resources because they are not allowed to develop intellectually. Or, perhaps their teachers were not aware of how to help them.

I'm a Chicana math teacher with a pledge to teach all students. I carry a flame—a flame that I hope will not only permeate my students but also spread throughout the teaching profession. I wish that my grandma could hear my short answer to her question about why I want to become a math teacher, "*Nina, p'os me gustan los números por que nos hacen PENSAR!*" Teaching, especially teaching mathematics, makes us think. Teachers of color and teachers of conscience must join together to enable all of our students to learn to think.

The passion and the promise that I have to fulfill my dream are guiding me as I begin my first year as a full-time mathematics teacher. I cannot change how students have learned in the past. What I can do today is attempt to uncover the means to improve how students learn. It is imperative for me to be prepared to better the educational system and give our youth the tools to learn how to be a learner within the mathematics classroom with confidence. Only a real "teacher" can do that. I have found that in most cases a teacher is committed to being a pivotal person in a young scholar's life. Today, I can confidently declare that I know that I have the calling, the determination, and the hope to contribute to improving the educational system to meet the needs of our diverse student population, and I know that I am not alone in this work.

CHAPTER 22

Educating a Profession for Equitable Practice

Linda Darling-Hammond

In the first chapter of this book, Todd Ziegler Cymrot observed how often he had heard the statement from teaching colleagues, "I just don't understand what this diversity thing has to do with me!" We hope that the answer to this question is clear to readers who have made it thus far. As Ziegler notes, diversity as a construct signifies a vast ongoing conversation about whom we teach, how we teach, and why we teach. Our relationship as teachers to the diverse students we teach and the institutions we help to shape causes us to have to examine and work on every aspect of who we are and how we practice.

Learning to teach for social justice is a lifelong undertaking. It involves coming to understand oneself in relation to others; examining how society constructs privilege and inequality and how this affects one's own opportunities as well as those of different people; exploring the experiences of others and appreciating how those inform their worldviews, perspectives, and opportunities; and evaluating how schools and classrooms operate and can be structured to value diverse human experiences and to enable learning for all students.

An "equity pedagogy" (Banks, 1993) also benefits from knowledge about how different children learn, and how teaching strategies can productively engage children who learn in distinctive ways. Finally, enacting an equity pedagogy requires an understanding of how to change one's own practice and how to work with others to change institutions. In combination, these understandings can enable a teacher to intervene in the relationship between schools and students in order to improve what happens for children.

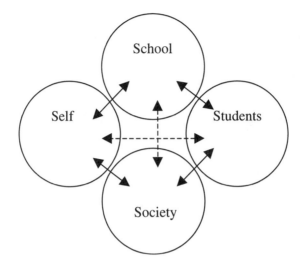

As the figure above suggests, examining oneself in relationship to society, understanding how society shapes students' lives and opportunities outside and inside of school (and how students respond to those influences), investigating students' relationships to school and classroom contexts (both how schools "frame" the possibilities for different students and how students construct their aspirations and efforts in the context of school) and then evaluating the relationship between oneself and the school are all part of the process of determining how a teacher can influence the school and the lives of her or his students.

The journey toward these understandings is intensely personal, and yet it is necessarily social—it has to be conducted in the company of others who teach us about their own experiences and who learn with us about how to build a common understanding that is greater than the sum of its parts. In *Democracy and Education*, John Dewey (1966) noted that "a democracy is more than a form of government; it is primarily a mode of associated living" (p. 87). He stressed the importance of creating circumstances in which people participate in a growing number of associations with others, noting that:

> In order to have a large number of values in common, all the members of the group must have an equitable opportunity to receive and to take from others. There must be a large variety of shared undertakings and experiences. Otherwise, the influences that educate some into masters educate others into slaves. And the experience of each party loses in meaning. (p. 84)

As Maxine Greene (1982) reminds us, if we are to create a public space for democracy, schools must consciously create community from the sharing of multiple perspectives. In a sense, this task of consciously creating community from the sharing of multiple voices is one of the first jobs of a teacher education program, and it is a continuing job of schools. Finding space for reflection and discourse about who we are, individually and collectively, in relation to one another and to society at large creates the initial foundation for all the other necessary work on social justice.

UNDERSTANDING SELF IN RELATION TO OTHERS

Many teacher education programs begin their work on multicultural awareness with autobiography, so that students can reflect on how the cultural context and conditions in which they grew up have influenced what they believe about education, learning, schooling, and teaching. Examining one's own experiences and their contribution to identity can be a powerful experience. Hearing about those of others and coming to understand how these experiences shape very different realities is equally powerful. In her chapter, "Can White Teachers Effectively Teach Students of Color?" Kristin Traudt recounts how an assignment that asked her to characterize her own identity sensitized her to the possibilities of stereotyping and the social consequences of labeling.

In addition, she notes that hearing her colleagues' stories brought new insights:

> For the first time I learned about struggles that minority students experience in classrooms across the United States, about ELD (English Language Development) "ghettos" that segregate English Language Learners in many high schools. Prior to STEP I had read about the disparities in treatment of African Americans, Latinos, and other ethnic groups in the United States, but it was not until discussing it with my colleagues that I began to picture the real pain and suffering involved in each case. After teaching students who fit these descriptions, I became aware of the unspoken privileges that I have had throughout my own education and life because of the color of my skin and my sexual orientation.... As we discussed teaching for diversity at STEP, I wondered how I was affecting my students' lives. Had I created a safe learning environment for them? Was I showing my students respect for their cultures, their individuality?

Asking these kinds of questions is the beginning of a process of reflection about one's identity as a teacher that, once begun, is not easily stopped. This process of identity development has implications not only for individual teachers but for the students they teach. As Robert Carter and Lin Goodwin (1994) noted in their seminal work on racial identity and education, the racial identity development of educators undoubtedly influences how they perceive and treat visible racial/ethnic group children. To be empathic and effective with all of their students, educators need to develop a sense of themselves as racial and cultural beings and to develop a sense of their students' experiences as well.

This requires a conscious effort to understand and embrace diverse perspectives. Lisa Delpit (1995) reminds us that "we all interpret behaviors, information, and situations through our own cultural lenses; these lenses operate involuntarily, below the level of conscious awareness, making it seem that our own view is simply 'the way it is'" (p. 151). Educators must develop a keen awareness of the perspectives they bring and how these can be enlarged if they are to avoid what Edmund Gordon (1990) calls "communicentric bias—the tendency to make one's own community the center of the universe and the conceptual frame that constrains thought" (p. 19). This bias limits understanding of those whom we teach and thus renders our exchanges less educative. The ability to appreciate different perspectives is an important aspect of both cognitive and social functioning; it is one of Piaget's indicators of higher stages of cognitive development as well as a goal of socially responsible education.

The capacity for perspective-taking develops through participation in a community in which diverse experiences and views are constantly elicited and shared within the group. This depends on what I think of as a "multidirectional pedagogy" in which teachers construct many opportunities for students to share what they think and what they know with one another as well as with the teacher. In teacher education programs, as in other settings, the use of the group as an educative body requires skillful management of discussions that can often result in the assertion of one view or one set of experiences over another and careful attention to the questions of standing, entitlement, and voice in the group.

It is not uncommon for those who have felt entitled in the educational system to be sometimes initially unable to hear the voices of those who have been marginalized. As Jen French and Paloma Garcia-Lopez described in the preface to this book and in their respective chapters, minority students and others who have had experiences outside the dominant culture often find themselves feeling marginalized even in their teacher education programs by those who do not understand their experiences or share the intensity of their commitment to changing a system that may have seemed to work well to those who were privileged by it. In "The Silenced Dialogue," Lisa Delpit (1995) describes how many teachers of color often feel they cannot be understood in conversations about race, class, and culture that are dominated by mainstream views. As one of her respondents put it, "I try to give them my experiences, to explain. They just look and nod.... They don't really hear me.... It just doesn't make any sense to keep talking to them" (p. 22). Another said, "Well, I don't know if they really don't listen or if they just don't believe you. It seems like if you can't quote Vygotsky or something, then you don't have any validity to speak about your *own* kids. Anyway, I'm not bothering with it anymore" (p. 21). These pained statements echo many I have heard from STEP students in my office after they have felt unheard or were stunned by insensitivity to their concerns in classes they have taken.

When this feeling causes students to shut down, they not only become disillusioned, but the group loses important opportunities for learning and growing. Like others in teacher education programs, we have worked to create increasingly open and inclusive dialogues by being clear about the value of diversity, insistent and persistent about the importance of hearing all voices, and dogged in returning to conversations about race, class, culture, and experience across multiple settings inside and outside of courses. There are substantial expansions in individuals' insights and steady growth in the social and cultural knowledge of the group as a result of these efforts. It is true each year, however, that some students at the end of the year offer the critique that we have focused too little on these issues and others complain that we have focused too much. It is important to recognize that the process of learning to teach for diversity cannot be accomplished without some discomfort and that views of what kind of discourse is useful and necessary will inevitably vary. But we take heart in the fact that, by the end of the year, there is a shared perception by students that they belong to a strong community of educators who are committed to ideals of equity and who have a cohort of colleagues to support them in their efforts at change.

Teachers do not have to be members of the same racial/ethnic community as their students to learn to teach them well. The fundamental idea of the common school was to create a public space within which diverse people could communicate and forge a joint experience that would allow them to build a broader community. The early university was designed to bring people together from around the world who could build knowledge by sharing different cultural experiences and areas of study. There is no doubt that this is uncomfortable and problematic: It is always easier to talk with those who think as we do, who have had common experiences, and who agree with us. That is one appeal of homogeneous neighborhoods, private schools, and tracking systems. A communication that is, in John Dewey's (1916/1966) words, "vitally social" and "vitally shared" is one that allows one person at least partially to experience the perspectives of another, and by that connection to develop understanding and appreciation for that person's experience and understanding of the world. In this way diverse individuals can create a space in which they can support each other in joint action.

UNDERSTANDING SOCIAL CONTEXTS

A second challenge is enabling teachers to understand the social context within which schools operate and students develop and learn. The fact that the U.S. school system is structured such that students routinely receive dramatically unequal learning opportunities based on their race and social status is simply not widely acknowledged, and few teachers will have had access to information about inequalities in schooling. Despite widespread stark disparities in school funding and radically different levels of educational quality available to students, the prevailing societal view is that if students do not achieve, it is both their fault and their sole burden to bear.

Much has been made in recent years of the relatively low performance of U.S. students on international assessments, especially in mathematics and science. Still more striking is the finding from the Second International Mathematics Study that, for U.S. students, the spread of achievement —and of measured opportunities to learn—was many times greater than that of other industrialized countries, and was comparable only to the level of disparity found in developing nations that do not yet provide universal access to education (McKnight et al., 1987).

It is important for teachers to have the opportunity to investigate the social context that produces these inequalities and to understand how opportunities to learn are constructed and distributed in schools. This can occur through school studies—for example, investigations of school programs and practices like those Erin Hays, Suzanne Herzman, and Laura Blythe describe in their chapters on tracking. It can also occur through examinations of what happens to individual students as they wend their way through schools, as in the case studies of students written by Roman Garcia, Leah Anderson, and Sandra Navarro. Coupling prospective teachers' investigations into the communities and schools in which they teach with readings that place their findings in broader social perspective (e.g. Banks, 1995; Darling-Hammond, 1997; Kozol, 1991; Nieto, 1999; Olsen, 1997; Tatum, 1997; Valdés, 1996) helps them to build an analytic understanding of the nature of the problem as well as an affective commitment to working toward reform.

An additional aspect of understanding social contexts for learning is appreciating the cultural contexts within which students develop and learn, and understanding how those contexts are tapped or ignored within schools and classrooms as well as how they influence students' experiences in society and school. In one sense culture is the foundation of all learning. As Jerome Bruner (1996) notes, "Learning, remembering, talking, imagining: all of them are made possible by participating in a culture (p. xi).... So in the end, while mind creates culture, culture also creates mind" (p. 166). When culture is ignored or misunderstood—or when it becomes the basis for prejudice—students' learning, identity development, and affiliation with school can be compromised.

Joel Spring (1997) has written about how schools can "deculturalize" in ways that result in minority students feeling they must place themselves in opposition to the school environment or that they must divorce themselves from their culture in order to achieve. Deculturalization can occur through segregation and isolation of minority students, forced change of language, a curriculum whose content and texts reflect only the culture of the dominant group, or a setting in which dominated groups are not allowed to express their culture or customs. Acceding to these forces can produce the psychological phenomenon Fordham (1988) identified as racelessness, when minority students "enter school having to unlearn or, at least, to modify their own culturally sanctioned interactional and behavioral styles and adopt those styles rewarded in the school context if they wish to achieve academic success" (p. 55).

The process of developing an understanding of the ubiquitous role of culture in society and the importance of its manifestations in schools is not straightforward. It requires a great deal of sensitization to the many ways in which cultural contexts matter to all of the people in them. Prospective teachers, especially those who are members of dominant cultures, may not initially realize the salience of race, class, and culture in students' experiences and in their own choices of content, modes of communication, and how they and others may see and treat students as well as how students may treat one another.

For example, in a discussion of readings by Carol Lee (1995), Deborah Juarez (1999), and Gloria Ladson-Billings (1992) about culturally relevant teaching, STEP students initially had very different reactions to the notion of culture and its relevance to them or to the classroom. A White male teacher of mathematics launched the discussion by commenting that the readings posed a lot of questions for him. He felt really "at a loss" about what to do in his classroom. There was "nothing culturally-relevant" for him in the articles—he was not sure about what to do about teaching "African-American math" or "Latino science."

A White teacher of foreign language noted that he felt that there was "only one culture" in his classroom—the culture represented by the country of the language he teaches. "As I read the articles, I just went" [he gestured as if to throw away the article]—"this is not useful for me at all." A White female teacher said that she "similarly struggled" and noted that perhaps the concept was to figure out what was it about the "kids' culture." It was important to figure out for her students where the links were to their lives. The foreign-language teacher responded, "to me, I see that as a no-brainer. That is just good teaching!"

An African American social studies teacher responded: "It really is NOT a 'no-brainer.' In my school, there are 139 African-American students. Only 19% of them scored at the 40th percentile or higher on the State test. The Ladson-Billings article was a very clear example that these students can learn. But obviously the teacher is doing something different than what we are doing in my school. For most teachers, it is NOT a no-brainer. My concern with the 'everybody has a culture' view is that for these students, what is being taught is not relevant to them, and the culture of the classroom is not relevant."

A White science teacher wondered if "it may be easier to make some subjects more culturally relevant than others." She wondered also if there were "only a certain amount of connections you CAN make for students."

A White social studies teacher noted that, "As a White teacher I really need to think about what my prejudices are, what I think, what I can do.... At the very core, we need to reflect on our teaching, what we value. We need to move past the idea of what is appropriate in math or other subjects and move on to the issues of how kids are treated in our classrooms."

A Latina Spanish student teacher working at a school ranking among the lowest on the state tests talked about the fact that at their last faculty meeting, teachers were given 20 pages of statistics about the school. "What do you see?" they were asked. Teachers replied that "70% of the school is Latino. More than half of the parents do not have an education beyond grade school." Some teachers said, "Well no wonder our scores are so low! The parents don't have an education!" The student teacher said to the class, "I don't want you to act surprised. Many teachers feel that way. They just don't all say it.... This is very personal for me; I feel like this is just like my school, and that these teachers are teaching my children, and that attitude comes across in the classroom.... Culturally relevant teaching DOESN'T exist in schools. How can we allow students to make connections to the material, to see how learning relates to them? These are the kinds of things we should be talking about today."

An African American social studies teacher commented that she "heard two themes" as she listened to the conversations about culture. One was the notion of culturally relevant teaching and the other was "increasing access." "It may not be totally clear how to make math relevant for all kids, but we are also thinking about 'access' and how to make our subjects accessible to kids." She noted that it was interesting that some people wrote about culture in a very abstract way, whereas she wrote about it very "personally."

A Latino social studies teacher commented that the difference in people's responses to culture may depend on who they are and what they've experienced. "For some people, culture may be more defined.... For me, aspects of culture play a really heavy role. How people perceive me is really important to how they treat me. For example, I have to convince people that I am a teacher. They think I'm an aide and I have to keep saying I'm a teacher. What about me makes me look like I'm not a teacher? When you have African American or Latino students, they're clearly defined by how they look. It's a part of everything they encounter."

There are a number of noteworthy aspects of this set of exchanges that occur in many others. First, the relevance of culture to teaching was differently viewed by students, in part as a function of their race: Students of color were much more likely to explain the relevance of culture to issues of student engagement, motivation, belonging, and achievement than were White students who raised early questions (although many later engaged these issues differently). Second, teachers appeared to respond differently in part as a function of their disciplinary areas. Some teachers of mathematics, science, and foreign language initially struggled to see what the concepts of culturally relevant teaching could possibly mean for them. They did not initially see how the examples they chose or the ways in which they communicated and worked with students could be fraught with cultural implications.

A third noteworthy aspect of this exchange *not* typical of many others I have seen was the vigorous participation of a number of students of color, who felt they could voice their views and even guide the discussion. Often students of color sit silently in discussions like this one, or give up after a comment or two that seems not to be heard or understood by a responding classmate, as Lisa Delpit described. In this case, I think one reason for students' participation was that I had asked a multiracial team of students to take charge of part of the class and plan several activities that would relate to the readings. By virtue of their standing in this class and the fact that they had thought through what they wanted to accomplish, they felt empowered to contribute to the discussion. This seemed to create a comfort zone within which other students of all races entered the conversation, including some who rarely spoke in the large group of 60 assembled for this portion of the class.

Finally, it is important to note that by winter quarter when this class took place, students had begun to develop more open and candid relationships and could sustain conversations in which they started at different places, shared their ideas, and arrived at different understandings by the end of a discussion. After this conversation, a free-write on "what culture means to you," a small group jigsaw and debriefing on the readings, and an activity led by the students in which groups traced the individual immigration patterns of each of their members (see Chapter 6), the class had a much greater collective appreciation of the ways in which social contexts influence us all.

UNDERSTANDING STUDENTS

A critical task in becoming an effective teacher of diverse students is coming to understand individual young people in nonstereotypical ways while acknowledging and comprehending the ways in which culture and context influence their lives and learning. This kind of understanding is to be distinguished from the romantic pity many people express for children who live in challenging circumstances—a sentiment reflecting merely a more well-intentioned blindness to who students really are. Instead, teachers need to develop both an empathy for what others experience and a capacity to perceive each student as a person and as a learner, with tools that reduce prejudicial filters and that enhance the accuracy of those perceptions.

One goal of this understanding must be to counteract stereotypes and subconscious expectations that most people will have developed growing up in a racialized society. For example, Jacqueline Irvine's (1990) review of 36 studies of teacher expectations found that most studies conclude that teachers hold more negative attitudes about Black children's personality traits, ability, language, behavior, and potential than they do about those of White children, and that most Black students have fewer favorable interactions with their teachers than do White students. Other studies have found that children of color are more likely to be punished for offenses that White students commit without consequence, and that Black students, particularly males, are more likely to be suspended from school than Whites who have engaged in similar behaviors (Carter & Goodwin, 1994; Fine, 1991; Nieto, 1992). Black students identified as "gifted" have been found to receive less attention, praise, and encouragement and more criticism than any other students, especially when they are boys (Rubovitz & Maehr, 1973).

To "see" students in another way, teachers need to learn to look and listen carefully and nonjudgmentally in order to understand who students really are, what they think, and how they make decisions about how they behave. Paolo Friere (1998) talks about the importance of preparing teachers for "reading" a class of students "as if it were a *text* to be decoded (and) comprehended" (p. 49), especially when teachers come from economic and cultural backgrounds substantially different from those of their students:

> Just as in order to read texts we need such auxiliary tools as dictionaries or encyclopedias, the reading of classes as texts also requires tools that can be easily used. It is necessary, for example, to *observe* well, to *compare* well, to *infer* well, to *imagine* well, to *free one's sensibilities* well, and to believe in others without believing too much what one may think about others. One must exercise one's ability to *observe* by recording what is observed. But recording should not be limited to the dutiful description of what takes place from one's own perspective. It also implies taking the risk of making critical and evaluative observations without giving such observations airs of certainty. All such material should be in constant analysis by the teacher who produces it, as well as by his or her students. (p. 49, emphasis in original)

These skills of observation and analysis are explicitly developed by some teacher education programs by teaching ethnographic skills of observation and recording to teachers, along with tools for interviewing, collecting samples of student work, and engaging in assessments of student thinking, learning styles, and performance. The practice of "observation and recording" and the application of these skills in a child case study has been a mainstay of child development courses in many early childhood teacher education programs; in recent years, the practice has spread to some secondary programs.

STEP teachers conduct many case studies of students to bring different bodies of knowledge and lenses to bear on their ability to look and listen. A literacy case examines the development of many kinds of literacy for a middle school student; a case of an English language learner develops multiple strategies for assessing language use and language learning; a case of a student receiving special education services examines strengths and needs and analyzes school services; an adolescent case study looks at a student's growth and development in family, community, and school contexts. In addition to observing, interviewing, and examining student work, the process of shadowing the student in school provides powerful evidence about how the student is treated and responds in different classroom and nonclassroom contexts. This creates a rich understanding of the many worlds of the adolescent, and provides insights into how teachers can support their developing identities and learning opportunities. Student teachers often find this one of the most eye-opening experiences they encounter, providing much greater insight into student lives and the possibilities for making a difference.

UNDERSTANDING AND TRANSFORMING
SCHOOLS AND CLASSROOMS

In order to be able to act on these evolving understandings of self, society, and students, teachers must have an opportunity to consider the kinds of strategies they can enact to support their students. These encompass all of the areas of multicultural education outlined by James Banks (1993): (1) integration of multicultural content into the curriculum; (2) construction of knowledge in ways that take account of multiple perspectives and frames of reference; (3) prejudice reduction; (4) development of an equity pedagogy; and (5) creation of an empowering and equitable school culture. Problematizing without providing a glimpse of the possibilities for schooling can be debilitating rather than motivating.

Fortunately, there are many more resources for learning about effective multicultural teaching than there once were. For example, a growing body of recent research has uncovered strategies that are effective with diverse students in a range of contexts. This research suggests that effective teachers of students of color form and maintain connections with their students within their social contexts. Such teachers do not shy away from issues of race and culture; with students of varying language backgrounds they allow the use of multiple languages; they are familiar with students' dialects even though they instruct in standard English; and they celebrate their students as individuals and as members of specific cultures (Cochran-Smith, 1991; Foster, 1993; Garcia, 1993; Irvine, 1992; Strickland, 1995), asking students to share who they are and what they know with the class in a variety of ways.

Jacqueline Jordan Irvine (1992), Gloria Ladson-Billings (1992, 1994), and Eugene Garcia (1993) have summarized research finding that effective teachers of students of color—who include White teachers as well as members of minority groups—are passionate about content and use an active, direct approach to teaching: demonstrating, modeling, explaining, writing, giving feedback, reviewing, and emphasizing higher-order skills while avoiding excessive reliance on rote learning, drill and practice, or punishment. They see the teacher/student relationship as fluid, humane, and equitable, and characterized by a sense of community and team. Their classrooms feature participation, cooperative learning strategies, and acceptance, while they de-emphasize competition. They express feelings of connection, affiliation, and solidarity with the pupils they teach; they link classroom content to students' experiences, focus on the whole child, and believe that all of their students can succeed, while carefully structuring learning to make good on these beliefs.

Many of the authors in this book describe their epiphanies in uncovering these various aspects of equitable teaching within the arenas Banks outlines. Winter Pettis-Renwick, Jennifer French, and Claudia Narez describe means for integrating multicultural content into teaching. Jennifer Steele, Todd Ziegler Cymrot, and Kristy Garcia discuss how to consider multiple perspectives in the construction of knowledge in the classroom. Carlo Corti, Ryan Caster, and Allison Rowland address strategies for the reduction of prejudice and oppressive discourse in the classroom. In addition to these authors, Susan Park and Ana Ruiz discuss critical issues in developing an equity pedagogy in the classroom. Sandra Navarro, Leah Anderson, and Roman Garcia describe the structural determinants of inequality and school failure for many students, whereas Suzanne Herzman, Erin Hays, Laura Blythe, and Paloma Garcia-Lopez deal with both the problems and possibilities of creating an empowering and equitable school culture.

Building a repertoire of strategies for equitable teaching depends not only on learning content-specific teaching strategies for students with different language backgrounds, learning styles, and experience bases; it also depends on working within a community of practice where new insights can be sought and found. No one person can ever learn all that is needed to teach all of the students she or he will encounter. Shared knowledge and experience is essential to the creation of equitable schools. This means developing cohorts of teachers within teacher education programs and schools who see it as their responsibility and privilege to engage in ongoing peer support through reciprocal observations and continuous problem solving about student learning and equity.

Learning how to work *together* toward social justice may be the most important learning of all. The work of achieving equity and opportunity for all students is long, hard, and difficult. There are few solid victories that, once won, are never again threatened. Thus it is critical that, as Langston Hughes put it, we build "a community of hands to help." As he reminded us in the great words of "Freedom's Plow":

> A long time ago,
> An enslaved people heading toward freedom
> Made up a song:
> *Keep Your Hand On The Plow! Hold On!*
> That plow plowed a new furrow
> Across the field of history.
> Into that furrow the freedom seed was dropped.
> From that seed a tree grew, is growing, will ever grow.
> That tree is for everybody,
> For all America, for all the world.
> May its branches spread and its shelter grow
> Until all races and all peoples know its shade.
> KEEP YOUR HAND ON THE PLOW! HOLD ON!

References

Banks, J. A. (1993). Multicultural education: Historical development, dimensions, and practice. In L. Darling-Hammond (Ed.), *Review of research in education,* Vol. 19 (pp. 3–50). Washington, DC: American Educational Research Association.

Banks, J. A. (1994). *An introduction to multicultural education.* Boston: Allyn and Bacon.

Banks, J. A. (1995). Multicultural education: Historical development, dimensions, and practice. In J.A. Banks (Ed.), *Handbook of research on multicultural education* (pp. 3–19). New York: Macmillan.

Berman, P., Minnicucci, C., McGloughlin, B., Nelson, B., & Woodwork, K. (1995). *School reform and student diversity: Case studies of exemplary practices for LEP students.* Washington, DC: National Council on Bilingual Education.

Berndt, T.J. (1996). Transitions in friendships and friends' influence. In *Transitions through adolescence: Interpersonal domains and context.* Hillsdale, NJ: Lawrence Erlbaum.

Bruner, J. (1977). *The process of education.* Cambridge, MA: Harvard University Press.

Bruner, J. (1996). *Culture and education.* Cambridge, MA: Harvard University Press.

Carter, R., & Goodwin, L. (1994). Racial identity and education. In L. Darling-Hammond (Ed.), *Review of Research in Education,* Vol. 20 (pp. 291–336). Washington, DC: American Educational Research Association.

Cochran-Smith, M. (1991). Uncertain allies: Understanding the boundaries of race and teaching. *Harvard Educational Review, 65*(4), 541–570.

Cohen, E.G., & Lotan, R.A. (Eds.). (1997). *Working for equity in heterogeneous classrooms: Sociological theory in action.* New York: Teachers College Press.

Crawford, J. (1999). *Bilingual education: History, politics, theory and practice.* Los Angeles: Bilingual Educational Services, Inc.

Darling-Hammond, L. (1995). Inequality and access to knowledge. In J.A. Banks (Ed.), *Handbook of research on multicultural education* (pp. 465–483). New York: Macmillan.

Darling-Hammond, L. (1997). *The right to learn: A blueprint for creating schools that work.* San Francisco: Jossey-Bass.

Delpit, L. (1995). *Other people's children: Cultural conflicts in the classrooms.* New York: The New Press.

Dewey, J. (1966). *Democracy and education.* New York: The Free Press. (Original work published 1916)

Diego-Vigil, J. (1988). *Barrio gangs: Street life and identity in Southern California.* Austin: University of Texas Press.

Donato, R., Henze, R., & Lucas, T. (1990). Promoting the success of Latino language-minority students: An exploratory study of six high schools. *Harvard Educational Review, 60*(3), 315–340.

Eccles, J.S., Midgley, C., Wigfield, A., Buchanan, C.M., Reuman, D., Flanagan, C., & MacIver, D. (1993). Development during adolescence: The impact of stage-environment fit on adolescents' experiences in schools and families. *American Psychologist, 48*, 90–101.

Erikson, E. (1968). *Identity, youth, and crisis.* New York: W.W. Norton.

Fine, M. (1991). *Framing dropouts: Notes on the politics of an urban public school.* Albany: State University of New York Press.

Fine, M. (1993). On equal educational opportunities and unequal educational outcomes. In *Beyond silenced voices : class, race, and gender in United States schools.* Albany: State University of New York Press.

Fordham, S. (1988). Racelessness as a factor in Black students' school success: Pragmatic strategy or pyrrhic victory? *Harvard Educational Review, 58*, 54–84.

Foster, M. (1993). Educating for competence in community and culture: Exploring the views of exemplary African American teachers. *Urban Education, 27*(4), 370–394.

Friere, P. (1998). *Teachers as cultural workers: Letters to those who dare to teach.* Boulder, CO: Westview Press.

Garcia, E.E. (1993). Language, culture, and education. In L. Darling-Hammond (Ed.), *Review of research in education* Vol. 19 (pp.51–98). Washington, DC: American Educational Research Association.

Gardner, H. (1983). *Frames of mind: The theory of multiple intelligences.* New York: Basic Books.

Gay, G. (1997, January/February). The Relationship between Multicultural and Democratic Education. *The Social Studies, 88*(1), 5–11.

Gordon, E.W. (1990). Coping with communicentric bias in knowledge production in the social sciences. *Educational Researcher, 19*, 14–19.

Greene, M. (1982, June/July). Public education and the public space. *Educational Researcher, 11*(6), 4–9.

Harter, S. (1990). Self and identity development. In S.S. Feldman & G.R. Elliot (Eds.), *At the threshold* (pp. 352–368). Cambridge, MA: Harvard University Press.

Henderson, V.L., & Dweck, C.S. (1990). Motivation and achievement. In S.S. Feldman & G.R. Elliott (Eds.), *At the threshold* (pp. 308–320). Cambridge, MA: Harvard University Press.

History-Social Science Curriculum Framework and Criteria Committee. (1997). *History–social science framework for California public schools: Kindergarten through grade twelve.* Sacramento: California Department of Education.

Irvine, J.J. (1990). *Black students and school failure: Policies, practices, and prescriptions.* New York: Praeger.

Irvine, J.J. (1992). Making teacher education culturally responsive. In M.E. Dilworth (Ed.), *Diversity in teacher education* (pp.79–92). San Francisco: Jossey-Bass.

Juarez, D. (1999). A question of fairness: Using writing and literature to expand ethnic identity and understand marginality. In S. Freidman, E.R. Simons, J.S. Kalnin, & A. Casareno (Eds.), *Inside city schools* (pp. 111–125). New York: Teachers College Press.

Kohl, H. (1994). I won't learn from you: Confronting student resistance. In *Rethinking our classrooms: Teaching for equity and justice.* Milwaukee, WI: Rethinking Our Schools.

Kozol, J. (1991). *Savage inequalities.* New York: Crown.

Ladson-Billings, G. (1992). Culturally relevant teaching. In C.A. Grant (Ed.), *Research and multicultural education: From the margins to the mainstream* (pp. 106–121). Washington, DC: Falmer Press.

Ladson-Billings, G. (1994). *The dreamkeepers: Successful teachers of African-American children.* San Francisco: Jossey-Bass.

Lee, C. (1995). A culturally based cognitive apprenticeship: Teaching African-American high school students skills of literary interpretation. *Reading Research Quarterly, 30*(4), 608–630.

Lindsay, R., Robins, K., & Terrell, R. (1999). *Cultural proficiency: A manual for school leaders.* Thousand Oaks, CA: Corwin Press.

McDonald, J. (1996). *Redesigning schools.* San Francisco: Jossey-Bass.

McElroy-Johnson, B. (1993, Spring). Teaching and practice: Giving voice to the voiceless. *Harvard Educational Review, 63*(1), 85–104.

McKnight, C.C., Crosswhite, F.J., Dossey, J.A., Kifer, E., Swafford, J.O., Travers, K.J., & Cooney, T.J. (1987). *The underachieving curriculum: Assessing U.S. school mathematics from an international perspective.* Champaign, IL: Stipes.

National Center for History in the Schools. (2000). *National standards for United States history:*

Exploring the American experience (grades 5–12, expanded edition). Los Angeles: National Center for History in the Schools, University of California, Los Angeles.

Nieto, S. (1992). *Affirming diversity.* New York: Longman.

Nieto, S. (1999). *The light in their eyes.* New York: Teachers College Press.

Olsen, L. (1997). *Made in America: Immigrant students in our public schools.* New York: The New Press.

Phelan, P., Yu, H.C., & Davidson, A.L. (1994). Navigating the psychosocial pressures of adolescence: The voices and experiences of high school youth. *American Educational Research Journal, 31,* 415–447.

Reynolds, A.G. (1991). The cognitive consequences of bilingualism. In *Bilingualism, multiculturalism, and second language learning.* Hillsdale, NJ: Erlbaum.

Rubovitz, P.C., & Maehr, M. (1973). Pygmalion black and white. *Journal of Personality and Social Psychology, 25,* 210–218.

Scott-Jones, D. (1995). Parent-child interactions and school achievement. In B.A. Ryan, G.R. Adams, T.P. Gullotta, R.P. Weissberg, & R.L. Hampton (Eds.), *The family–school connection: Theory, research, and practice* (pp. 75–107). Thousand Oaks, CA: Sage Publications.

Simmons, R., Burgeson, R., Carlton-Ford, S., & Blyth, D. (1987). The impact of cumulative change in early adolescence. *Child Development.* Minneapolis, MN: The Society for Research in Child Development.

Spring, J. (1997). *Deculturalization and the struggle for equity* (2nd ed.). New York: McGraw-Hill.

Stanford Working Group on Federal Education Programs for Limited-English Proficient (LEP)

Steele, C. M. (1992, April). Race and the schooling of Black Americans. *The Atlantic Monthly, 269*(4), 68–78.

Strickland, D.S. (1995). Reinventing our literacy programs: Books, basics, balance. *Reading Teacher, 48* (4), 294–302.

Students. (1993). *Federal education programs for limited-English proficient students: A blueprint for the second generation.* (Online: http://www.ncbe.gwu.edu/miscpubs/blueprint.htm)

Takanishi, R. (1993). Changing views of adolescence in contemporary society. In R. Takanishi (Ed.), *Adolescence in the 1990s: Risk and opportunity* (pp. 1–7). New York: Teachers College Press.

Tatum, B.D. (1997). *"Why are all the black kids sitting together in the cafeteria?"* New York: Basic Books.

Tharp, R. G., & Gallimore R. (1988). *Rousing minds to life: Teaching, learning, and schooling in social context.* New York: Cambridge University Press.

Trueba, H. (1989). *Raising silent voices: Educating the linguistic minorities for the 21st century.* Cambridge, MA: Newbury House.

Tuan, M. (1995). Korean and Russian Students in a Los Angeles high school: Exploring the alternative strategies of two high-achieving groups. In R.G. Rumbaut & W.A. Cornelius (Eds.), *California's immigrant children: Theory, research, and implications for educational policy.* San Diego, CA: Center for U.S.–Mexican Studies, University of California.

Valdés, G. (1996). *Con respeto: Bridging the distances between culturally diverse families and schools.* New York: Teachers College, Columbia University.

Vygotsky, L. (1978). *Mind in society: The development of higher psychological processes.* Cambridge, MA: Harvard University Press.

Wiggins, G., & McTighe, J. (1998). *Understanding by design.* Alexandria, VA: Association for Supervision and Curriculum Development.

About the Editors and Contributors

Leah Anderson currently teaches ESL and Spanish at International Studies Academy, a small public high school in San Francisco. She completed her M.A. in Education at Stanford University. Prior to her graduate work, she taught Spanish in private schools for 4 years. In addition to teaching, she enjoys coaching, getting students involved in community service, and taking students on outdoor expeditions. In her free time, she often explores the outdoors with her husband and works on art projects.

Grace MyHyun Bang graduated from UC Berkeley in August 1997, with a B.A. in Rhetoric and History of Art. Prior to STEP, she worked as an English instructor for a university in Northern China, volunteered in East Africa for 5 weeks, and was an active youth mentor at her local church. She is proficient in Korean and French, enjoys singing, and values art education. She currently teaches English at Los Altos High School in Los Altos, California.

Laura Blythe enjoyed her undergraduate school experience at Stanford, where she received a B.A. in English, an M.A. in Education, and a teaching credential in English. She now has the pleasure of teaching World Literature to sophomores of the Silicon Valley and putting some of her theory to practice in coordinating an English Language Development program and teaching ELD 1 and 2.

Ryan Caster was an English teacher at Mountain View High School in California, teaching Freshmen Survey of Literature and American Studies. Before teaching, he earned his bachelor's degree at Emory University and master's degree at Stanford University. Tragically, Ryan was killed in an accident in the summer of 2001, just as this book was going to press. This book is dedicated to his memory.

Carlo Corti teaches economics, government and world history at Aragon High School in San Mateo, California. When he's not planning lessons or reflecting on those he has already taught, he is an avid reader and water sports fanatic. He is a Gemini, loves Italian food, and enjoys leisurely walks in the park.

Linda Darling-Hammond is Charles E. Ducommun Professor of Education at Stanford University and faculty sponsor for the Stanford Teacher Education

Program (STEP). Her research, teaching, and policy work focus on teacher education, school reform, and educational equity. She received a B.A. magna cum laude from Yale University and served as a teacher's aide and a teacher at the elementary, middle, and high school levels in a number of urban school settings before completing her doctorate at Temple University in Urban Education. She recently helped to start a public charter high school in East Palo Alto, California, and feels privileged to work with dedicated and committed teachers and other school leaders who are launching reforms in the Bay Area and around the country.

Jennifer French teaches English and Social Studies at Tennyson High School in Hayward, California. Before teaching she was a social worker in the domestic violence movement and an environmental educator in the Americorps program. She balances her teaching by enjoying the amazing art, music, food, and landscape of the Bay Area.

Kristy Garcia received a B.A. in English Literature from Harvard in 1998, and an M.A. in Education from Stanford in 2000. She taught for a year and a half in Palo Alto, California before moving East. Currently, Kristy lives and teaches in the New York City public schools.

Roman Garcia graduated from Humboldt State University with a B.A. in Social Science Secondary Education in May 1999 and received an M.A. from Stanford's Teacher Education Program in 2000. He is committed to working in bilingual classrooms in economically disadvantaged communities and has 5 years experience in various leadership positions of the Educational Opportunity Program; he continues to work with youth from underserved communities to increase their academic achievement. He currently teaches at Frontier Continuation High School and resides in Oxnard, California.

Silvia Paloma Garcia-Lopez is a graduate of Stanford University with a B.A. in international relations (1997) and an M.A. in education (2000). She spent most of her childhood in La Paz, California, where her family worked closely with the late Cesar E. Chavez. She has dedicated the bulk of her volunteer time since 1990 to Future Leaders of America, a Latino youth leadership organization, as a staff member and director of workshops and conferences. She recently completed her first year as a U.S. History teacher and Razas Unidas-Latino club and Service club advisor at Santa Clara High School in Santa Clara, CA. In her spare time, Paloma dances ballet *folklorico* as a member of *Raices de Mexico* in East Palo Alto, California. Her future plans include teaching at a charter school and eventually developing her own school targeting minority students in underprivileged neighborhoods.

Erin Hays is a 1994 graduate of the University of California, Santa Cruz with a degree in Sociology. After her undergraduate studies, Erin moved to Spokane, Washington where she worked as an Americorps VISTA volunteer. In 2000, Erin obtained a master's degree/teaching credential through the Stanford Teacher Education Program. Outside of school, Erin loves to travel and participate in outdoor recreation, especially with her golden retriever in tow.

Suzanne Herzman teaches English at Albany High School in Albany, California. Prior to obtaining her M.A. from the Stanford Teacher Education Program, she worked as an Americorps VISTA Volunteer at the East Bay Center for the Performing Arts in Richman, California, and subsequently worked for the Center as the Academic Coordinator. A graduate of New York University, with majors in French and Fine Arts, she also studied at the NYU program in Paris. Suzanne's interests include hiking and travel.

Claudia Angelica Narez is currently teaching Spanish for Native Speakers and advising the Future Leaders of America Club at Oxnard High School, Oxnard, California. She graduated from UC Berkeley with a B.A.in Spanish Language/Literature, Latin American Studies, and a minor in Education in May 1999. Her interests lie in research toward establishing more effective ESL/Bilingual education programs in urban settings, as well as mentoring and tutoring these students to succeed. She has experience as a teacher's assistant in an Oakland high school, creating web pages based on student's family history, and serving as mediator between minority families and access to information technology.

Sandra Navarro received her B.A. in 1998 from UC Berkeley in Chicano/a Studies and Sociology. She has years of experience working in Oakland Public Schools K–12 community where she coordinated a high school ESL Stay In School Program, and a *Dia de Los Muertos* program at the Oakland Museum. Sandra currently teaches social studies at Tennyson High School in Hayward, CA. She continues to be an innovative, dynamic, spirited, self-motivated young educator who believes in the human potential of all children to learn and succeed given the *opportunity*.

Susan Park graduated summa cum laude with a B.A. in English from UCLA in May 1998, and an M.A. in Education in June 1999. She did her student teaching in San Lorenzo, California and was a literacy instructor teacher's aide for second grade for Americorps. Susan has also tutored international students from South Korea and worked as a UniCamp summer camp counselor for low-income children. She strives to raise literacy levels and to build lifelong learning through developing independent, interested, and informed readers.

Winter Pettis-Renwick continues to grapple with what she feels is the need for a more inclusive understanding of American culture in education and the media. She works in the areas of education and curriculum design. Most recently, she worked at the Martin Luther King, Jr. Papers Project at Stanford, where she was a coordinator for the Liberation Curriculum Project, a program to create interactive web-based learning materials from the works of Dr. King. Winter lives in the Bay area with her husband Ron.

Allison Rowland is a high school teacher in San Francisco. She received her B.A. in biology from Williams College in June 1995. Prior to graduating from STEP in 2000, she was an Integrated Science Teacher at a public continuation high school in San Francisco for a year, an ESL Teacher in Chile for 5 months, a counselor at a residential home for adolescent girls with addictions, and a volunteer in English classes at School of the Arts in San Francisco. In her free time she plays soccer and dances, and someday would like to have a dog named Gecko.

Ana Louisa Ruiz received her B.A. in Mathematics/Hispanic Studies from Mills College in May 1999 and an M.A. in education in June 2000. After completing the Stanford Teacher Education Program, she has returned to high schooled fueled with *ganas y conciencia* to teach ALL students. Ruiz is currently teaching high school mathematics at San Lorenzo High School, near her Oakland home. Her next professional goal is to pursue a doctorate degree.

After finishing her M.A. in English at Georgetown University and working for several years in for-profit education, **Jennifer Steele** earned her teaching credential and M.A. in Education at Stanford University. She currently teaches English in San Diego, California.

Kristin Traudt is a 1996 graduate of Lake Forest College, Lake Forest, Illinois. While education and literature are her first loves, Kristin ventured into the corporate arena for 3 years before obtaining her master's degree and teaching credential at Stanford. Kristin is grateful for the fabulous experiences she had as a student teacher at Independence High School in San Jose, and as a full-time teacher at Wilcox High School in Santa Clara. Outside of the classroom, Kristin enjoys outdoor sports, dancing, and spending quality time with family and friends.

Todd Ziegler Cymrot graduated from Brown University in 1996 with a major in American Civilization. Todd taught for three years at Community Preparatory School in Providence, Rhode Island, where he learned more than he could have possibly given back to his students. Todd graduated from the Stanford Teacher Education Program in 2001. He currently lives with his wife in Washington, D.C. where they both teach high school social studies. Todd recently joined the faculty of Thurgood Marshall Academy, a brand new charter school.

Index

Achebe, Chinua, 69
African Americans, 10, 28, 31, 44, 72, 73, 83, 95, 96, 159, 160
  cases, 90–91
  conflict with Latinos, 121–122, 131
  expectations regarding, 209–210
  in history curriculum, 35–37
Anderson, Leah, 90–91, 103–115, 206, 212
Asian Americans, 72, 73, 74, 83, 95, 96

Bang, Grace MyHyun, 41, 71–78
Banks, James A., 10, 35, 86, 201, 206, 211, 212
Berman, P., 181, 182
Berndt, T.J., 135
Blyth, D., 138
Blythe, Laura, 150, 151, 171–183, 206, 212
Brown, Claude, 96
Bruner, Jerome, 101, 206
Burgeson, R., 138

California Standards for the Teaching
    Profession, 32, 88, 177
Canon
  reconstructing, in social studies curriculum, 30–38
Carlton-Ford, S., 138
Carter, Robert, 203–204, 210
Case studies, 7, 84–86, 89–147, 206, 210–211
  academic literacy, 93–102
  culturally relevant curriculum, 139–147
  "doing good in school," 103–115
  drop out/push out, 128–138
  immigrant student in American middle
    school, 116–127
  tracking, 167–169
Caster, Ryan, 41, 66–70, 212
Check-in(s), 187, 188–190, 191
Cisneros, Sandra, 100
Classroom(s), 151
  acknowledging diversity in, 18–21
  controversy in, 142–145
  environment, 11, 138, 139, 146, 157
  examining cultural assumptions in, 22–29

management, 186, 194
  power in, 26–27
  student motivation to succeed in, 162
  transforming social dynamics of, 52–58
  understanding and transforming, 211–212
Cochran-Smith, M., 211
Cohen, E.G., 84
Community building, 184–191
  of teachers of conscience, 198–200
Community youth organizations, 128–138
Conciencia (consciousness), 192–200
Corti, Carlo, 41, 52–58, 212
Crawford, J., 178, 179
Cross-cultural exchange vs. cultural warfare,
    14–16
Cultural assumptions, 22–29
Cultural relevance, 121, 125, 139–47, 166,
    206–207, 211 and teaching, 32, 95, 207–209
Cultural warfare, cross-cultural exchange vs.,
    14–16
Curriculum, 30, 160–161, 183
  culturally relevant, 139–147
  ELL, 177–179
  gays/lesbians in, 62–65
  and identity development, 138
  inclusive, 34–37
  multicultural, 11, 32–33
  social studies, 30–38
  watered-down, 87, 174, 178
Curriculum design, 46–47, 186

Darling-Hammond, Linda, 1–7, 9–17, 89–91,
    149–152, 201–213
Davidson, A.L., 14, 73, 77, 127
Delpit, Lisa, 2, 96, 100, 204, 209
Democracy and Education (Dewey), 202
Developmental needs, 124–126
Dewey, John, 202, 205
Diego-Vigil, J., 131, 136
Difference(s), 18, 71
  bridging, 184–191
  learning, 10, 103–115, 194
Discrimination, 2, 79–88, 142, 143–144, 145

Diversity, 1, 6, 7, 10, 15, 26, 48, 201
  acknowledging, 18–21
  analyzing, 44
  beliefs about, 23–24
  in curriculum, 37–38
  effect on education, 49–51
  guidelines for, 32
  lack of, in English departments, 76–77
  in teacher education programs, 28
  teachers and, 16–17
  teaching for, 46, 48, 51, 205
  what it is, 9–17
Donato, Ruben, 179, 183
Douglass, Frederick, 96
Dropping out, 128–138
Dreamkeepers, The (Ladson-Billings), 31
Dubois, W.E.B., 37
Dweck, C.S., 114, 123

Eccles, J.S., 85, 106–107, 130
Emotional support, 165–166, 169, 170
English Language Development (ELD)
    Programs, 44, 46, 140, 158, 159, 163–169,
    170, 203
English as Second Language (ESL), 119, 125,
    130, 164–165, 175, 176, 179, 180
  federal policy, 178
English Language Learners (ELL), 44, 87,
    150–151, 163, 164–165, 166
  curriculum, 177–179
  meeting needs of, 171–183
  programs for, 171–175, 176, 177, 178,
    180–181, 182, 183
Equitable practice
  educating profession for, 201–213
Equity, 40, 41, 199
  in school reform, 171–183
  teaching for, in mathematics classroom,
    194–197
Equity-based teaching, strategies, 48–51
Equity pedagogy, 1, 150, 201, 211, 212
Erickson, E., 104
Ethnic conflict, in school(s), 121–122

Fences (Wilson), 20
Fine, Michelle, 82, 210
Fordham, S., 207
Foster, M., 211
"Freedom's Plow" (Hughes), 212–213
Freire, Paolo, 210
French, Jennifer, 2, 34, 39–42, 59–65, 204,
    212

Gallimore, R., 111
Garcia, E. E., 211–212
Garcia, Kristy, 11, 22–29, 212
Garcia, Roman H., 91, 116–127, 206, 212
Garcia-Lopez, Silvia Paloma, 2, 9–17, 34, 41,
    79–88, 204, 212
Gardner, H., 147
Gay, Geneva, 38
Gays/lesbians, 41, 59, 60–65, 83, 188–189
GLBT (gay, lesbian, bisexual, transgendered)
    students, 59, 61, 62–65
Goodwin, Lin, 203–204, 210
Gordon, Edmund, 204
Greene, Maxine, 203

Harlem Renaissance, 35, 36–37
Harold Wiggs Middle School, 181
Harter, S., 123
Hays, Erin, 150–51, 163–170, 206, 212
Henderson, V.L., 114, 123
Henze, Rosemary, 179, 183
Herzman, Suzanne, 150, 153–162, 206, 212
History, 30–31
  multicultural curriculum, 32–33
  as place where students find/lose themselves,
    33–38
  as study of all peoples, 37–38
History-Social Science Framework for
    California Public Schools, 32
House on Mango Street, The (Cisneros), 100
Hughes, Langston, 37, 212–213
Hurston, Zora Neale, 36, 37

"I Won't Learn From You" (Kohl), 101
Idealism, and reality, 59–65
Identity(ies), 7, 42, 47, 64, 77–78, 140, 141, 142,
    203
  acknowledging, 187
  in adolescent development, 132
  assumptions about, 22
  development, 128, 138, 203–204
  dialogue on, 39–40
  influence on pedagogy, 39–42
  multiple, 71–78
  building amid assumptions, 24–25
Immigrant students, 116–27, 129–138
Inclusion/exclusion, 18, 19, 33–34, 57
Individualized Education Plans/individualized
    help, 112–113, 115, 125–126, 164, 170
Irvine, Jacqueline Jordan, 209–10, 211–212

Juarez, Deborah, 142, 207

KBLs (Kick Back and Learn), 136–137
Kim, Helen, 34, 35
Kingston, Maxine Hong, 95
Kohl, Herbert, 101, 186–187
Kozol, J., 206

Ladson-Billings, Gloria, 31, 50, 95, 96, 100, 140,
    207, 211–212
Language, 66, 123, 136, 141
    homophobic, 69–70
    power relationship in, 68
    use of, 66–67, 68, 70
Latinos, 28, 44, 83, 85–86, 88, 95, 96, 141–142,
    121–122, 143, 159, 160, 208
Learning, 5, 9, 11, 136–137
    culture foundation of, 206–207
    students taking charge of, 151
    to teach, 186–87
    teaching and, 101–2, 186–187
Learning differences, 10, 103–115, 194
Lee, Carol, 141, 145, 207
Lee, Harper, 70
Lindsay, R., 85, 86
Lotan, R.A., 84
Lucas, Tamara, 179, 183

Made in America (Olsen), 120
Maehr, M., 210
Malcolm X, 74, 95
Marginalization, 2, 75–76, 204–205
Mathematics teaching, 192–200
McDonald, J., 183
McElroy-Johnson, B., 18
McGloughlin, B., 181
McKnight, C.C., 206
McTighe, Jay, 34
Mexican Americans, 10, 24, 41, 80–81, 140, 144
Minnicucci, C., 181
Minorities, 23
    in curriculum, 62–63
Minority students, 44, 79, 149–150
    deculturalization, 206–207
    discrimination against, 79–88
    marginalized, 204–205
Mongia, Lydia, 34
Multicultural education/multiculturalism, 3, 22,
    26, 30, 62, 64, 86, 203, 211, 212
    curriculum, 11, 32–33

Narez, Claudia Angelica, 34, 91, 139–147, 212
National Standards for United States History, 32,
    33

Navarro, Sandra, 91, 128–38, 206, 212
Nelson, B., 181
Nieto, Sonia, 11, 206, 210

Oakland Blueprint for Youth Development,
    129–130
Olsen, L., 117, 120, 121, 123, 124, 206
"On Equal Educational Opportunities and
    Unequal Educational Outcomes" (Fine), 82
Other People's Children (Delpit), 96

Park, Susan, 90, 93–102, 212
Pedagogy, 165, 204
    influence of identity on, 39–42
Phelan, P., 14, 23, 77, 127
"Premio, El" (Salinas), 142, 144

Reynolds, A.G., 136
Robins, K., 85, 86
Rodriguez, Luis, 95
"Rose for Emily, A" (Faulkner), 20
Rowland, Allison, 151, 184–191, 212
Rubovitz, P.C., 210
Ruiz, Ana Louisa, 151, 192–200, 212

Salinas, Marta, 142
San Francisco Unified School District, 184
SAP (Student Assessment Program), 125
School reform, equity issues in, 171–183
Schools
    educating low-income and minority stu-
        dents, 149–150
    failure as equitable institutions, 15
    social and emotional development in context
        of, 122–124
    understanding and transforming, 211–213
Scott-Jones, Diane, 105
SDAIE (Segregated Specially Designed
    Academic Instruction in English), 85,
    86–87, 164, 166, 167, 169, 174, 178, 180
Second International Mathematics Study, 206
Self
    in relation to others, 203–205
    sense of, 31
"Silenced Dialogue, The" (Delpit), 204
Simmons, R., 138
Skills class, 154, 155–159, 162
Smith, Frank, 14
Social change, 6–7, 62, 151
    supporting learning to teach for, 4–6
Social development, in school context, 122–123
Social dynamics, in classroom, 52–58

Social justice, 40, 86, 88, 212
   learning to teach for, 1–7, 39, 201
   mathematics teaching as path to, 192–194
Social studies curriculum, 30–38
Spanish Immersion Program, 119, 123, 125
Spring, Joel, 206
Staff development, 182–183
Stanford Teacher Education Program (STEP),
      1–3, 4–6, 10, 13, 22, 44, 46, 47–48, 49, 50,
      82, 83, 89–90, 155, 203, 204–205
   case studies, 210–211
   culturally relevant teaching, 207–209
Stanford Working Group on Federal Education
      Programs for Limited-English Proficient
      Students, 179
Steele, Claude, 83
Steele, Jennifer, 10–11, 18–21, 212
Stereotypes, 26–29, 44, 48, 60, 69, 71, 74–75, 76,
      83, 188, 203, 209–210
Strickland, D.S., 211
Student needs, 156–158
   meeting, 90–91, 103–115
Students, 89–91
   of color, 79
   immigrant, 76–77
   teachers of, 211–212
   treating as individuals, 26–29
   understanding, 209–211
Success, 123
   confronting realities of, 97–99
   depending on, 93–102
   examining meaning of, 99–101
   and failure, 169–170
   meaning of, 94–95
   redefining, 101–102
   in spite of system, 128–138
Support, 79, 163, 165–166, 170, 180, 181
   emotional, 165–166, 169, 170

Takanishi, R., 131
Tan, Amy, 99
Tatum, Beverly, 27, 72, 73, 74, 77, 101, 121, 206
Taylor, Lynda, 34
Teachable moments, 66, 69, 70, 100, 187, 189,
      197–198
Teacher education programs, 1, 39–40, 44, 48,
      59, 61, 82, 151, 186–187, 191
   diversity issues in, 28
   group in, 204
   multicultural awareness, 203
   observation and analysis skills, 210
   silencing in, 2, 3

Teachers
   and diversity, 16–17
   with *conciencia* (consciousness), 192–200
   knowledge and skills, 150
   peer support, 212
   role of, 196–197
   as students, 47–48
   of students of color, 211–212.
   See also White teachers
Teaching, 2, 91, 151, 157
   as cultural exchange, 12, 14, 17
   and diversity, 10
   equity-based, 48–51, 212
   and learning, 101–102, 186–187
   mathematics, 192–200
   multicultural content in, 212
   questioning, 45–46
Terrell, R., 85, 86
Tharp, R.G., 111
Things Fall Apart (Achebe), 69
To Kill a Mockingbird (Lee), 70, 157
Toomer, Jean, 37
Tracking, 149, 150–151, 153–162, 163–170, 177
Traudt, Kristin, 40–41, 43–51, 203
Trueba, H., 123, 180
Tuan, Mia, 76

Valdés, G., 85, 206
Vision statement, 175–183
Voice, 26
   student, 145–146
Volunteers, 182
Vygotsky, L., 113

Warfield, Benjamin B., 43, 44
White teachers
   culturally relevant teaching, 207–208
   teaching students of color, 43–51, 184–186
*Why Are All the Black Kids Sitting Together in the
      Cafeteria?* (Tatum), 27, 72, 73, 101
Wiggins, Grant, 34
Woolwork, K., 181
Words, 41, 56, 66, 69, 70, 71–78

Yu, H.C., 14, 73, 77, 127

Ziegler Cymrot, Todd, 10, 12, 13–17, 201, 212